Dennis Skinner is the son of a miner sacked after the 1926 General Strike. Skinner, to the distress of his mother, and despite passing his 11-plus at the age of 10, followed his dad down the pit. He was a Clay Cross and Derbyshire councillor before winning Bolsover for Labour in 1970, a seat he's held ever since. A former chairman of Labour and member of the party's ruling National Executive Committee, Skinner's Parliamentary heckles and interventions are legendary. He has been expelled so often from the Commons that suspension has become an occupational hazard.

SAILING CLOSE TO THE WIND

Reminiscences

DENNIS SKINNER

Quercus

First published in Great Britain in 2014 by Quercus Publishing Ltd

This edition published in 2015 by

Quercus Publishing Ltd
Carmelite House
50 Victoria Embankment
London EC4Y 0DZ

An Hachette UK company

A CIP catalogue record for this book is available
from the British Library

PB ISBN 978 1 78429 123 5
EBOOK ISBN 978 1 78206 158 8

Typeset in Minion by IDSUK (DataConnection) Ltd

Printed and bound in Great Britain by Clays Ltd, St Ives plc

For all my friends and family, past and present.

CONTENTS

FOREWORD

In producing this book I have finally succumbed to the demands of all those Labour and trade union friends up and down the country to provide them with a few written reminiscences.

Whenever I have addressed meetings I've heard a familiar question: 'When are you going to write a book?' My answer for the first thirty years was always something like: 'Thanks, I will think about it.' I always knew I could tell a good story on a platform, in a room of trade unionists or sometimes in Parliament. There is, however, a vast difference between making people laugh, cry and think at a Labour movement function and on the printed page.

But in the last ten years the social media phenomenon has turned those requests into a clamour from people who could not understand my reluctance to put pen to paper.

I know in my heart that I cannot make words as exciting on the printed page but I've made a decision to relate a few stories that characterise my upbringing; my time on Clay Cross council; some of the more exciting moments in the Palace of Varieties; and, most important of all, my involvement in the trade union and Labour movement rallies, meetings and strikes!

FOREWORD

This book is not intended to be anything other than a response to that clamour, to the din and demand from friends near and far who believe I should heed their requests.

Dennis Skinner, 2014

CHAPTER ONE

Good working-class mining stock

The place is Clay Cross, a small pit town in Derbyshire. The year is 1932 and I was born on 11 February in a long terrace of two up-two down houses, a tin bath hanging from a nail in the backyard, on Waterloo Street. The street was known, for some unfathomable reason, as Monkey Hollow. When I was still in the pram, we moved to John Street at the other end of the pit tip.

My mother, Lucy, always had a song on her lips. She took in laundry and cleaned for other people to scrape a living. My father, Edward, who was also called Tony for reasons I never quite fathomed, was a coal miner, as I was to become. A resourceful man, he'd been blacklisted for six years when I arrived. The pit bosses branded him a troublemaker after the General Strike of 1926 and Dad wasn't allowed to go back down a mine and earn a wage packet until the thirst for energy to power British rearmament against Hitler meant the employers couldn't sustain their discrimination against him. He was a union man, but like all union men he was a grafter, instilling in all of his children a strong work ethic.

At the corner of John Street, the pit tip soared more than 150 feet into the sky and, on most days, would be partly enveloped by a yellow sulphurous cloud that blotted out the summit. Over the road, pollution burst out of the coke ovens at the Clay Cross Works many times each day, floating past the football ground and over our house before enshrouding the tip. You could smell it, taste it, almost physically feel the gas which tinged the air. How we yearned for the wind to blow the cloud towards the home of General Jackson, owner of the coke plant and seven collieries within a five-mile radius. Needless to say, General Jackson didn't live on John Street. He resided in an extremely large house a mile away from the pollution factory while his kids, including Guy Jackson who captained Derbyshire at cricket, and Bridget, who stood for Parliament as a candidate of the Conservative Party, lived even further away.

The rock and slag from the nearest pit were carried in massive industrial buckets hanging on cables in the air, crossing the football field before dumping the waste on the top of an ever-expanding pile. These vast metal containers would criss-cross their way back and forth noisily all day long and, naturally, there would be a spillage from time to time. When, much later, I discussed planning applications and health and safety issues as a local councillor, I'd often reflect on my early childhood. I'd recall the buckets that occasionally turned over and dropped debris where people walked or played. The influence of General Jackson's Clay Cross Company was an early lesson in the power that money can buy. The firm possessed real muscle in the town and almost certainly Whitehall too, a firm used to getting what it wanted. No wonder that in those days the common phrase 'Where there's muck there's brass' sounded as if it had been coined for General Jackson's empire.

When I was old enough to get out of the pram, that pit top was to become my adventure playground. With other lads on the street, I climbed regularly to the summit. We sledged down in winter when it snowed. After the Second World War began, we played soldiers in the 200-yard-long trench dug across the top by the Home Guard to fight the Germans on the beaches, on the landing grounds, in the fields and in the streets and on the slopes and summit of Clay Cross pit tip. When finally the company was required to dismantle the pylons and the buckets, they deposited the industrial waste on another tip 300 yards away. The western side became covered in gorse, blackberry bushes and willow herb. Linnets nested and we enjoyed butterflies in abundance. I knew every inch of the hills. When I became a school cross-country champion, I owed a lot of my stamina to running – yes, running – up and down that pit tip.

This is my story, the tale of a man whose life was shaped by the pit environment and the Second World War. I grew up in a mining community as Hitler hammered on Britain's door. From the age of 10, I did a newspaper round every day. I devoured every one of the eight pages that each wartime title was permitted. I scoured the *Empire News*, *Sunday Pictorial*, *News Chronicle* and the rest before pushing them through the doors. I wanted to discuss the progress of the war, particularly with friends of my parents. I vividly recall saying excitedly to Bal Parker, a workmate of my father: 'We've captured Benghazi!' He answered dourly: 'Yes, Son, but we'll lose it next week.' And we did.

Naturally, I discussed the football results in the North and South Leagues which operated during that period. The horserace meetings too, limited to five racecourses with the rest requisitioned by the RAF or used for other activities to boost the war effort. Taking in all this information, and discussing it with adults, was an education in itself and developed my good memory. I was to pass the 11-plus at the age of 10 and found myself told to stand in front of the class to recite times tables backwards. Reading the papers and debating issues in my early years, particularly with my father, also helped me recognise that things didn't have to be the way they were. That we could improve lives and create a better world.

The Great Depression was still around when I drew my first breath. My two elder sisters, Joan and Hazel, are sadly no longer with us. Joan was to go on to be a floor manager in Woolworth's, Hazel a shopworker. The three of us were born before mother was 20. I often wonder what the *Daily Mail* would've made of her. They'd probably have had a pop. The paper would hate a woman who gave birth to three kids in her teens and nine children in all. How wrong they would be, as usual. She was a wonderful woman – caring, hardworking and always singing. It was a reasonably happy childhood. Our lack of material possessions didn't leave us a sad family. We made the best of it.

After me, along came Gordon (now dead too), Donald, Graham, David, Gary and Derrick. Gordon, Graham and David were to follow Dad, as I did, into the pit. Gary went into the building industry. Derrick, the baby of the family, was the only one of us to go to university, getting a degree in Sheffield. He represents claimants at tribunals against Atos, the French company given a contract to persecute Britain's disabled. Donald, the fifth of my mother's children, lasted only a few days. It was during the war and his death must have been traumatic for my parents, although they did their best not to show it. I was young, yet old enough to realise the baby we'd looked forward to so excitedly was swiftly taken away from us. I kept asking Dad what the boy had been called and, upset, he didn't want to talk about it. I pestered and pestered and in the end he replied, gruffly: 'Adolf'. It was to shut me up. The war was on. Uttering Hitler's first name was a strained joke from a parent bottling up grief.

My parents had been lodging in John Street at number 27 with a Mr Bexton. Later, when he died, we took over the tenancy and rented from a charity, paying the rent at the office in Broadleys in the middle of Clay Cross. It was near a shop selling paraffin called Kenning's, expanding from those humble beginnings into the huge national motor dealership of that name. Thankfully, the charity agreed we could take over John Street if we promised to pay the rent on time. The house had two and a half bedrooms, one so small you couldn't really call it a full bedroom. You couldn't swing a kitten, never mind a cat, in it. The place was cramped, though I don't remember my parents moaning. We got on with life, making the most of what we had.

I shared a double bed with Gordon, sleeping top to bottom. Joan and Hazel were crammed in the box room. My other brothers, as they came along, started out in my parents' room before they'd join us in an increasingly crowded boys' room. Downstairs there was a kitchen with a coal oven and boiler to heat hot water. In a second room we'd sit at a table to eat, although to call it a dining room would be misleading. It was neither large nor grand. There was also a front room with a three-piece suite where we'd listen to the radio.

My father's blacklisting guaranteed we ate politics with our breakfast, dinner and tea. We didn't have much in terms of material possessions and weren't encouraged to expect much, what with my father denied the right to work for the early years of my life while my mother hardly earned a fortune as a washerwoman. With money tight, there were few presents on birthdays and Christmas. One year I asked my father: 'Santa Claus doesn't come here to our house, does he, Dad?' He replied: 'No, we've got the bloody economic Santa Claus, son, and he doesn't bring many presents for the likes of us.'

Yet if we were poor, and we were, we didn't starve. We always had enough to eat. What we didn't enjoy were the extras, treats like ice cream. Other kids might be bought a vanilla slice but there were so many mouths in our family, and so little money to fill them, that we had the basics and nothing else. Hardship encouraged enterprise. Every week a fruiterer's cart would trundle over the stony, rough road that was the street. A few of the John Street gang, the sons of miners I played with, would pat the horse while a couple of us would hang about the back, waiting to grab an apple or two when serving customers distracted the man.

Lots of kids in a small house meant we had to play outside in all weathers. It was the era before TV and computer games, so we occupied ourselves. My mother would shoo us out, remarking how we cluttered up the place. The aim of whatever game we played was not to be caught. Going where we shouldn't was exciting. Clay Cross coke works was a favourite haunt. We ignored the Keep Out signs and kept an eagle eye open for Bobby Starling, the works' fearsome bobby. If Bobby Starling grabbed you it was the thump of summary justice, and trouble with your parents. Whingeing to them didn't get you anywhere when you'd been where you shouldn't.

The Home Guard trench along the top of the tip was a wonderful adventure playground. We built what we imagined to be a castle with pieces of corrugated iron. We'd play soldiers, the British against the Nazis. The aim was to control the castle. Those of us in Clay Cross lived the nearest so we'd get there first and children from other rows of housing would come and try to take it over. A few stones would be thrown. It was great fun.

One idiot, who was three years older than the rest of us, insisted we call him the Field Marshal. I wasn't a big lad for my age and, aged five or six, I'd be chased by older boys waving penknives and shouting: 'Skinner bob a rabbit.' They were threatening to skin me alive. It was a rough game of chase, really, and they wouldn't – I trust – have really cut me if I'd been too slow. As it was, I was never caught. And nobody called social services or the police. I became quite nippy and those early years, fleeing in terror, were good training for later cross-country running. I learned later, too, how to stand and fight my corner.

I was pretty handy at making things, particularly carts. I'd find a big plank, two smaller bits of wood across the front and back, then fix on wheels from an old pram. Coming down a steep tip on that was fast and frightening. We also played in the country-side surrounding Clay Cross, roaming the fields and hanging a rope from a tree in the woods to swing over the stream. The aim was to get across to the other side without falling in and hope some other boy would slip and be drenched. If you pushed straight, whoever was clinging onto the knot at the bottom might make it across but eventually someone would be pushed at an angle and that would be that. It happened to me, coming home soaked and trying to hide the fact.

The Field Marshal was dangerous and could've blinded me. I was walking near the corner flag on the Clay Cross Welfare foot-ball pitch, and could see a little crowd near the goalposts. I heard the Field Marshal shout: 'There's Skinner coming.' At almost the same moment I felt this incredible pain on my left ear. A warm liquid flowed down my face. I'd been shot with a pellet in the lobe. It bled like merry hell, only a few inches from my eye.

It transpired one of the dads who served in the Army had brought a captured German rifle home to Britain, and his son had taken it out to play with. The Field Marshal – and I'll spare his family's blushes by not naming him – liked to impress younger kids instead of hanging out with teenagers his own age. He'd swung round the gun and shot me in the ear. My father hated the man who'd smuggled the weapon into England. He went round to sort it out in the time-honoured fashion of mining communities. The damn gun never reappeared.

The Field Marshal, who really was as mad as a hatter, went on to join the Army, then the Navy. His rank was never as elevated as that he conferred on himself to play with us younger kids. By the time I was 18, nobody wanted anything to do with him. On a Bonfire Night, 5 November, a gang of us were going to the Victoria Dance Hall in Chesterfield. The Field Marshal, home on leave, wanted to come. He was no longer able to impose himself because we were all working, but still he tagged along. At the dance, daft lads started throwing exploding jumping jacks on the dance floor. The compère announced from the stage that if there were any more fireworks the band would play the National Anthem, in other words the last tune, and the dance hall would close. The Field Marshal, who was 21, shouted: 'Play the King!' He chucked a lit jump jack into the middle of the room. He was less popular than ever when we were all sitting gloomily on the early bus home to Clay Cross.

The Field Marshal did a silly, boyish thing on that dance floor. By then we were 18 and working down the pit. We'd matured. He was 21 and still acting like a juvenile. He'd never grown up and we had.

It's not until later in life that you appreciate the lessons you learn as a kid. One Sunday, I arrived home from sliding down the pit tip on a piece of corrugated iron to find Hazel and Joan had gone to Sunday School in the Methodist chapel. On a whim I set off to join them, even though I was never usually up for Sunday School. I ran over the hills for a short cut. When I arrived, it was packed. Everybody else was in their Sunday best. I was as scruffy as the Artful Dodger: grimy hands and face, in grubby clothes covered in dust from the pit tip. I went upstairs to find somewhere to sit and all the pews were crowded. As I was trying to find a space on the end, Teddy Thompson, the local milliner, appeared. He must have been a churchwarden or something. 'Come, me lad,' said Thompson, 'I don't think you should be here.' He kicked me out because I was dirty. And I suppose, if I'm charitable, because I didn't usually attend Sunday School. It hurt.

I repaid Teddy Thompson with interest over the years, making him pay for the slight. He would come knocking on our door for his clothes money, my parents buying what we wore on tick at a shilling a week (5p) because they didn't earn enough to purchase it outright.

My mother would whisper: 'Quick, it's Teddy Thompson. Tell him I'm out. Don't let him in.'

He'd bang on the door and I'd answer: 'Yes?'

He'd say: 'Is your mother in?'

'I don't think so.'

'Are you sure, my lad?'

'Yes, I'm sure.'

'Are you really sure?'

'Yes, I'm really sure. Are you calling me a liar or what?'

And away he'd go, without his shilling from our house.

When the weather was bad, we'd stay in. To keep out the cold, the doors were kept shut and the radio would be turned on. That meant that someone in the house, meaning Joan, Hazel, Gordon or me, would have to go to Wardle's shop to get the heavy accumulator, a big battery, charged. It was a walk of a mile there and back to Market Street. We would listen to the news and Arthur Askey, and at the same time make another rug for the floor. We'd cut up rags into 4-inch pieces, sharpen a wooden peg and proceed to 'peg the rug', as it was called, by making holes in a thick piece of cloth and pushing through the rags. Sometimes my mother and the girls would knit and sew. I saw how they did it so often that I could cast on, cast off, knit one, purl one. Throughout it all my mother would be singing songs from the shows, nearly always including Gracie Fields. I heard them so often I can still remember all the words. I'm really the only one of the nine who followed mother's lead and sang in the house, in a choir and on a few occasions even the stage.

As I said, it was a reasonably happy childhood. We hadn't got two pennies to rub together but, particularly during the war, we supplemented rations with Dad's allotment near the Ashover light railway. What's often overlooked by people from outside mining areas is that most pits are in semi-rural areas rather than cities. Miners by and large worked cheek by jowl with farmers. Father had an allotment, like lots of miners. To keep the unemployed off the streets and give them a chance to feed their families, the jobless in our patch of Derbyshire were allowed to rent a smallholding of a few acres by the Land Settlement Association. The government scheme in the middle of the 1930s was a lifesaver for us. On the plot they erected several triangular chicken pens. The hens supplied us with eggs and a little meat, Dad selling birds to get a bit of cash. As a little kid I'd go with him, he in his cap, me carrying a bucket of corn, to feed the chickens. We grew broad beans, carrots, cabbages, lettuce, radishes and potatoes. He was fit and healthy, a strong man. He could dig and turn over the soil. The injured, sick and frail in depressed areas were less fortunate. Their stomachs would've been empty.

He'd supply chickens to a Miss Kirkham, headmistress of the local school, to bring in a little money. She lived in a big house and Miss Kirkham would say: 'Tony, I have got company coming. Could you let me have two or three fowls for the weekend?' I recall Bal Parker, a neighbour, stopping me and sneering: 'You want to ask your dad about those dead fowls and Miss Kirkham.' Puzzled, I ran home and asked my father what he meant. The response – 'You tell Bal Parker to shut his bloody mouth' – heightened my interest. Dad's way of preparing the birds was to kill the chickens, then bury them in rags for a few days. It was an unorthodox method he wisely declined to share with Miss Kirkham. She was happy in her ignorance. 'The meat drops off your fowls,' I heard her tell him. 'It's delicious.' She probably would've delivered a different verdict had she known they'd been interred for two or three days. Bal Parker was upset, I worked out, because he never received a lucrative order from Miss Kirkham. Serving buried birds didn't do her any harm, I hasten to add. She lived to 88.

During the war years, Dad banned me one evening from going to the allotment with him, which was unusual. He whispered he had a little job to do with Char Butterworth. When we were served pork for dinner a few days later, I sussed out their scam. A group of pitmen had been keeping pigs and four or five secretly shared one between them, depriving the Ministry of Agriculture of an animal. You weren't supposed to eat these animals yourselves. Ducking and diving made life bearable and was the only way to beat the system. The incident lacked the humour of *A Private Function*, the Michael Palin film about killing a pig. When you were hungry, you weren't sentimental.

Dad would keep going to the pits in search of work but he was well known in the area and repeatedly rejected by managers. To be a trade union activist was to be labelled a troublemaker, a mark of Cain. Pit owners operated by paying men as little as they could get away with in dangerous conditions. I may have been only five years old, but I remember vividly him rushing into the house and shouting: 'You'll never believe it, Luce. I've got a job at Morton Colliery on the afternoon shift.' It was 1937. Hitler was beginning to pound the drums of war in Germany. In Britain, the government was starting to recognise it had to respond. Rearmament meant more munitions. Building weapons required energy and in Derbyshire the increased output of coal translated into work for a previously blacklisted pitman. Industrial militants like my father, who had been refused work for many years, were allowed to bring home a wage. Miners were breaking production records under the Essential Work Order, a 1941 regulation banning strikes and giving Ernie Bevin, the Transport and General Workers' Union general secretary co-opted into the wartime coalition government and a future foreign secretary in Clement Attlee's first Labour government, the authority to direct workers – the Bevin Boys – into the mines. Building tanks, guns, ships and aircraft required energy and coal was the source. After the end of the war a few miners, the Bevin Boys, were given a medal but the majority of miners, pitmen who had put forty years of their life to the industry, received not as much as a thank you. Don't get me wrong here. Tony, my dad, would never have taken a medal but I know of retired miners who are aggrieved to this day that their war efforts were overlooked.

My father, however, did win a few prizes when the war ended. Within a week of VE Day it was announced that Clay Cross Works would allow its sports field (which we played on as if it was our back garden) to be used for celebratory games for all the men, women, boys and girls of the Egstow area of the town at the bottom of the tip. There were prizes worth winning. National Savings Certificates of 10 shillings (50p) would be awarded to the winners of the 100-yard foot race, sack race, egg and spoon and many more contests.

Tony was first up in the 100 yards and he realised his biggest threat was from a man who lived at the bottom end of John Street who turned up in running spikes. 'He's a professional in those shoes. He should start further back so it's a fair race,' Dad insisted to the organisers. And the man in the spikes was placed two yards back. The Skinners enjoyed a good day. Dad finished in front of Mr Running Spikes to win his 100-yard dash. Joan, Hazel, Gordon and I were victorious in our respective age races.

Later in the afternoon, Gordon triumphed in the sack race by entering in an exceptionally large sack instead of the small ones handed out, enabling him to sort of skip rather than hop along the course. He collected another 10 shilling certificate in the egg and spoon with potatoes substituting for eggs because of rationing. With a little bit of lateral thinking and physical strength it was possible to see how bending a spoon around a raw spud ensured it couldn't fall out. We sailed close to the wind but our family set a games record.

The Skinner *pièce de résistance* was to come on the evening of the VE Day Olympics. A fancy-dress competition was held outside John Street Working Men's Club and a late entry appeared when Dad arrived dressed in a tigerskin rug usually found on Mrs Langley's floor. The sight was too much for me. I ran behind the club to hide my embarrassment. The judge, a member of the Jackson family we regarded as political enemies, awarded first prize to the Wild Man of Borneo, i.e. my father. I shudder to think what my dad's mates down the pit said, no doubt pulling his leg mercilessly. I'm sure he had an answer as well as the prize. The money for the certificates came from the profits of the company that owned the pit so they'd all contributed, unwillingly or otherwise.

I think of my parents often. My mother, Lucy, never outwardly complained about her life and nor will I about mine. Her singing filled the house. She sang in the kitchen when she did our washing, cleaning and cooking and, as a sideline, the washing of Mrs Langley, a local shopkeeper, whose house she also cleaned. Mother was from a large family – 12 in all – and there is another book to be written about all her brothers and sisters. Perhaps the most disappointing thing in her life was, as she told us more than once, that when she won a scholarship aged 11 to go to a 'higher grade' school, what we might call a grammar school, her parents couldn't afford to let her attend. She had a hard life, especially in those early years, but she was proud of us all for our work in the trade union moment; the political battles we fought and in particular the Clay Cross rent strike against Ted Heath's dictatorial declaration that every local authority would impose central government rent increases. She, like every other council tenant in Clay Cross, told Heath's housing commissioner to get lost. For a whole year he collected nothing and went back to Whitehall without a penny. Sadly, no other council managed to hold the line and Clay Cross Urban District Council stood alone for a full year before the Law Lords declared 11 councillors bankrupt and banned them from holding office for 14 years.

When my mother became ill with dementia it was a shock to us all. It happened so suddenly that most of the family could not believe what the medical authorities were saying. Then we quickly realised they were right: Lucy's short-term memory was rapidly fading away. It was heartbreaking to see our mother leaving us the way she did. We decided quickly that she should leave her three-bedroom house, with its stairs, and go into a small bungalow. It didn't work out. The unfamiliar surroundings made things worse. Inadvertently I learned a political lesson. I voted in Parliament against the Conservatives' bedroom tax, and Ed Miliband has promised that Labour will abolish it. Although the Tories currently exempt pensioners, who knows what that lot will do in the future. She would often walk out of the bungalow and try to find her way back to 41 Meadow Road, where we'd moved after John Street. I dread to think what could happen to someone with dementia walking the streets because of the bedroom tax.

Soon she couldn't even remember any of the family's names. Anybody who has been through this with a parent or another loved one will know the pain. To those who haven't, I can only say I hope you never do. When she was ailing, I decided to take her to the miners' welfare grounds, where we used to play football and cricket. On a park bench I sang to my mother to see if she could remember her favourites when she was bringing us up. I started with one of the Gracie Fields songs, 'Sally', that constantly filled our house. 'Sally, Sally, pride of our alley,' I sang, 'Sally, Sally . . . Don't ever wander, Away from the alley and me. Sally, Sally . . .' It worked. Her memory jogged back. For half an hour, on the deserted Clay Cross Welfare ground, we sang to our hearts' content. 'Sally' was followed by 'At 17 He Falls in Love', 'The Biggest Aspidistra in the World', 'If Those Lips Could Only Speak', 'My Heart and I', 'The Little Boy that Santa Claus Forgot' and 'I Like a Nice Cup of Tea'. For those precious 30 minutes she was with me again.

There is no doubt that all the great medical minds accept that singing comes from a different part of the brain to the areas ravaged by dementia, but in the late 1980s it was not generally recognised. I told my brothers and sisters and, despite some scepticism, we agreed that when we got the chance we would share what had happened on Clay Cross Welfare ground with a wider audience in the hope our experience would assist families facing similar challenges. Soon enough, in early 1990, I was asked to go on *Desert Island Discs*, Radio 4's show in which you're asked to pick eight tunes as if you were a castaway marooned on an island in the middle of an ocean. The first record I chose was Peter Dawson's 'If Those Lips Could Only Speak', a number my mother must have sung every week. The plan was for members of the family to sit with Lucy around the radio when it was broadcast. I asked the presenter, Sue Lawley, to play my first choice. The words and tune came out of the wireless and my mother, who could barely communicate with us, joined in to the very end. It was a day for us all to remember. She'd entertained us and raised our spirits so often and there she was, in her 79th year, still topping the bill.

I've never forgotten that little experiment and I sing to the residents when I visit old people's homes in the Bolsover area and invite them to sing along. It works so well that in Shirebrook the Shire Vale Centre started a regular early dementia class with singing at its heart. It goes without saying we need money spent on a dementia cure instead of wasting billions of pounds on wars.

Mother was to die in Clay Cross Hall, General Jackson's grand old home. The house, where we'd sing carols on Christmas Eve for a 12-cornered threepenny bit, was taken over by the county council in the 1960s and converted into a pioneering place for the vulnerable and elderly. We planted a tree in the garden when she died and long after she'd gone I returned. Remembering how she liked to sing, I sang to the residents who joined in. There was a man who was silent. The staff said he'd lived in Derbyshire for some time but was originally from London. 'I bet you know this one,' I told him, and began 'Maybe It's Because I'm a Londoner.' He did and joined in.

It was 1948 when we left John Street for a council semi at 41 Meadow Road in Holmgate, Clay Cross. Our new house was bigger, if still cramped because there were so many of us. It had proper bedrooms. Initially four boys – Gordon, Graham, David and me – shared two beds. But the beauty of Meadow Road was that we had a brand-new council house and, what is more, Joan, Hazel and myself were all working and bringing home a wage. None of us were employed by agencies and none of us were on zero-hours contracts.

So this is the start of my story, reminiscences from the boy born into poverty who, via a good education, 22 years down the pit and ten years as a councillor, was elected a Labour MP in 1970 and 11 general elections – and eight prime ministers – later is still representing Bolsover in Parliament, fighting for socialism. I've been lucky along the way, I'll admit. I'm aware age doesn't travel alone. I was fortunate to escape serious injury or the dreaded lung disease, pneumoconiosis, in the mines. The NHS, a wonderful Labour creation, was there for me when I needed a heart bypass and I was diagnosed with cancer. And I was blessed with an incredible memory for names and incidents – a boon for speeches on public platforms or in the House of Commons.

Before that first general election 44 years ago, I was sent a form to complete by *Who's Who*. I suppose the publisher wasn't expecting any surprises in a rock-solid Labour seat like Bolsover. The compilers recognised that I, barring disaster, would be the MP. It was like no form I'd completed before, the questions obviously designed for titled blue bloods rather than the horny-handed likes of me. I took it to the council and filled it in with my friends. I was asked by *Who's Who* which clubs I was a member of. I realised this section was the place to list the Pall Mall boltholes of a ruling class, the posh centres of power where a tiny, wealthy, privileged elite endured, over gin and tonics served to them by liveried flunkies as they luxuriated in deep leather armchairs. I'd thought of chucking the form in the bin, then on second thoughts had decided I'd reply honestly. I didn't write the Athenaeum, Carlton, Beefsteak, White's, Reform, Garrick or, if you've read P.G. Wodehouse, the Drones. At that stage I'd never even heard of the Bullingdon Club. But I was a member of Bestwood Working Men's in Clay Cross and numerous miners' welfares in Derbyshire. So I put them down.

The form asked about my pedigree. I don't recall the exact wording, but it was another blue-blood question. The only honest reply I could give was to tell *Who's Who* that I was from good working-class stock, good working-class mining stock. I am what I was made all those years ago, a product of the pit and the war. We were dealt a tough hand by a political and economic system which treated us as cheap, disposable labour. Everything we achieved as individuals, families, communities and as a class we had to battle hard to win. We reaped the gains of past victories and strove to improve the lot of the present and future generations. We laughed when I wrote the answers down, and didn't expect *Who's Who* to put them in. I was surprised when they did.

If my mother, Lucy, and my father, Tony, were here with us today they would marvel at iPods and iPads but they'd be familiar with the grotesque poverty and despair which scar our communities and blight lives, wasting potential and creating misery. From generation to generation we must stop passing on what is wrong – inequality, injustice – and sustain what is good – a sense of decency, fairness, concern, solidarity – to transform our country and the world for the better.

I've always heeded the advice of my father to stick to my guns and treat the Houses of Parliament as a place of work, a building where the people of Bolsover send me to do a job for them. I don't regard it as a cosy club where MPs, of all parties, gather to eat and drink together, to enjoy a comfortable life instead of representing those who put their trust in us through the ballot box.

I distrust patronage and put my faith in elections, declining offers of this, that and the other. The prime ministers who command authority by hiring also hold the threat of a firing to guarantee docility and loyalty, as I told the Labour Prime Minister Jim Callaghan when he offered me a job. Tony Blair should've known better when he complained I would've made a good minister if I'd accepted what he called responsibility. I call it the servitude of patronage.

I've also retained a belief and faith in the power of extra-parliamentary action, particularly through the trade unions. The 650 MPs in the Commons do not have a monopoly on political wisdom, as decisions taken regularly prove. I've been on more picket lines, marches and demonstrations, and spoken at more rallies and meetings than I can count. I've heard more truth, honesty and sanity from people outside Parliament than some of those inside. For 40 years and counting, I've listened to people and disagreed with opponents, particularly Tories.

I am proud to stand up for my class, to say publicly that I am from good working-class stock. I am proud to be a trade unionist, to be a member of the Labour Party and to be a socialist. I stick to my principles. I know no other way in politics. I make mistakes, everybody does. Nobody is perfect. I have no monopoly on the best way of being an MP. I try not to let anybody down. I've sailed close to the wind in my life but always for the good of the cause, to champion those at the bottom of the pile who deserve better.

I am proud, too, of my own children Dawn, Dennis and Mandy and all four grandchildren Matthew, Tom, Hannah and James. Raised in an era when men were taught never to show emotion publicly, I am what I am.

So here goes. It was all to start with a good education.

CHAPTER TWO

Mrs Langley's books

War was fascinating, even exciting, for a schoolboy. I was just seven years old when, on 3 September 1939, Prime Minister Neville Chamberlain announced on the wireless that we were at war with Germany because Hitler had ignored the ultimatum to withdraw from Poland. I was going down Market Street in Clay Cross not long after the announcement on the radio. 'Did you hear it, then?' I overheard a man asking a passer-by nervously. 'We are at war.' And so we were.

I recall sandbags being filled and placed across the windows in Clay Cross school, protecting the glass should bombs fall. I remember carrying a gas mask in a little square cardboard box, the inventor devising a container so awkward to carry it was a pain to cart about and often left at home. My parents shared none of my innocent excitement. Memories of the slaughter in the First World War were fresh for them. Mam and Dad knew that young men would be going off in the armed forces and dying. Our next-door neighbour, a Mrs Topliss, told mother she was very worried. Her two sons were in the Territorial Army. Her gravest concern was for the son 'ordered across the water', as she put it. We thought the poor lad must be heading to a ship, embarking for France or some other foreign shore. It subsequently emerged he'd been transferred from Grimsby to Hull, manning guns across the Humber.

As the war progressed, we were to spend many a night crammed in the cubby hole under the stairs, eight of us packed into what was a cupboard. Not far away the steel city of Sheffield was bombed incessantly. We stitched blankets together to black out doors and windows so not a chink of light escaped the Skinner house to guide the Luftwaffe navigators. We'd hear the siren warning the Heinkels were approaching overhead, a frightening wailing you didn't dare ignore. We'd pile into the cubby hole until the wonderful, sweet, mellow all-clear was sounded. Whoever devised the two tones, the harsh air-raid warning and the inviting all-clear, must have had a fine musical ear.

Any bombs not dropped on poor Sheffield would be dumped on Clay Cross, German pilots aiming for the railway junction where the lines from Nottingham and Derby joined or separated, depending on the direction you were travelling. On the morning after the night before, I'd go off with my dad to inspect craters. You could wait days to learn where the bombs had dropped, the sites and damage largely kept out of the papers and off the radio to avoid assisting navigators and bomb-aimers. In Tupton a couple were killed in Wingfield Road, about half a mile from the railway. There was a lot of tutting and muttering about how unfortunate they were.

It would be naive to think that, as an optimist, there wasn't part of me that believed from the beginning that we'd win in the end. It was our side or Hitler. As an avid newspaper reader, I totted up the losses on both sides during the Battle of Britain.

'Dad, we must be winning,' I insisted. 'I've counted all the German aeroplanes we've shot down. They can't have many of theirs left in the sky and we've lost hardly any.'

'Son, I don't think you should believe all that crap. It's wartime propaganda,' he replied, wearily.

He was right, of course. Winston Churchill could teach a thing or two to modern spin doctors when it comes to deceit. But reading about the battles was exciting. It started to be one-way traffic in our favour after El Alamein and Tobruk. I don't recollect much about General Montgomery when it turned his way in North Africa. I suppose the personality cult surrounding Churchill didn't leave room for anybody else. To me the Russian breakout from Stalingrad, breaching the German lines, was as thrilling as winning the FA Cup. Stories about Cossacks taking the lead conjured magical, if inaccurate, images of fierce warriors on horseback destroying Hitler's Panzers.

The war also introduced the great leveller that was rationing. I can't think of a fairer system in my lifetime for distributing food and necessities. It was a practical form of socialism. From sweets to clothes, we were for the first time guaranteed a share. Some capitalists exploited it – those with money were able to buy extras. But the black market was mostly a city curse. In rural areas there was a true spirit of camaraderie. It was as far as you could humanly get from the contemporary culture of instant gratification, symbolised for me by a DFS sofa sale with families offered it all and promised it now.

I'd been sent to school from the age of four in September 1936 because my mother was pregnant with brother Gordon and there was a place. I enjoyed attending Clay Cross infants and juniors. The classrooms were austere, pretty chilly. Since we knew no better school to compare it with, we were happy. As they usually were in that period, the toilets were outside at the bottom of the schoolyard. In winter the hard playground froze into a giant ice rink. The trip to the lavatory became a skate downhill with a slippery return.

I was born with the head start that is a good memory, an enviable capacity to absorb and recall huge amounts of information without breaking sweat. By the age of five I could name every capital in the world. I learned reading, writing and arithmetic with reasonable ease. My horizons were extended by listening to the wireless in the front room. Newspapers were a window into the world, transporting me from Clay Cross and beyond Chesterfield to the rest of Britain and then abroad.

Yet I recognise that everybody, including me, benefits from lucky breaks in life should they come your way. If my first was a useful memory, the second was Mrs Langley's books. Mrs Langley was the shopkeeper whose washing my mother took in to clean, dry and iron. Mother also did her house, scrubbing and polishing to keep it spick and span. This Mrs Langley was a kindly woman. She'd bought a shelf of books in the hope of landing her daughter a scholarship to Tupton Hall, a local 'higher grade' school that was similar to a grammar. To the disappointment of the Langley family, the plan failed and Mrs Langley's daughter didn't get her scholarship. But I was given her books. Mrs Langley, hearing from mother how much I loved to read, parcelled them up and they were brought to John Street.

I'd spend hours reading about geography and history, my nose stuck in Mrs Langley's books. I was receiving an education far beyond what was provided at school. Teachers noticed that I was improving, coming on in leaps and bounds. My memory was soon exploited to encourage other pupils. I'd be instructed to stand in front of the class and the teacher would chalk a poem on the blackboard. By the time she'd finished writing it, I'd have memorised all the lines. So I was ordered to speak the lines instantly. My memory has come in handy in the decades since, serving me well as a union representative, councillor and then MP. As a kid I was being exploited, forced to perform when all I wanted was to be part of the crowd. I didn't like what was happening but as a young kid you are powerless to do anything about it.

I was really motoring at school thanks to the boost from Mrs Langley's books. I was never aware of my parents pushing me, wanting me to do particularly well at school, until, aged 9, I was entered by my teacher, Mrs Bainbridge, for the 11-plus to win a free County Minor Scholarship to Tupton Hall. I was in what would now be called Year Five instead of the top primary class, Year Six, which usually supplied the candidates for the exam. Mrs Bainbridge thought I was ready and put down my name. I remember little of the exam except I passed. Had I failed I'd have had another crack the following year. But I was in. I later discovered this was the moment when my mother was willing me to do well at school, for her son to go to Tupton Hall. As I mentioned earlier, she'd also passed the 11-plus as a child but, one of 12 children, the family was too poor to send her to the school. The sadness of that missed opportunity drove her on. Mother was absolutely determined that I wouldn't suffer the same fate.

Many in authority expected the working class to know and keep its place. My success was swiftly followed by a rare visit to our house by the head of the juniors. He came not to praise but to caution. As a miner's son, he argued, I wouldn't fit in at Tupton Hall. The scholarships were precious and might, he counselled, be wasted on a street urchin with the bottom hanging out of his trousers like Dennis Skinner. He tried to force my mother to recognise there were more deserving cases than me. When I think back, it is hard to imagine a head could behave like that. He did, believe me. I'm not blaming him. He was as much a creation of circumstances as I.

I recall the whispering and hostile looks between my mother and the head as they disagreed over me, hushing their voices to debate my future. I failed to grasp the significance of what was going on, a naive child bewildered by the very presence of the head in John Street. Home visits weren't usually paid by such a remote figure. A formidable woman when riled, my mother wasn't intimidated. She wasn't having him come to our house and tell her to deprive her son of a place in a school. I'd won that entry to Tupton Hall on merit. He departed with a flea in his ear, never to return. And I, in 1942, at ten years of age, enrolled at Tupton Hall.

The school was mixed, educating boys and girls, which was unusual in those days. Other than that it had a very traditional ethos. Most of the pupils paid fees, we scholarship kids being the exception rather than the rule. We didn't consciously separate along class lines at Tupton Hall but we tended to mix naturally with people like ourselves; the wealthier kids, offspring of solicitors and doctors, would hang about together while I instinctively felt most comfortable with the sons of workers in Clay Cross.

We were each designated a house within the school. I was in Cavendish. I was to receive another lesson at Tupton Hall on what a marvellous leveller wartime rationing could be. With clothing in short supply, the uniform was pared down to a cap. Green rings signified I was in Cavendish House. I'd stick it in my pocket and put the thing on my head when I neared the school. But apart from that we could wear what we wanted. No regulation tie, shirt, jacket, trousers or shoes were stipulated. Had the family been presented with an expensive list to be bought from a gentlemen's outfitters in Chesterfield or some such place, social apartheid would've locked the gates to the likes of me. Apart from the cap, the only thing I needed was a school bag. Good old Mrs Langley returned as a fairy godmother, presenting me with her daughter's leather satchel.

In lessons the memory I'm blessed with was again a great boon. Latin, hated by many pupils, was simple if you could remember how to conjugate the verbs: amo, amas, amat, amamus, amatis, amant – I love, you love, he loves, we love, you love, they love. My Latin marks were always 90 per cent and upwards. I was good with numbers so maths wasn't a problem, a Tupton Hall education handy for the Killer Sudoku in *The Times* I do every day. History and geography were my type of subjects and I could write a decent essay. We studied Shakespeare and learned by heart long passages from *The Merchant of Venice*, *Macbeth* and *A Midsummer Night's Dream*. I'll admit I'm no fan of the Bard, his language unnatural in our era. I'll take the vivid descriptions of Charles Dickens over Shakespeare any day.

I was no stranger to trouble at Tupton Hall. Argumentative, unafraid to challenge accepted wisdom, I'd clash with teachers. Detention was a familiar partner in my school life. Drabble, the headmaster, once announced: 'Skinner! You wouldn't respond, so there is no point beating you.' As a result I was regularly made to stay behind after school. The punishment was lines, copying out the same repetitive sentence – 'I will behave in future', 'I will respect teachers' – over and over. Michael Gove, the Tory kid with the moist lower lip who was David Cameron's education secretary, is clueless when he bangs on about returning to traditional discipline and punishment. It didn't work then and it wouldn't work now. Lines were easy for me – scribble, scribble, scribble until allowed out. The only lesson it taught me was that dull, boring, mundane sanctions are a waste of time and fail to change how pupils behave.

Sport was a big part of Tupton Hall, the old building surrounded by playing fields. All that running up and down the pit tips, chased by older boys shouting they'd skin me like a rabbit, gave me the lungs and legs for cross-country. I was to be the school champion, able to keep on running when others were collapsing exhausted.

During the spring, summer and early autumn, I walked to the school. From John Street I'd trudge alongside the railway line past the coke works and the pit tip to the edge of the school grounds with the school building another half a mile on. In the winter or when the rain was torrential, I caught a double-decker bus in the green livery of Chesterfield Corporation. You could set your watch by them, they were so punctual. On the bus in the morning the other kids would borrow my memory on the way to school. I didn't see anything wrong in them copying my homework. I've always believed in the value of sharing.

Tupton Hall was very ambitious for most of its pupils, although we didn't all share the same academic goals. I smile when I remember the headmaster demanding to know what we wanted to be in life. I, in common with many of my age and class, didn't have much of a clue. I had experience only of the world in and around Clay Cross. One lad, Bill Leivers, had a dream. 'Professional footballer, sir,' he answered. Mr Drabble, the head, replied sternly: 'So you have wasted your time here.' That wasn't fair or accurate. Bill proved the head completely wrong. He lived the dream and was a professional footballer. The Clay Cross lad played for Chesterfield and won the FA Cup with Manchester City in 1956 when they beat Birmingham 3–1 at Wembley. The final is remembered in history as the final in which City's German goalie, Bert Trautmann, played on with a broken neck. I recall it as the day Bill from Tupton Hall won a medal. You could see he was a pretty good player at an early age. He was lucky he could play a bit because, as Bill would admit, he wasn't cut out for studying.

The war ended in 1945 and a couple of years later I passed my School Certificate. My mother and father hoped I would go to university. Dad pressed home how I'd had a great start to life as far was education was concerned. Tony Blair inadvertently misjudged my parents and schooling when I was a Labour backbencher and he was prime minister. He thought I was in the same boat as John Prescott, his deputy and my old flatmate, who'd failed his 11-plus. 'Dennis is', Blair wrote in *A Journey*, his autobiography, 'a really brilliant guy – first-rate mind, great wit, huge insight into people – but was brought up in the days when exceptionally clever people were regularly failed by the education system, or just fell between the cracks of poor schooling, and the narrow-minded views of parents and communities.'

I wasn't failed by the education system, although I could see the teachers pushed the kids harder from homes with money and raised their expectations higher. The working-class boys, including me, were proud to be at Tupton Hall, aware we'd worked our passage because our parents couldn't afford a ticket. Nor were my mam and dad narrow-minded – they valued good schooling. I was lucky. That I knew. My objection to the grammar system, and why I believe in comprehensives, is I was one of a lucky few when the majority would be wrongly written off by an 11-plus system unfairly dividing kids into sheep and goats. Everybody develops at a different age and everybody deserves a fair crack of the whip. In later years when a councillor, I was chair of governors when Tupton Hall and Clay Cross schools merged into a comprehensive. I ensured it was no takeover, teachers from both obtaining jobs in the new Tupton Hall. I know what a top school it remained from the experiences of my own children. Dawn, Dennis and Mandy thrived at the new Tupton Hall and all graduated with degrees from Manchester University.

Yet I wasn't interested in trying for university. To me, Oxford or Cambridge were hoity-toity. Universities as a whole were unappealing, alien. Peering back, I was already increasingly politicised. In 1944, when 12, I'd gone to hear the declaration of Harold Neal's Labour victory in a wartime parliamentary by-election triggered by the death of the party's MP George Ridley. The following year, aged 13, I went to listen to the Clay Cross result as Clement Attlee's Labour Party swept the board and pushed Winston Churchill out of Downing Street. I'd been assured by Dad that Attlee would be prime minister, defeating the war hero Churchill. We'd fought and dug for victory, benefited from rationing and didn't want to wind back the clock to the Depression. I'd also never stopped playing football and cricket with the kids from Clay Cross secondary.

Away from Tupton Hall, every evening and weekend I headed down to the miners' Welfare with its football and cricket pitches. As a schoolboy I kicked or hit a ball with the lads from the bottom end of Clay Cross. Later on, we would be joined by the young men from the Long Rows – two strips of forty-four houses each, including the birthplace of my mother – in the heart of the town. Many of them had already started work in the local Parkhouse Colliery. They acted like they were part of a close-knit society. They talked about the life underground and their language was about the world of work. I noticed the blackened fingernails. I still wore a Tupton cap with the Cavendish colours. They were not asking for help with their homework. They were busily painting a picture of an exciting, albeit dangerous, life underground. I had a Sunday paper round but they had a proper wage and, like my father, were members of the National Union of Mineworkers (NUM).

I joined the crowd and swapped studying for a wage and a proper job. Mam and Dad were devastated. I was rejecting an opportunity they never had for a new life. But their eldest son, at 16, wanted only to follow his father down the pit. It was to be the biggest education of my life.

CHAPTER THREE

Never show you're scared

I want to be absolutely honest: I don't remember my first day down the pit. I can't recall anything, really. I have a decent memory so it must have been a non-event, no big deal. When I look back, I see clearly lots of moments, incidents, during a defining 22 years of my life underground but not, genuinely, that first day.

And I'll tell you another thing. I never, ever romanticise life in the pit. I was there and it was a hard, dirty, noisy, tiring, dangerous job in a confined space. Only those who didn't do it could put an attractive gloss on backbreaking toil in the bowels of the earth. Yes, pound for pound there was more camaraderie in the pits than any other walk of life except, possibly, deep-sea fishing. Everybody knew they depended on everybody else. That carried through into the communities because we lived cheek by jowl with one another. But romantic? No.

Because going down the pit wasn't like walking into a factory or shop. We went into a very dark world where there were no toilets or running water to drink or wash with. The facilities were non-existent underground. There was no popping up for a breather, let alone lunch or a cup of tea and a fag. I ate what we called snap, a sandwich in a metal tin, with grubby hands wherever I happened to be. And it was thirsty work. Some would take three or four pints of water in a cylindrical metal bottle to keep them going.

Depending on the depth of the pit you were in, it was very cold or very hot. Parkhouse, my first colliery, was a shallow mine, just 120 yards under the surface. It was cold. In Parkhouse you could still be shivering two or three miles from the bottom of the shaft despite the physical exertion. Glapwell, the colliery I was transferred to in 1962 when Parkhouse shut, was deeper at 800 yards down and hot. To give you some idea of how warm it was, the cheese in our sandwiches would melt into the soggy bread. So that is the world I entered on leaving behind studying at Tupton Hall, and possibly university. Instead I chose a life battling against Mother Nature underground.

Parkhouse and Glapwell were just two of the ten collieries within a five-mile radius of our house in Clay Cross. There were also Morton, Shirland, Holmewood, Grassmoor, Williamthorpe, Ramcroft, Alfreton and Swanwick. I heard I'd get a start at Holmewood, but my dad knew the industry like the back of his hand and it had no baths. He told me Parkhouse, the pit he'd moved to from Morton, did have baths so I wouldn't come home filthy. Parkhouse, originally owned by George Stephenson, the railway pioneer who discovered coal digging the Clay Cross rail tunnel, lost 45 men and boys in an explosion in 1882. There's a stone memorial of a weeping widow in Clay Cross cemetery listing the dead, aged from 15 to 53.

When I started work at Parkhouse in 1948, the training lasted three months. I spent one day a week down Williamthorpe pit, a day at technical college in Chesterfield and three on the pit top at Parkhouse. I also went down Ramcroft during the period. It wasn't the cleverest thing I ever did. A surveyor needed another miner to help him to test the airflows with a wind gauge. I thought I'd like a crack at that and volunteered. I ended up carrying his bag all day long!

Clement Attlee's Labour government had nationalised the mines in 1947 and the National Coal Board didn't take over the pits until 1 January 1948, so safety standards were very limited. Pit boots, for example, weren't supplied, never mind compulsory. Some of the men wore wooden clogs. Pit ponies were widely used, about 20 stabled underground at Parkhouse. Some of the lads would ride them. The roadways weren't high enough so they'd hang on the side, like you see in Westerns.

As trainees we were put on what were called the coal screens to pick out pieces of rock as the coal rumbled past on conveyor belts. It was hard work grabbing the heavy pieces of stone. Nobody wanted to do it. Nor were we supplied with gloves. Your hands were cut raw. And we trainees, the fresh-faced new recruits, found ourselves working alongside miners crippled in accidents underground. There were several who'd suffered serious accidents, transferred to the screens on the surface to keep a job by standing all day on the remaining leg. It was brutal. My immediate reaction was 'Let me get that rock, it's heavy' and I'd stretch for the rock. The maimed miners were victims of an industry with a reputation as a killer. When I joined there were 700,000 miners in the country and every year between 500 and 700 pitmen lost their lives. Contrast that with the 148 workers killed at work in the whole of Britain, according to the Health and Safety Executive, in 2012–13. The 148 remains far too high, yet it underlines the extent of the carnage underground when I started.

When we went underground at Williamthorpe pit we were taught the rudimentary skills of the trade such as how to shovel coal, put down rails for the coal tubs to move on, and how to move it on bogies. There was a spot of bother when the gaffer tried to pull a fast one, using the apprentices to do the jobs of paid miners rather than training us. We weren't going to be exploited so we had what I suppose now would be dubbed a lightning strike, but at the time didn't feel significant. The others, who weren't very happy at the way we were used, wanted somebody to take the lead. We were spending hours shifting materials from one part of the pit to another. So we walked to the pit bottom. The pit bottom was where the cage lifted us back to the surface. The apprentices, 20 of us, walked along the roadway and sat down in protest. The gaffer ordered us back. We weren't shifting. Realising we weren't moving and therefore wanting us out of the way, he rang us off – pressed the button to call the cage. Up we went. On the surface we walked to the cricket pavilion which was used as the classroom for training purposes.

The next day I was called in to see the general training manager.

'You're the one who went to Tupton Hall,' he said, glaring at me. 'You're the opposite of the kid in the film.' He was referring to *The Guinea Pig*, a movie then just out about a tobacconist's son given a scholarship to a public school and starring Richard Attenborough. It was a cheap shot intended to hurt.

'I'm nothing of the sort,' I replied. 'We're members of the National Union of Mineworkers. I know the difference between training and using us as cheap labour.'

The manager wanted to bang on about how my education made me privileged, that I could've been a Clay Cross working-class guinea pig at university but chose to conform by following my dad and mates into mining.

'I come from a big family,' I told him, 'and know nothing about the middle-class rubbish you are spouting.'

The truth is I was a year older than the other trainees and therefore confident to challenge the gaffer. The lesson I learned was they never stepped over the mark again, replacing training with work. The manager knew we were in the right so tried to change the subject to middle-class guinea pigs. I wasn't having it. I knew it was stand up for yourself or they walk all over you.

At the technical college we learned, amongst other things, about the dangers of gases – methane, carbon monoxide and carbon dioxide, etc. – which were a miner's perpetual enemy. Sitting at the back of the class, I was next to a big lad called Darra Green. Big Darra, whose first name was actually George, had missed a lot of school. He could shovel coal forever, yet sadly couldn't read or write. The teacher asked me to spend my time helping him to read and write. I'd go through the alphabet with Darra, showing him how words made sounds. He was eager to learn and picked it up. Six months later, I rode past Darra at the pit gate on my bike. It was six in the morning and he was shouting the odds from Templegate, the *Daily Herald*'s horseracing tipster, the sport a big topic of conversation underground. Darra wanted everybody to know he'd mastered reading and numbers. Happy for him, I smiled as I cycled by.

The training officer at Parkhouse, Horace Reeves, predicted if I worked hard at the pit exams I could become an official or even a manager because I was quick on the uptake. I dismissed that as pie in the sky, a cushy job I didn't aspire to. My sole ambition was to work with my mates and stay with the NUM.

I'm willing to admit it could be very frightening underground until you became used to the routine dangers. Not that anybody confessed to fear. It was considered shameful to show you were scared. But the noise of the weight of the roof coming onto the creaking supports, pressing down on metal arches helping prevent millions of tons of earth from crushing us to death, was terrifying until we became used to it. So were controlled explosions to blast coal. Try to imagine thunder in a tunnel with everybody outwardly pretending they weren't bothered.

I felt the tension most of all in the cage taking us down the shaft. The winding gear at Parkhouse was steam-driven so we descended in silence slowly, struggling to avoid thinking about the awaiting dangers. Glapwell was electrically powered so we flew down, but that meant if it was stopped midway our metal lift would bounce violently on the cables. Nobody uttered a word, but we were all wondering what was wrong and there were cases of cages plummeting to the bottom. They talk about the stiff upper lip of public schoolboys, but we wouldn't twitch a muscle, including when we feared our number was up.

One of the great ironies was if you were fortunate enough to avoid accidents and the dreaded lung disease pneumoconiosis, the pit life was heavy physical work, often bent double with a shovel, heaving coal on to a conveyor belt, which kept you superfit. It's no surprise the Derbyshire mines produced strong, fast bowlers, great cricketers such as Cliff Gladwin, Les Jackson and Bill Copson. Miners were either knackered or crippled by the job, or still fit in their later years.

The worst I suffered was a broken ankle from a dropped block, which meant a few weeks off work, but there was another occasion during my time at the pit that I found myself in hospital. I'd been knocked down on the way to Parkhouse. I was waiting for a bus with a mate outside the Clay Cross Woolworth's when this lorry veered across the road and knocked us into the doorway. I was taken to hospital unconscious, but remember coming round to find the ward empty except for us. It had been cleared for victims of a mining disaster in Creswell, a town in the Bolsover constituency I was to represent. The pitmen never came. Eighty of them died, suffocated behind a fire sparked by a jammed conveyor belt on the night shift. Rescuers couldn't reach them. Disaster was never far away. We knew that.

So I survived the pits in good nick. Others weren't as lucky. A good runner, when somebody needed to be carried out on a stretcher I'd be put on the front to run backwards, quickly, for a couple of miles to watch the stretcher didn't come off the rails that usually carried coal tubs.

The tradition when there was a fatality was for a union man and a coal board official to break the news together. In the 1960s I was given this uncomfortable task after a pitman, aged 63 or 64, had died underground of a suspected heart attack in Glapwell pit. What happened next remains with me to this day. I went in the manpower officer's car to the man's home, a small terrace row near a Norman church in North Wingfield. As we approached the door, I felt the manpower officer hanging back. I knocked and the door was opened by a woman about to be told by two strangers that she had just become a widow. I can still vividly see the checked cloth stretched on a table, on top a porcelain jug of what I soon discovered was beer. It was like a scene out of D.H. Lawrence's *Sons and Lovers*. Her husband was late back so I think she knew something was wrong. I told her he wouldn't be returning, the suspected heart attack killing him. The official, Griffiths I think his name was, nodded in sympathy. How do you leave a house after that? Boy was it difficult.

Over the years I was drawn into the NUM and, thanks to the union, received my second education. Dad was the Parkhouse delegate to the Derbyshire NUM. The area's secretary was Bert Wynn, a wonderful man to whom I owe a lot. He was a Marxist who quit the Communist Party over the Soviet Union's 1956 invasion of Hungary. Very intellectual and attuned to the idea that knowledge is power, Bert created day-release courses for miners to study industrial relations, economics and politics. He persuaded the Coal Board to stump up half the cost, the NUM covering the other half.

The day-release courses for Derbyshire and Yorkshire miners were a model of progressive education for trade unionists. I'd troop off to Sheffield University's extra-mural department between 1956 and 1959. I was reading and learning about working-class culture and analysing capitalism. The tutors were first rate. John Hughes went on to be principal of Ruskin College in Oxford. Royden Harrison stepped into E.P. Thompson's shoes as a professor at Warwick University. Economist Kenneth

Alexander became Sir Kenneth. Another tutor, John Mendelson, had a clipped accent and he'd talk about his friend who was a Tory MP in the City of London. I thought Mendelson, elected Labour MP for Penistone in a 1959 by-election, a pedant. I was wrong. He taught me how to be precise, to get my facts spot on, to strengthen an argument.

Not everybody could write the essays set for us. One of my close friends, a miner married with children, always complained he lacked the time and energy to do the essays. He could talk the hind legs off a donkey. The problem was, essays weren't his thing, so for several weeks I'd write a second essay for him on John Stuart Mill or, on one occasion, Karl Marx. I would always write a couple of pages for my mate and probably half a dozen for myself. Naively I believed the tutor would not know that I had written both. Harrison wasn't fooled. He told us he was fed up reading the same essay twice every week. The trouble was I could see only one right answer, the conclusions identical however expressed. Sadly, I'm afraid my friend quit before the end of the course.

Industrial relations were a constant battle and Dad had drilled into me the value of miners standing together, although he was sacked in 1953 and blacklisted a second time. He had a row with the manager, Carter, at Parkhouse. They wanted him out of the way and seized the chance. He was given an ultimatum to grovel or be fired following a confrontation over working conditions. 'It's like asking me to put my head in the oven,' he said. The manger knew Dad couldn't. The word went round locally not to employ trouble-maker Tony Skinner. He eventually made a second comeback a couple of years later when, five miles away, Shirland needed miners.

*

I won a pithead ballot to be the Parkhouse delegate to the Derbyshire NUM by a convincing majority of 440 of the 600 votes cast by the men at the pit: I'd demonstrated that, like Dad, I could win an argument. I forced myself to read the 1954 Mines and Quarries Act so I knew as much as the manager. Pitmen thought because I'd been to Tupton Hall I must also be clever. My formidable memory helped, and I'm absolutely sure a lot of my votes were because I was my dad's son, judging from the number of miners who constantly called me 'Tony Skinner's son' instead of Dennis Skinner.

When Parkhouse closed in 1962 I was transferred to Glapwell pit. In 1964 I was elected Derbyshire vice president, then president in 1966, aged just 34, the youngest in the area's history. The duties included chairing the council meeting, every month, of delegates from all the pits in the Derbyshire area in the union's headquarters in Saltergate, Chesterfield. The pay of miners had fallen relative to other workers. It took the successful national disputes in 1972 and 1974 to restore parity. The presidency put me on a committee overseeing NUM investments. Royden Harrison's tutoring in Sheffield, including how to read the *Financial Times*, came in handy. Plus I made sure we didn't touch oil or apartheid South Africa.

In 1966 I was persuaded to stand for the Derbyshire NUM as compensation agent, a full-time paid post concerned essentially with wages. There were thirteen candidates and in the pithead ballot I led until the last, when I was pipped at the post by Peter Heathfield. He went on to be the area's secretary, then the union's national general secretary shortly before the start of the 1984–5 Strike for Jobs. I'm not the type to dwell on how life might have changed had I won. I was regularly speaking at meetings in pit canteens and I also represented injured miners at tribunals in Nottingham, mistaken for a lawyer by claimants as I learned how to refine arguments and craft a winning case.

The papers were studied the night before and I'd pop off to Nottingham where the tribunals were held. I'd meet the miner, then make an argument to the panel as to why the injured man should receive financial support. I was given some of the harder cases and had a pretty good record, but you couldn't win them all. Gordon was a miner who'd injured his right arm. He was also a good darts player in an era when the sport was really popular, with a team in every pub, club and miners' welfare. The tribunal hearing was to consider an application to increase Gordon's compensation. I went through the case beforehand with him, and in we trooped.

The award should be raised, I argued, because it wasn't only Gordon's ability to work that was damaged but his darts. He'd nearly made the county team, I said, and now found it difficult to throw a dart straight. I asked Gordon to show the panel how his dart arm was impaired. He raised a shaky limb to half the height required to play before dropping it, in pain, to his side. The chairman of the panel was wily. A director of Sheffield United, he knew his sport. He engaged Gordon in a discussion about darts, asking if Gordon had met the big names in the game the chairman had seen on TV. The pair were having a good old chat when the chairman said it must be awful that Gordon couldn't play properly any more, and he asked him to show how he threw a dart before the injury. Gordon fell for it and raised his right arm to give a perfect demonstration, as if he was on the oche and throwing for double top to win a tournament. It was like a scene in *Columbo*, when Peter Falk's detective would spring a final question to catch the criminal. Gordon was chalked down as a defeat.

Playing an ever-greater role in the union saw me sent on a few delegations abroad. There was an anti-nuclear weapons protest in Paris, and we paid a solidarity visit to the international miners' conference in Moscow. I skipped the visit to peer at Lenin in his Red Square mausoleum. Displaying a dead body is not quite my style. But I wasn't a great one for these travels. It wasn't my scene.

I learned a lesson in 1959. I had been dispatched on an NUM delegation to a World Youth conference in Vienna. Derbyshire voted to send Eric Varley, a future Labour energy secretary, and me. The conference was organised by the World Youth Council. We were taken to a football stadium on the outskirts of the Austrian capital where the organisers spent the entire time shouting slogans, calling on us to join the chanting. They'd shout and the idea was we would shout back. I said to Eric: 'Have we come all this way to do this?' It went on for hours. I got fed up and left to walk around Vienna. I believe in speaking out, arguing, debating. This was yelling the same slogan again and again. Bonkers.

They were heady industrial and political times when I was at the pit. I saw miners picketing away from their own collieries for the first time in 1969 during a strike over the poor pay of surface workers. Derbyshire pushed for industrial action and there were walkouts in Wales, Scotland, Yorkshire, Kent and Durham as well as Derbyshire. Glapwell was a two-pit complex with a deep colliery and a shallow drift mine. On a Monday morning men from Shirebrook and Warsop arrived to help us cover all the entrances. Miners doing the same in future disputes would be called flying pickets.

I'd joined the Labour Party in 1956, aged 24. The NUM was a pillar of the party, affiliated to Labour. Both the union and party existed to improve the lot of the working class. As with the union earlier, I was becoming drawn into the Labour Party, attending meetings and annual conferences.

In 1960 I saw a notice in the pit canteen about writing an essay of 2,000 words for a scholarship to Ruskin College, the trade union education institution linked to Oxford University. I wrote the essay and I was offered the Robert Smillie scholarship, in memory of a remarkable trade unionist, Belfast-born and one of a family of fifteen. Smillie was a socialist miner in Scotland and contemporary of Labour's first MP and leader Keir Hardie, who battled tenaciously to improve terms and conditions. I wrote the essay on the industrial relations and economics in the mining industry, but had to turn down the place I was offered. On top of my union duties, I'd been elected to Clay Cross council in 1960 and couldn't see how I could do both jobs and spend weeks away at Ruskin. The Tupton Hall boy who'd rejected university for the pit now put politics before college.

My overlapping involvement in the union, and increasingly the party, resulted in a peculiar brush with notoriety during the 1964 general election campaign which ended in Labour's Harold Wilson defeating Old Etonian Alec Douglas-Home to end thirteen years of Tory rule. Bert Wynn had joined Labour after leaving the Communist Party and asked me to help Wilson's deputy, George Brown, win in Belper. Bert picked me up and we drove to

Crich, a town in the Peak District famous for its inland light-house. Brown was late, as usual. Bert kicked off the rally, with me coming in when he flagged. When Brown eventually arrived, we legged it to the next meeting in Lea Green. Brown had made us late and the man holding the fort was glad to see us. Bert opened, then gave me the nod. I was extolling lessons a Labour government could learn from Clay Cross, particularly the building of houses for families and the elderly. Brown appeared and I shut up and gave him the floor. Brown announced he was glad I was talking about mortgages. I wasn't. He was close but not quite there. Brown, destined to be Wilson's secretary of state for economic affairs, was determined to concentrate on mortgages. He dropped a bombshell by announcing he thought interest rates should be cut to three per cent, a two per cent reduction.

The press pack trailing Brown scribbled furiously. The papers were full of the controversy. The statement was interpreted variously as a huge gaffe and a calculated attempt to switch the debate away from nuclear weapons. Newspapers began running around to track down everyone at the rally. Bert told them I was called Charlie Makepeace to throw them off the scent when he was pinned down. Peggy Robinson, a reporter on the *Daily Express*, called at our house and asked my wife, Mary, if she had a photograph of me. The only picture was in the passport I'd used for the Vienna conference. Robinson, a go-getter of a journalist, tracked me down to the Furnace Inn where I was sheltering with Charlie Bunting, a miner and future Clay Cross rent rebel. I was sitting behind a vase of chrysanthemums when Robinson marched in. She saw me behind the flowers and came over.

'Where were you on Saturday night?' she demanded.

I turned to Charlie. 'Where was I, Charlie, on Saturday night?'

'He was propping up this bar with me,' answered Charlie, not entirely accurately.

'Well, I have reason to believe that you were campaigning with George Brown.'

I didn't reply. She departed, vowing to write the story. She had my photograph in her bag. I hatched a plan with Peter Heathfield. He rang the *Sunday Express* posing as my lawyer. With me prompting him in the background, Heathfield told the paper: 'You acquired a passport and photograph without the permission of the holder. You're not entitled to publish this or any part thereof.' It was legal mumbo-jumbo we concocted to get out of a tight spot. I mean, why would a paper want to publish 'part thereof' of a passport photo?

It must have done the trick. My picture didn't appear and I dodged the fallout, but the *Express* papers ran the story for a few days. According to the authoritative David Butler guide to the 1964 election which resulted in a Labour marginal win, Labour secured the victory by concentrating on important domestic issues instead of defence. So the *Express* episode left me without a passport in exchange for a Labour win. Not a bad swap.

CHAPTER FOUR

More to lose than their chains

My time as a councillor almost ended before I'd really got started.

Electioneering was planned as if it was a military campaign after I was asked, as a reasonably well-known union man, to help oust the Tories dressed as Independents who sneakily took control of Clay Cross Urban District Council under false colours towards the end of the 1950s. We had to fight back.

Clay Cross Labour Party asked me to be editor of the *Clay Cross Clarion*, with Bill Lander as deputy. Running to just four pages, it didn't match the *Daily Mirror* and nor was I Lord Beaverbrook, but we asked difficult questions of the council and printed the answers under the headline The Truth. We handed out copies in the marketplace and pushed it through letterboxes. A few small shops took out adverts to raise a little bit of money to cover our costs.

I'd knock on doors and hold street-corner meetings, pitching up with a loudspeaker to make a speech and take questions from the crowd. We did this day after day. It worked. I won and Labour took control of the council in 1960 with a majority of one. We knew we needed to keep our promises to replace slums by building houses, with bungalows and wardens for the elderly, as well as opening Darby and Joan clubs so they had places to go.

Elections in Clay Cross were on Saturdays every year, with a third of the seats up for grabs in a three-year cycle. Elections in neighbouring Chesterfield were on Thursdays, so we'd go and help them out and they'd return the favour on Saturdays. I nearly came a cropper when, in one contest, a feller drove over in a minibus from Chesterfield to give us a hand ferrying the infirm and elderly to the polling stations. When we'd finished, he dropped me off at home. It was just him and me in an empty bus. The following day, there was this loud knock on the door. I answered and a copper was standing on the doorstep. He said I'd been seen using a minibus with a Public Service Vehicle (PSV) licence in the election and that was unlawful. What? I didn't even know what a PSV was. 'Is this another Tory trick?' I asked, interpreting his refusal to respond as an acknowledgement. I realised it sounded serious, so minded my Ps and Qs.

I was charged with illegally using a hackney carriage to carry electors, or their proxies, to and from the polls. I was summonsed before an election court and threatened, if guilty, with all sorts of punishments including fines and a ban from elected office. To give myself a fighting chance, I obtained a copy of the relevant act to study every single clause. The outcome rested, as far as I could see, on whether I had 'knowingly' used a PSV vehicle. The court found against me in September and I was fined a hefty £620 – more than 20 weeks' wages – and ordered to pay another £65 13s 6d in the old money (£65.68) in expenses, plus 12½ guineas (north of an extra £13) in legal costs.

I felt a furious grievance and went back to the act to read and re-read each line until I knew every word, comma and full stop. I appealed. The hearing was in Derby that November in the magistrates' court. I rehearsed the arguments in my head on the bus there. Hiring a barrister cost £30, over a week's wages then. He'd no experience of a case like mine so I found myself educating him. The appeal hinged on an exchange with the prosecutor over this question of 'knowingly' using it.

'Mr Skinner, you're vice president of Derbyshire NUM and the union has two holiday centres. Is that correct?'

'Yes. In Skegness and Rhyl.'

'And miners fix a week's holiday to stay in one or the other?'

'Aye, that's right.'

'And a lot go on minibuses?'

'Yes, though many go on travel buses with thirty or forty seats.'

'And have you been to Skegness or Rhyl in one of these minibuses, which surely you would know must have a licence?'

'I can put your mind at rest because I've never been to Skeggy or Rhyl miners' camps for a holiday.'

'So you're the vice president and you haven't visited two union holiday centres?'

'You might find it hard to believe, but no, I haven't. Nor have I been on holiday with my mother and father. We've never had the money. Putting food in our bellies was more important than holidays in our house.'

The court ruled on the 'knowingly' issue that 'after considerable heart-searching we are not sure that he did', which smacked of disappointment on their side. That sentence said more about the magistrates than me. Had I lost I would've been barred from the council. Who knows if it would've stopped me becoming an MP. All I knew was my innocence and hatred of losing.

I was to sit on Clay Cross council from 1960 to 1970 and Derbyshire County Council from 1964 to 1970. I was put up for Derbyshire to defeat a local doctor, Dr Hammerton, who won with patient support. It said Independent on his ballot paper but I found he'd been slipping into Tory group meetings. Nobody could shift him: he'd always topped the poll. I must have seen more of his patients than he did as I relentlessly knocked on doors and held street-corner meetings.

We knew we had to keep on delivering, ahead of future Liberal Democrats, when it came to pavement politics. We had Ashover Road paved, to the delight of residents who'd fought fifteen years for a footpath. We introduced free chiropody for the old and infirm of Clay Cross, Danesmoor and Holmgate at the Clay Cross clinic. We obtained £750,000 for an extension to Tupton Hall comprehensive which became a showcase in the county. We fought hard for Clay Cross but we were never blinkered.

We also felt a strong bond with other mining areas. The year 1966, when England won the football World Cup at Wembley, was also the year disaster struck at Aberfan in South Wales. I'll never forget the time and date. At 9.15 a.m. on Friday, 21 October, a pit tip slid down the mountain and engulfed all in its wake. A junior school was in the path of the avalanche of mining waste and 116 children perished. It took nearly a week to recover all the bodies, 144 in total including 28 adults.

Everyone in Britain, especially those of us in pit communities, was horrified. An Aberfan Fund was set up and as the then chair of Clay Cross council, I announced that I would contribute the £25 chairman's allowance. Someone muttered that we should keep part, but I insisted we donate the lot. I wouldn't be spending it anyway. 'The people of Aberfan need it more than we do,' I told councillors. The fund raised £1,750,000 – equivalent to more than £20 million today – and the local people erected a beautiful memorial in the cemetery with part of the money. However, that wasn't the end of it for Clay Cross and, indeed, many mining communities across the country.

In August 1967, following the inquiry into the Aberfan disaster, every area with pit tips overlooking built-up areas was asked by the Labour government to consider if there might be any danger to 'people and property'. The pit tip I'd played on was inspected by, in our case, a retired officer from the armed forces. We decided amongst ourselves the tip could be dangerous even though the tip's profile hadn't changed since the Home Guard dug that trench to fight the Nazis. The fact is we wanted it gone, the land levelled, so we could build houses and factories. It might have been an adventure playground when I was young, but residents complained it was an eyesore and interfered with the TV signal. Nobody wanted *Coronation Street* to be hazy.

We drew up a plan of action. It was agreed that a couple of councillors together with Joe Rysdale, the council surveyor, would escort the Colonel, as we called the inspector, up the tip so he could be shown the possible danger. On the day of the visit we climbed up the tip and the Colonel asked about the risk of spontaneous combustion because he thought he could see smoke as he neared the top, fearing smouldering coal underneath might erupt into an inferno. It wasn't smoke, but nor was it in our interest to contradict him. Earlier in the day it had been raining heavily and it was in fact steam as the water evaporated in the sun. Nobody challenged his theory. He poked about near the top for a while before we descended and, when he got his breath back, declared that because of the close proximity to houses and the smoke coming off the tip, he was declaring it unsafe. Within weeks we were awarded a government grant to remove it. The people in the town were, in the main, overjoyed at the prospect of improving the Clay Cross landscape, and gratefully gave us another resounding Labour victory at the following election.

The Civil Service issued us with a list of possible contractors to flatten the pile. We rejected the names of large national and multi-national companies and put the project out to tender. The lowest bid, of less than £70,000, was accepted. Some officials cautioned the bid was so cheap for the amount of work that we should seek a meeting with the firm. A visit was arranged and when we walked into the yard we could see state-of-the art machines.

'How could your bid be so much lower than the firms on the official list?' I asked.

'Simple,' the contractor replied. 'We're working on the M1 and the contract is completed. We've another job in two months and instead of leaving our machines and men idle, we can flatten your tip and spread out the waste in the surrounding area, providing you with an industrial development area before we resume our normal business on the motorway.' They sold it to us.

We all heaved a collective sigh of relief and reported back to the council, confident the task would be completed on time. It was, and in the next six weeks hundreds of retired miners and others watched all day long as they saw the giant machines change the Clay Cross landscape for ever. Now it is known as the Bridge Street industrial estate, with more than a dozen businesses operating at any given time.

Forty years later, in Parliament I asked Chancellor Gordon Brown for more than £30 million to flatten the Shirebrook and Markham pit tips so that they could be turned into industrial sites so vast that upwards of 8,000 people would be employed. I obtained the money and, as of now, more than 2,000 people work on the sites. Had it not been for the global financial crash and world recession in 2008, my guess is that the figure would be double that now.

The Markham development also provided me with another parliamentary idea: what about a motorway link straight off the M1 into the old pit yard? When I called in the chamber of the House of Commons for the new junction, 29A, on the M1, I was initially told to forget it. I wasn't going to give up that easily. I persuaded transport ministers to examine the idea; then finally after nearly two years of questions to ministers in various departments, a junior minister in the Department for Transport, Plymouth MP David Jamieson, gave me the thumbs up and announced 29A had got the go-ahead and would be known as Skinner's Junction. The whole area is now changing. Something like 3,000 miners worked in the three Markham pits and workshops and post-recession the site, together with the adjacent Coalite site, could provide well in excess of 6,000 jobs. All we need now is a change of government and the replacement of austerity economics with a ten-year growth plan.

All the growth, however, has to be accompanied by a totally new employment strategy. The Labour government has to get rid of zero-hours contracts and agencies that exploit the workers and effectively outlaw trade union membership, refusing to hire anybody who joins a union. Let us get back to the days when the Labour Exchange or Jobcentres provided people with work, and employment agencies didn't short-change and abuse people. Men and women today are worried about being undercut by foreign labour. The real problem is that agencies act as middlemen, taking a cut of wages. When I worked in the coal mines in the late 1940s, Poles and Ukrainians were employed in nearly every pit. They were regarded as displaced persons after the war. I can't remember any serious objections. And why? Simply because a) they were not employed by agencies, b) they were paid the same wages as us and c) they were all members of the NUM or the appropriate trade union! Today these lessons should be learned and practised in every private or public firm in Britain.

I sailed close to the edge more than once in those days. During the late 1960s we heard much about an age of leisure which never arrived, but Harold Wilson appointed the first Minister for Sport, Denis Howell, and created a Sports Council to improve facilities. I was interested in sport, having played football and cricket, and enjoyed cross-country running. The Sports Council in the East Midlands called a meeting in Leicester 1966 and I was the obvious choice for Clay Cross. I've always been punctual and set off early on the train. It paid off.

The Sports Council had a big map with blue or red flags stuck in towns. I saw Clay Cross was flagless. I asked a Sports Council official next to the chart: 'What do these flags mean?' Blue were for proposed golf courses, red for prospective swimming pools.

'Why isn't there anything in Clay Cross?' I inquired.

'We understood it already has a miners' Welfare swimming pool,' he shot back.

I had to improvise. 'My information', and that was the term I used, giving me room to wriggle if I bellyflopped, 'My information is it's closed or closing. The pits are shutting too. Clay Cross has had a pounding for a few years now. It could do with a new baths.' Believe it or not, he took another red flag out of a box and pinned it on Clay Cross.

I caught the train back to Clay Cross to tell the chair to call an immediate extraordinary meeting of the Housing and Public Health Committee. I explained we might get a new baths if we shut our dilapidated pool there and then. We only needed to meet for five minutes or so. Frank Green, the council officer in charge of the old baths, looked askance. More and more chlorine had to be put into the pool and he knew it couldn't go on forever, but this turn of events was sudden.

Frank pulled the plug and we did replace the baths with a new Rykneld pool named after the old Roman road. I pushed my luck. But I didn't lie. We didn't have a pool by the time the Sports Council gave us the green light and the money to help build the replacement. At a meeting in Clay Cross YMCA, 500 or 600 came to hear our plan to construct the new baths and we thought there'd be trouble about the cost until I said we had to put only one old penny on the rates and the rest of the money would be given to us. Most of the the audience cheered and we knew we were on our way.

I recounted this story recently to a grandmother, a constituent, who was telling me she takes her disabled granddaughter to the Rykneld. She laughed. I don't know if she believed me but it's true, although I'm pretty certain we wouldn't get away with the same stroke today because central government has cut local council finances by 40 per cent and more.

We rooted the council in the community, drawing strength from working people and serving those we never forgot were in charge via the ballot box. To symbolise change, we moved Clay Cross Urban District Council's headquarters to new offices in the old Victoria Buildings on the High Street. The place was roomy, with large cellars. I joked at the official inauguration in July 1965 that we hoped to avoid any Guy Fawkes activities. 'The public will be the openers of the new offices,' I said at the ceremony. 'If public service is presented properly, the people will take an interest.' And they did, with the turnout in council elections topping 70 per cent as we were returned with thumping majorities.

I had no interest in the fripperies of office – I wanted to *do* things. My election in 1966 to chair Clay Cross Urban District Council created a series of events which saw the law changed. Traditionally the chair was expected to wear a gold chain of office of the heavy type that might dangle from a mayor's neck. I objected on principle. I was a miner and would not be placed above other people. There was a fierce private argument among Labour councillors, delaying the public meeting of the council. I walked in and the clerk of the council, with great solemnity, opened a wooden box to produce a glittering chain known as the badge of office. He then tried to hang it on me. 'I'm not putting that on,' I declared. He, admittedly in a tricky position, muttered something like 'Perhaps on another occasion' and put it back in the box. I was elected to represent people – not dress up.

I wanted the chain melted down and the money deposited in the housing revenue account to build new homes. The redundant jewellery was instead donated to what is now the People's History Museum in Manchester, although I heard the municipal ornament was either lost or stolen.

I also stopped people standing up when I entered the room. I sat on what was known as the Scarsdale Valuation Panel. Named after a member of the aristocracy, it set the rateable value for properties and businesses. We'd hear appeals from people claiming they were paying too much. I stepped in for the chair and when I entered the room they all stood up. 'Hey, what are you doing?' I asked. 'You're not standing up for me. Sit down.' I was there to hear arguments, not to be shown a deference I disliked.

The chain wasn't all I rejected as chair. The post came with an additional position as a Justice of the Peace. How bloody ridiculous can you get? The idea you were appointed automatically as a magistrate because you chaired a council was ludicrous. It smacked of an era when worthies would ride around Derbyshire or other counties locking up striking miners on the say-so of the mine owners. So I rejected the seat on the bench on the grounds that magistrates should be properly trained.

There was the predictable fuss. I was called a wrecker, destroying traditions. I thought it had died down until a meeting at the newly merged Tupton Hall comprehensive. I chaired the governors to guarantee all the jobs didn't go to grammar school teachers so staff at Clay Cross secondary had a look in.

The head, Mr Rice, smiled and said: 'You've made it, Mr Skinner.'

'What?'

'You're in *The Times*.'

'Oh, I'm always in the *Derbyshire Times*. They hate my guts.'

'No, *The Times* in London.'

I didn't read that *Times*. I was aware of the controversy generated locally and hadn't fully appreciated how it rippled far wider. It wasn't until recently that I saw that editorial from May 1966 in *The Times* of London rather than the *Derbyshire Times*. The position I took as chair of an urban district council covering 10,000 people contributed to a change in the law on magistrates. Under the headline More to Lose than their Chains, *The Times* thundered:

Mr Skinner, chairman of the Clay Cross urban council in Derbyshire, deserves a round of applause for declining to wear his chain of office because he feels that it is old-fashioned and apt to promote self-importance. Not many councillors are likely to join his campaign to persuade mayors of the world to unite against pomposity – having, as they were once reminded, nothing to lose but their chains. That was an over-simplification. The spirit should nevertheless be encouraged.

The royal commission on local government is on its way mainly because of the Minister of Housing's belief that the British people are right in suspecting that the present system is wholly out of date. There have always been trenchant critics of the pretensions of local government: but the critics have become louder as local government has had to cope with more and more detailed planning and administration. A preoccupied manner becomes rather more fitting that a benign, dignified air.

The prophet from Clay Cross is even sounder about his refusal to serve on the local bench of magistrates merely because, as chairman of the council, he can claim such as position by virtue of tradition. The views of Lord Gardiner, the Lord Chancellor, about ex-officio magistrates are well known: he wishes to discourage such appointments. They derive from the infancy of British legal history, and have precious little relevance to the duties of magistrates in modern times.

The local bench has an armoury of punishments and remedial treatments at its disposal, and they are the second line of defence against crime. The knowledge (or ignorance) of current penal methods and thought which they bring to their duties could have a profound effect upon criminal behaviour. The work of the magistrate is, of necessity, becoming more specialized and more difficult. It requires training of a kind not inevitably acquired in the service of local government. As mayors, too, are getting busier, the time has come for the two offices to be separated.

I'd convinced the Establishment of magistracy madness! It doesn't rank up there with the fundamental legal reforms of Wilson's Swinging Sixties, however. The Lord Chancellor, Lord Gardiner, legislating to require magistrates be trained wasn't abolishing the death penalty, decriminalising homosexuality or permitting women to control reproduction. But down the pit we laughed at what one of the lads called the Skinner Act.

I finally went to Ruskin in 1967 for two ten-week terms on a political course. By this stage a little older and much wiser, realising I could be a councillor, NUM representative and a student, I went home to Derbyshire most weekends as well as for important meetings. I'd hitchhike or a group of us would hire a car, me getting out in Clay Cross, mates Bob Jones going on to Goldthorpe and Jock Milne to Sheffield. The tutors liked my essays but complained

I didn't, as they put it, give answers 'in the round'. What they meant was to reflect the views of Conservatives and assorted right-wingers. I replied they enjoyed enough coverage in the Tory press and I considered issues from a socialist perspective. I also learned to play tennis, a game I grew to really enjoy.

I attended trade union schools in Wortley Hall, a trade union centre near Barnsley. One of the lecturers was Ralph Miliband, Marxist father of Ed and David. He was part of a left-wing crowd radicalising the NUM. In the 1950s and 1960s it wasn't a left-wing union. That changed to some extent in the 1970s. But the union was never as far or as firmly on the left as the Tories and their propagandists in the newspapers claimed, either through ignorance or deliberate distortion.

I was fulfilled as a union representative and councillor. I was married with three children. The involvement of my brothers in politics saw Clay Cross referred to as Skinner Town. I was pretty contented with my lot. Then I was asked by the NUM to run for Parliament to stop somebody else.

CHAPTER FIVE

'Why tha' waddling tha' bloody arse?'

'Eey up, Tony, that lad of thine has passed our house three times this week waddling his bloody arse.'

Miner Tommy Lunn's ribbing of Dad was my first taste of how much of a stir my road walking was causing in our corner of Derbyshire. I discovered I'd been spotted when I was sitting innocently at the dinner table after coming off my shift.

Father piped up: 'Ey up, thee. I want to ask you something. What tha' doing at night? Tommy Lunn stopped me twice. Twice I have been asked why tha' waddling tha' bloody arse.'

Mam was listening and jumped in to defend me. 'You were complaining when he was going in the pubs,' she scolded him. 'Now he's changed his life. Leave him alone.'

I had changed my life. I was shocked when my Uncle Nip was killed after he came out of the Elm Tree pub on Christmas Day and was hit by a car. I was keeping out of pubs and had started running to get fit. I saw an advert in the *Sheffield Star* over Easter 1956 for the Star Walk on Whit Tuesday. This was a big road walk race with a huge field, a heel-and-toe competition famous in

Yorkshire and beyond. Sheffield steelworkers were given the Tuesday off and as many as a quarter of a million people would line the route. I decided to enter.

Roland Hardy had won in a previous year. He was already a legend in Derbyshire. Hardy was British champion and held the 10km world record. He'd been well placed in the 1952 Olympic Games in Helsinki before he was pulled up for what is known as 'lifting', failing to keep a toe or heel on the ground. The ruling was a massive shock at the time because Hardy had such a lovely, smooth walking style and it was difficult to imagine him putting a foot wrong.

So I told Dad I was training for the race, and he wasn't at first what you'd call enthusiastic.

'You mean tha' going in a walk that Roland Hardy won? What can tha' do in that walk against him? He was in the Olympics.' Dad's tone was I'd finish down the field, that I didn't have a chance. The Skinner family way was to be in it to win it and he feared I'd be hammered.

'Tha' might be interested to learn,' I responded, pushing my luck, 'Roland Hardy can't go in it after winning it. The top three can't enter again.'

Tommy Lunn had picked up on the unusual style of road walkers. My hips would waggle in an exaggerated style because I needed to swing them to reach a fair pace. I'd build up such a momentum that when I finished I'd keep on going for 20 yards before I stopped. It sounds weird but it's true. I was up to 7.5 miles an hour when I was really shifting, which was a fair old pace for walking.

Later it turned out Tommy hadn't seen me himself but his son had. That was bad luck. I didn't strip off and train in shorts. I always wore long trousers because, I suppose, I was embarrassed and didn't want to cause a stir by being a spectacle. To avoid detection I'd take a gentle stroll through Holmgate in Clay Cross as if I was out for a little walk. When I arrived at the country lanes, and I'd made sure nobody was about, I'd check the watch and set off. If I saw anybody approaching, I'd slow down and resume strolling. But on the way back from a session I must have passed Tommy Lunn's son's house, going full pelt, without spotting him.

The Whit Tuesday arrived and I caught a bus from Clay Cross to Chesterfield, then another to Sheffield. I changed into my shorts, vest and running shoes and a number was pinned to my chest. Then we were off. Scores of us were doing the race around hilly Sheffield. Thousands of spectators cheered and clapped as we passed. I tore through the field, feeling as if I was walking on air. I was in the front pack and doing brilliantly, going like a train downhill on the Whitley Road. Until I encountered Roland Hardy. He was standing on the side, shouting encouragement. 'Save yourself for Barnsley Road,' he advised me, urging me to slow. I thought: Maybe he's right, he knows what he's saying.

So I slowed. Fatal mistake. I hadn't gone round the course in advance to check what it was like, and I thought Barnsley Road must be this massive hill if a road walker as renowned as Roland Hardy was telling me to save energy to conquer it. When I got on Barnsley Road I found it wasn't as steep as Slack Hill on my training route between Chesterfield and Matlock. I'd lost ground with a tactical mistake. The finish was outside Kemsley House where the *Sheffield Star* and *Morning Telegraph* were printed. I finished a disappointed second in 1 hour 42 minutes and 55 seconds. I felt I had the energy to go round the course again. I kicked myself. The bloke who finished ahead of me collapsed over the line. It was a case of what might have been, how I might have gone one better if it wasn't for Roland Hardy.

I couldn't say anything publicly or it would've smacked of sour grapes. But I knew inside that I hadn't done myself justice. I collected the runner-up cup and a prize of a leather case with a shaving razor in a ceremony in Davy's cafe before heading home on the buses. I arrived back in Clay Cross at what must have been four or five in the afternoon.

As soon as I was in the house, mother said: 'Oh, didn't you do well.'

I replied: 'I could have done better. Anyway, how do you know?' This was before the age of Twitter or anything like it. And don't forget there was no phone in our house. I don't think we had a television, not that the walk would have been on the telly if we had.

It turned out Dad had come up the pit early and caught a bus to Chesterfield to visit the miners' offices on a pretext. He'd really gone to buy a copy of the *Sheffield Star*. The headline in the Stop Press box for the latest news was 'Holmgate man stars in Sheffield walk'. Dad never said anything but I think he changed his mind about my waddling my bloody arse. He was proud. Yet we weren't a family for displaying our emotions in public. As a Skinner, I couldn't afford to do other than well. He was secretly pleased. When I watched the father come round in *Billy Elliot* I glimpsed how Dad must have felt.

My success in the Star Walk earned an invitation to sign for Sheffield Walking Club but I only went a few times. It was two buses there and two buses back. I was involved with the union and played football anyway on Saturday afternoons. I twisted my ankle at work, hurting it while jumping off a coal conveyor belt (we weren't supposed to travel on them but it was two miles from the face to the pit bottom so we'd lie on them. The ground was uneven, rocky, and I turned the ankle) and I stuck to marathons when it healed. I enjoyed running and legging it up those spoil heaps had proved great for breathing, muscles and stamina. I could complete 26.2 miles in under three hours, which wasn't bad going. These days I settle for watching the London Marathon on TV, then diving out of the flat to see them go by on Birdcage Walk, not far from the finish.

The years of training came in handy for a round-the-town walk in 1960 as a freshly elected councillor. The day smiled on the Skinner family, as the local newspaper acknowledged. I was the first man home in the 9-mile trek in 1 hour 22 minutes with brother Graham 19 minutes behind in second place. Joan, our sister, was second woman home to complete what was the greatest sporting day in the history of the Skinners.

Being good at running meant I could fly down the wing at football. I was useful rather than good, better in the second half when my fitness told, though I was let down by my ball control. I played on the left wing, appropriately enough, or inside left. I won a couple of trophies with Pilsley Miners' Welfare and turned out a few times for Clay Cross and Danesmoor Welfare in the Central Alliance league when they were short.

I got my first game for Pilsley when they were a man short. They were top of the league. There was a knock on the door. One of the lads was at a wedding so I was asked if I fancied a game. I borrowed a pair of boots and scored a hat-trick in a 4–2 win, one of them going in off my nose after I mistimed the jump. The three goals meant they couldn't drop me but as I wasn't regis-tered as a player I appeared as the mysterious A.N. Other in the *Green 'Un* evening sports paper on the Saturday. Pilsley had some top players and a couple were watched by West Bromwich Albion.

The game was very different to today. I only tackled when it was absolutely necessary. There was none of the tracking back. I wore heavy leather boots and the leather ball was heavy, nobody wanting to head it in the rain because the thing was soaked and weighed a ton.

If not playing we'd watch Chesterfield some weeks and I won tickets in a raffle for the 1961 FA Cup Final at Wembley. Tottenham Hotspur, who'd already won the League, beat Leicester 2–0 to pull off the first double since 1897. It was a spectacular event but you don't see it all, and though I feel guilty saying this after what was an historic occasion, you do see more on TV.

Nowadays I support whichever northern team is playing a club from the south. It's a natural preference I can't shake. I admired what Brian Clough did at Derby County and Nottingham Forest, twice winning Europe with Forest. I'd bump into Cloughie some-times on the train. He'd be in First Class with some of the MPs, with me talking to them from the end of the carriage because mine was a Second Class ticket. 'Eey up, Skinner, come in 'ere and have a chat,' Cloughie would say. He was good company – when it suited him. I didn't know anything about the drinking then, and that may explain why at other times Cloughie would ignore you. When you did talk with him, he loved politics and was a big Labour man. So is Alex Ferguson, who has never forgotten he was a shop steward in Glasgow. Fergie's a member of the Labour Party and I looked out for his results to see if Manchester United had beaten the London teams such as Tottenham, Arsenal and Chelsea.

When a kid and a young man I played cricket as well as football. We had some exceptionally gifted cricketers in the Parkhouse Colliery youth team who went on to play in the Derbyshire league. We skittled out one team for 14. Twice. I could bowl reasonably fast. Fitness told again and I would send them down over after over.

My enjoyment of cricket led to a slightly bizarre chance encounter with a few of the best-known names in the game. I was passing Westminster Abbey on an errand to the shops when I saw this big crowd. The women were all well dressed, wearing big hats. It reminded me of an Ascot parade. This feller suddenly exclaims: 'Thank God there is another socialist here.' I'm trying to think on my feet, wondering: 'What's going off here?' Then I remembered. Denis Compton, a fabulous cricketer, had died. I was walking past the memorial service for the Brylcreem Boy, as he was called. Compton was a hugely popular cricketer in his day, the grand turnout witness to that.

I'm about to resume my errand when another feller says to me: 'Oh, we're going in now.' The crowd starts moving slowly towards the Abbey's impressive wooden doors and I'm thinking: What am I doing here? But, I'll admit, I was curious. The other feller, the bloke who originally grabbed me, was certain I was part of this ensemble. I was musing on how it might be interesting to go inside. I'd seen Compton in his prime. He'd scored 18 centuries in 1947 when I was a schoolboy. Nobody has got near him as a cricketer since. His 3,816 runs in a season has never been beaten. So we shuffle as a pack to the doors where a man checking invitations says: 'Where's your ticket?' I haven't, naturally, got a ticket because I wasn't invited. Thankfully a woman in a great long black church gown steps in to announce: 'He doesn't need one.' I'm in! I don't believe in God so it couldn't be divine intervention. I'll put her presence down to luck.

I was escorted to a seat next to Henry Blofeld, the cricket commentator. I'm glancing around the Abbey and see lots of worthies, including John Major. Blofeld looked startled I was sitting alongside him.

'Dennis, Dennis Skinner?' he asked in the booming voice of his. 'Are you a cricket fan?'

I explained I'd watched Compton score one of his astonishing 18 centuries for Middlesex at Derbyshire and how in that magical season Bill Edrich, a teammate, scored 12 the same summer.

Blofeld, astonished I was there, was slyly testing my cricket knowledge. I told him I'd played in Derbyshire and used to head regularly to Queen's Park in Chesterfield to watch Derbyshire, although now I mainly followed the game on telly and in the papers.

'What did you think of Denis Compton?' Blofeld enquired.

I replied straight off the bat: 'He was the cavalier of cricket – everything Geoffrey Boycott isn't. He'd play extraordinary shots. He'd go in at number four for Middlesex and England and had an impressive record.' I still remember the look of surprise on Blofeld's face – surprised I did know my cricket.

The hymns started and I knew them, singing without the book. Blofeld noticed that too and asked if I'd been in a church choir. I did sing in a choir but it was at Tupton Hall, occasionally stuck out at the front to do solos. I picked up singing, as you know, from my mother. I noticed Blofeld, an engaging Old Etonian, read the hymn book.

We went outside at the end and were milling about. John Major was in the middle of a group of Ascot-type women. The people in the flowery hats saw me surrounded by journalists and cricketers, who I reckoned had been told by Blofeld I was an unlikely cricket fan. The women came over to ask for autographs. I'm positive some didn't know me from Adam but a huddle attracts a bigger crowd.

I was invited by Blofeld to chat with him about cricket in the 'View from the Boundary' slot on *Test Match Special*, when a commentator discusses the game with a fan. Off I went on a Saturday to the Oval when England were playing the West Indies. We had a great time. Blofeld wanted me to have lunch with John Major but I excused myself, telling him: 'No, I'm sitting with the mere mortals.' In fact I was put in the press box and had a couple of sandwiches. I'd never had such a good seat and could see the ball swing a foot. Until then I'd thought commentators exaggerated the movement generated by bowlers. I don't doubt them after watching it with my own eyes. In the interview on the radio I put a few political points across, criticising the sale of school cricket fields. Cricket's a brilliant game. It should be taught to children in every state school rather than letting it be dominated by private schools.

I discovered tennis at Ruskin. I've in the past joked I read tennis at the college. There's some truth in it. A lad from the NUM didn't have anybody to play with so I went up against him and loved it immediately. One of the obvious advantages is you require only two players so it's easier to organise than football or cricket. Back in Clay Cross, I played at the YMCA. Brothers Gordon and David and I would play doubles matches with Keith Bradshaw, secretary of the Clay Cross Labour Party. We fought like Kilkenny cats, disputing if the ball was in or out. Genteel we were not. I taught my own children how to play and took them for coaching. Now all my grandchildren play sports, including tennis.

I'm a strong advocate of the benefits of sport, at whatever level, both for enjoyment and general fitness. The Skinner family, including me, helped organise an annual sports day in Clay Cross in the late 1950s and early part of the 1960s. It was a large event at the miners' welfare. We had a grass running track and a grass-banked cycle circuit. We erected between 2,000 and 3,000 seats. Marquees had to be put up and bales of straw laid around the cycling to stop riders crashing into spectators. And I helped enrol competitors, the events attracting big names such as Ron Hill, who won gold in European and Commonwealth marathons, and Dorothy Hyman, a sprinter who took Olympic silver in the 100 metres.

I found it hard work, particularly when secretary. As a family we knew nobody could criticise you politically if you did your bit in the community. I also stumbled on a social distinction between cycling and athletics in that era. Cycling is traditionally more working class, a more cosmopolitan sport. I was transported back in time watching on TV as Bradley Wiggins became the first Briton to win the Tour de France. There he was, on the Champs-Élysées, joking and enjoying himself – not sticking on a stiff upper lip.

One of my jobs ahead of the sports day was to obtain handicaps for the entrants so the races were competitive. We were instructed to go to Sheffield to visit a Mr Garner. He came to the door in a blazer with the badge of the Amateur Athletics Association (AAA) on the breast pocket. By the superior look on his face we spotted instantly that he thought he was a cut above us. He led us through the house to the back where he put us into a conservatory. The first conservatory, incidentally, that I'd ever been in. We weren't offered so much as a glass of water or a cup of tea. The AAA tie-and-blazer left us twiddling our thumbs while he went into the front room to mark, in secret, the handicaps. When he'd finished, we were handed the results and shown out.

The difference in the welcome couldn't have been starker when we arrived in a pit village near Doncaster to have the cyclists handicapped. Ike Delbridge was the man from the British Cycling Federation. I heard he was 100 recently. On that day I didn't know him from Adam. He opened the door and cheerily greeted us with a 'Come on in, lads.' He had a flat cap on the side of his head, like my dad. We followed Ike into the front room. He told us to sit ourselves down and studied our list of names. Ike took out a pencil and started marking the handicaps. In front of us, not in private. Every now and again Ike would mutter 'He's been swapping prizes' and punish the cyclist with a handicap so he'd start a certain distance back.

'What do you mean,' I asked innocently, 'swapping prizes?'

'You'll know what I mean when you've done this job,' came back Ike, who carried on marking the card.

This was the age of amateur sports. We weren't allowed to offer cash prizes to athletes or cyclists. Instead we sent somebody to a 'cash and carry' warehouse in Sheffield to buy electric blankets, a dozen watches and a pile of other stuff for the winners. In complaining about 'swapping prizes', Ike was condemning cyclists who let another rider finish first because they'd already won, say, a kettle and wanted the iron for second place. We were permitted in that era, however, to pay expenses. I never ceased to be amazed how some runners we'd invite would answer they were on holiday in Cornwall but could travel back if given cash for a rail ticket. Funny how they were always on holiday as far as you could travel from Derbyshire. I don't remember a single one camping in the Peak District. Today they'd claim an airfare from Benidorm or Ibiza but, as we know, they are all professional now.

CHAPTER SIX

To the Palace of Varieties

Miners' business took me to Parliament several times before I was elected an MP, so I knew exactly what the place was like and it didn't overawe me. If you could speak and control heated debates in the Derbyshire NUM council chamber in Saltergate, with as many as 150 pitmen crowding into the room during a dispute, 50 of them delegates from the pits with the right to speak, the floor of the House of Commons held no fears.

I'd watched Harold Macmillan (plodding) and Harold Wilson (sharp as a knife) at the despatch box before I visited in 1967 to listen to a debate on the Labour government's prices and incomes policy. I handed in a green card in Central Lobby to pass a message to Tommy Swain, an ex-miner who was MP for North East Derbyshire, that I'd like him to get me in. Tommy wasn't always in Parliament but, while I was kicking my heels, as luck would have it, John Mendelson, my old Sheffield tutor who'd won Penistone, came into the lobby and sorted me out.

I was put in a seat under the gallery within touching distance of the chamber floor. I sat listening for a couple of hours before I felt peckish. I'd been to a miners' meeting earlier so hadn't eaten dinner. I had a sandwich in my pocket that I'd made before leaving home. I started chewing it and Eric Varley, who'd been sitting nearby on a bench, lurched towards me.

'What are you doing?' he wailed, looking worried.

I said: 'I'm just having a sandwich.'

'You can't do it in here.'

'Well, Eric, nobody can see me. You only did because you were up close.' I was nearly finished anyway and there was no point stopping, particularly when I was causing no harm.

I had no idea when I was listening and eating that I'd end up in the place. I had no career plan. My work was in the pit and the union. I wasn't on the National Union of Mineworkers political panel at the time. I was in many ways an accidental MP, persuaded to stand to stop an interloper. Looking back I'm glad I did.

Naturally, the National Union of Mineworkers wanted miners in the House of Commons to represent pitmen, the union and communities. It was shaken when Peter Heathfield failed to win the Ilkeston nomination and concern spread when we got word that a big BBC name was being hawked as the answer to Bolsover's dreams. His name was Keith Kyle, a presenter on the BBC TV *Tonight* show, a forerunner of *Newsnight*.

Bolsover has only had two MPs since the seat was created in 1950: Harold Neal and me. Neal won the 1944 Clay Cross wartime by-election and as a young lad I'd gone to the count. The name changed to Bolsover when the boundaries were redrawn. An ex-miner and vice president of the union, his politics weren't mine. He'd go on free holidays to Fascist Spain, then return and sing the praises of General Franco. Wilson's 98-seat majority in March 1966 meant the next election could be as far away as 1971, but Neal let it be known in early '67 he'd be off.

There was no urgency until late that year when Leo Fretwell, the delegate from Shirebrook Colliery, took us all by surprise at a Derbyshire union meeting. Leo announced he had it on good authority that a man backed by Transport House, the party headquarters in London, was being carted around Bolsover as a candidate.

'I have to tell you that there's a man from the BBC called Keith Kyle,' Leo declared out of the blue. 'He's being picked up at Nottingham station and taken to meetings in different parts of the constituency. Unless we buck up our ideas and get our skates on, it'll be too late.'

How Leo knew was a mystery. But he was right. There was a kerfuffle as the penny dropped. The union realised another seat could slip from our union's grasp. Immediate calls were heard to consult branches, to seek nominations. Leo, the man in the know, intervened again:

'There is no time to ask for nominations. We have to get a move on and make a recommendation today. There is only one man who can beat Keith Kyle and that is you, Chairman.'

My instant thoughts were: What's Leo's game? What's he up to? Is he trying to get me out of the chair? His politics are in the middle of the union, well to the right of me.

The truth, as I came to appreciate over the years, was that Leo was as genuine as the day is long. He was a member of the Labour Party and wanted to secure the Bolsover seat for the NUM. He was a stalwart in 1972 and 1974 pit disputes and the great Strike for Jobs in 1984–5. I gave the oration at his funeral. Back at that meeting, however, I was confused.

The meeting sided with Leo and I went home a putative if unlikely parliamentary candidate. I harboured doubts too about whether I wanted to do it, yet I knew that if I was running I had to do it properly. Letters were sent to every union branch seeking nominations and I secured the backing of 17 of 18 pits in the constituency.

My main rival, Kyle, enjoyed a superficial glamour from television. He wasn't what you'd call a conviction politician. He started as a Liberal, ratted to the Conservatives, re-ratted to the Liberals after the 1956 Suez invasion before ratting yet again to join the Labour Party. When he subsequently joined the SDP, he had a political royal flush. The *Derbyshire Times*, a local Tory rag, went out of its way to try and halt me in my tracks. The paper was no fan of mine or of any left-winger for that matter. The editor published an editorial urging everything be done to stop me. The only thing it predicted correctly was I'd turn up at the selection meeting in a black suit and red tie. Kyle and the *Derbyshire Times* lost and in 1969 I was selected as the Labour Prospective Parliamentary Candidate for Bolsover. Mam and Dad were proud. I like to think it made up a little for the disappointment at the end of Tupton Hall.

Bolsover was a safe seat but I campaigned as if it was a marginal. Neal, in his later years, had taken his foot off the pedal. I put my foot on the accelerator and drove the campaign hard. Bolsover's a big semi-rural constituency, about 25 miles north–south and 18 miles east–west with 14 small towns and largish villages. We visited every one, several times. I had a van with a loudspeaker and would shout the usual – 'Vote Labour', 'Vote

Dennis Skinner' – while cracking a few jokes. I copied the soapbox street-corner five to ten minute meetings I used in Clay Cross, across the constituency. I took questions in public, although I found then, as now, most people prefer to speak to me quietly rather than in front of a crowd. My pitch was working-class solidarity versus greed and the Establishment. 'It's not the Reds under the beds you should worry about,' I'd shout. 'It's the Lords on them you should be afraid of.'

My instruction that we'd have lunch in the nearest pit canteen didn't excite the canvassers initially. The tradition under Neal was to retire to a cosy pub for a long lunch, the Shoulder of Mutton in Hardstoft a favourite. I put a stop to that. The food was cheaper in pit canteens, and we could canvass the votes of the miners while we ate our dinner. I'm not a great one for fancy food. My palate was formed in the austere 1930s and the war years when the lives of merchant seamen weren't risked in a boatload of spices. I've never eaten a curry.

The Bolsover count wasn't until the Friday morning and I knew by then that Ted Heath had the removal men packing his stuff to move into Downing Street, with Harold Wilson on the way out after falling short. I was angry at the prospect of going to Parliament to fight the Tories because the Labour Cabinet, and Chancellor Roy Jenkins in particular, had failed to give enough people reasons to go out and vote Labour. Bad trade figures, later revised upwards, didn't help. Nor did England losing 3–2 to Germany in the World Cup quarter-finals in Mexico. So it was against that miserable backdrop my result was announced in Bolsover Assembly Rooms at lunchtime. I won 28,830 votes with a healthy 20,459 majority over the Tory, a man called Humphrey, polling 77.5 per cent of the votes. I was heading to a Parliament with a 31-seat Conservative majority.

On the Monday after the weekend I'd heard nothing from London about my new job and I wasn't sure when I'd start receiving pay. So I got up, put on my pit clothes and went to work at Glapwell.

One of the lads shouted: 'Hey, what you doing here? I thought you were an MP.'

'I am,' I said back, 'but I mightn't be on the books yet.'

Later that day I got hold of Tommy Swain. 'Tommy – what do I do?' I asked. Tommy explained I'd be paid after I was sworn in but the money was backdated to the election. So I waited until the following Monday to head down to London.

The advice of my father was to treat Parliament as a workplace and to keep my eyes on what the others were up to. I affirmed with the Speaker in preference to swearing an oath of allegiance to the Crown and the wages started. In 1970 there were no induction courses, no guides with clipboards waiting to give you a tour. You sank or swam. You didn't even get an office. I'd hang my hat and do the mail in the trade union room used by Labour MPs, working alongside Tommy Swain, Don Valley's Dick Kelley, another miner, and Ted Garrett from Wallsend. A few years later I started using a joint office shared by Michael Foot, who was to be a Cabinet minister and leader of the Labour Party, and Norman Atkinson, another left-winger and party treasurer. I work with all Labour MPs but most closely in Parliament with others on the Left, and to that end I was to help found the Socialist Campaign Group of MPs in 1982 as an alternative to a Tribune Group taken over by MPs who weren't on the Left.

I started in those early days as I was to continue and still do. I like to get ahead of the game, getting in early. Parliament in those days didn't sit until two-thirty in the afternoon, then went on into the evening and, when the Labour Opposition was attacking the Conservatives, into the small hours of the following day. I got in for eight or eight-thirty in the morning when it was quiet, replying to letters and writing notes. I collect the mail from the Post Office and set to work. I write replies or ring people up, finding numbers in telephone directories if they've not written them on letters. I've an office now near Big Ben. Thousands of people in Bolsover must have heard the chimes while we were talking on the phone. I'm still in early. I don't send emails because it would open a Pandora's Box. Lois, my assistant and, after my marriage to Mary ended, my partner, deals with that side of the office.

With Dad's advice ringing in my head, I arrived determined not to be seduced by the Palace of Varieties. I was in Parliament to represent miners and Bolsover, to fight for working people and socialism. I knew I'd be a small cog in a great big wheel but I was determined to do my bit as best I could and not let anybody down. There are, I acknowledge, a thousand and one different ways to do the job of an MP. Everybody does it differently. I make no claim to have a monopoly on the right way to do this job. I've learned along the way. At the outset, however, I adopted three resolutions. I've stuck to them for 40-odd years. And I've never found these three resolutions irksome.

The first was never to be involved in the racket of pairing. MPs may secure a night off to miss votes by linking up with a Tory pair. In my book it's nothing less than organised absenteeism. In the pit, if I didn't go to work I didn't get paid. Can you imagine

Louis van Gaal ringing up Manuel Pellegrini and proposing Manchester United didn't play a left-winger so Manchester City needn't bother to put out a right back? It isn't in my DNA to pair with a Tory. When it was suggested I find a pair, I told the party whips that I wasn't interested in a deal with a Tory. The whips were surprised. They said I was cutting off my nose to spite my face, that I'd be stuck in the building until late every night by the voting. Good. That was one of the reasons I was there.

In the back half of 1970 we were debating the Family Income Supplements Bill, which was a poor Tory answer to the needs of kids in homes with next to nothing who deserved better. This Tory MP came up to me and asked: 'Have you got a pair?' I answered, truthfully: 'Why? Do you want to go?' Grinning like a Cheshire cat, he replied: 'Yes', and off he went for a nice dinner in a restaurant in the West End. I didn't tell him I wasn't going. I didn't tell any lies. His desire for a night off led him to interpret my question as consent for a deal. My vote and his absence reduced Ted Heath's majority. The following morning I was collared by Bob Mellish, Labour's chief whip.

'I hear reports that you paired and voted. That is definitely not allowed,' said Mellish.

'No, I never paired,' I explained. 'He just wanted to get away and I didn't say' owt to disappoint him.'

Mellish delivered a little lecture, but it was water off a duck's back. I understand why whips argue pairing is beneficial to both parties. I just happen to disagree. It can make us look as if we're adopting club rules, behaving as if we're all pals together when Tories are imposing vicious cuts and cruel policies which hurt those outside in the real world.

Mellish, by the way, was a bitter man in later life. He turned on the Labour Party and the Left. Thatcher performed somersaults to give him a nice number at the London Docklands Development Corporation as Baron Mellish. I recall the 1983 by-election he triggered in Bermondsey to dress in ermine. Mellish supported his friend, John O'Grady, who was standing as Real Bermondsey Labour candidate against our candidate Peter Tatchell in a campaign disfigured by crude anti-gay slurs. The beneficiary was Simon Hughes, the Liberal. I bet Mellish was pleased.

My second resolution was never to accept junkets, the free trips and dodgy visits to nice places overseas. I've noticed over the years how most of the jaunts are between the Tropics of Cancer and Capricorn. Cold, wet and windy destinations lack appeal. Too many of these trips sound like jolly boys' outings, the MPs in it together. The threat is a muddled consensus emerges, blunting politics. The friendliness operates against the interests of those we represent, people who expect us to take a position and keep it. Straining to accommodate the other side is dangerous when they are wrong. Anyway, I find it no hardship to refuse to go on holiday with Tories. The very idea appals me.

In my book the same rule applies to all-party groups. I don't want to befriend Tories. There's a whiff over the way many of the groups are financed, vested commercial interests footing the bill. These bodies spread like wildfire. If Syria split permanently tomorrow, there'd be two all-party groups within twenty-four hours – both finalising visits.

The third resolution was to keep out of the bars. We didn't have bars at the pithead. I'm not puritanical. I used to enjoy a drink, although as I mentioned I rarely bother now. Uncle Nip, a desire to turn my life around and an ulcer I developed while in the pit made it an easy decision to enforce. I've no objection to people enjoying beer or a glass of wine. I go into pubs and clubs for meetings and the occasional sing-song. I intend no criticism of others using the bars in Parliament. I made a choice about how I work, not how they should work. Early on, when I'd been in Parliament only a few years, I popped my head round a door to ask the barman if someone was in. He didn't recognise me and said only MPs were allowed in the bar so I had to get out.

I've witnessed good, principled people brought low by alcohol. Lawrence Daly steered the National Union of Mineworkers during national strikes in 1972 and 1974 when Joe Gormley was a right-wing president. Lawrence, the general secretary, had a brilliant mind and was one of the finest orators I've heard. I'd met him in 1962 at a Scottish NUM school in Dunoon. One of his problems in office was his gregariousness. I'd go up from Parliament to the union's headquarters on the Euston Road at noon to keep him company for a few hours. Sadly, Lawrence had some problems in later life.

Life in Parliament was a breeze after the pit. I took my children to the place and told them their dad had landed on his feet. I know my parents were proud, yet we weren't a family to make a fuss. Asked if she was pleased I was the Bolsover MP, my mother told the interviewer she had seven other children! My dad usually kept his emotions buttoned and was justly as proud of his other children too. He came to London only the once to see me in Parliament. Looking back, it may have been a blessing in disguise that he didn't visit more often.

Father attended during the prolonged fight over the 1972 Housing Finance Act. The legislation was an unprecedented intrusion into local government by forcing councils, including Clay Cross, to put up rents by £1 a week. We'd frozen rents for the preceding ten years. We were proud of our record of clearing slums and building decent homes. We weren't going to be pushed around by Heath. Dad turned up to listen to a debate of the standing committee scrutinising the bill. Brothers Graham and David were on Clay Cross council, so the family was heavily involved. Tory MP Spencer Le Marchant, Sir Spencer, an Old Etonian who was Conservative MP for the High Peak in Derbyshire, was also on the committee. Marchant repeatedly tried to intervene while I was speaking. I wouldn't give way to the supercilious Tory, knowing he'd have nothing sensible to say. Dad, listening in the public seats, shouted: 'He's told you once. He's not giving way, so shut your bloody mouth.' Marchant got the message and shut up.

On the Labour side we opposed the nauseating bill every clause of the way. In terms of hours of scrutiny, it was said at the time to be a record. The Tories were determined not to impose the guillotine, a procedure to cut short discussion. To curtail debate was considered weak, a defeat in itself. Since that era all of the governments, Labour, Tory and Conservative–Liberal Democrat (ConDem) coalition, have shown no such compunction. In one significant week we kept the Tories up for four continuous nights, the MPs allowed out on breaks to eat, go to the toilet and wash. We took time out for Prime Minister's Questions, then held twice a week for fifteen minutes on Tuesday and Thursday afternoons, before trooping back into committee room 10 to continue the argument. Julian Amery, an unpleasant right-winger, led for them as Minister for Housing and Construction. Tory MPs were under strict instruction to avoid intervening in an effort to speed proceedings along. We had plenty to say, so gagging them left the floor open for us. Tony Crosland, a frontbencher whose intellect I respected, led for us. One day I saw him at the taxi rank, nipping home to change his shirt, in his carpet slippers. So tired and worn down was Crosland by our war of attrition that that he'd forgotten to put on his shoes when he left home the previous morning.

Eventually, when Heath realised we weren't going to give up, he imposed the guillotine. It was a loss of face for the Conservatives and a pyrrhic victory for us because we knew they had the votes lined up in the chamber of the House of Commons, never mind the hereditary peers slumbering in the House of Lords, to ram home higher council house rents.

Yet the battle wasn't over. Outside Parliament, a magnificent eleven Clay Cross councillors, including my two brothers, refused to impose the rent rises. Other local authorities vowed to fight alongside, until they melted away. When we continued to refuse to raise rents, Heath appointed a Housing Commissioner, Patrick Skillington, a retired civil servant from Henley-on-Thames who'd probably never seen the inside of a council house, to do the dirty work. He came in October 1973 and left six months later without collecting a single extra penny.

I spoke at demonstrations in Clay Cross and was the parliamentary arm of the campaign. Ultimately the Clay Cross Eleven were barred from office and bankrupted, judge Lord Denning in the Appeal Court typically siding with the Establishment and sneeringly ruling that they weren't fit to be councillors and the sooner they were disqualified the better. All that was missing was his black cap. Bankruptcy left the 11 unable to obtain credit except at the Co-op and another store. Graham's Ford Escort was seized by the bailiffs despite Derbyshire county council, where he worked as a surveyor after leaving the pit, saying it was a 'tool of the trade' and therefore exempt as essential to his job. Before the bailiffs arrived to drive it away, he swapped the new wheels for older ones so somebody on the National Coal Board estate where he lived would benefit from his misfortune. Poor George Goodfellow, a school caretaker, lost his holiday money. He'd booked a first trip abroad for him and his wife, a cleaner. The travel agent taking them to the Black Forest in Germany collapsed and when he received compensation the receiver grabbed the cheque.

We took a principled stand on rent rises and the resistance was heroic. Support locally in Clay Cross was tremendous. When the eleven were disqualified, the Labour Party re-won ten of the seats and missed out on the eleventh by a measly two votes. After Wilson returned to Downing Street in February 1974 without a majority, then secured a four-seat cushion in October of that year, I demanded in the Commons and at the party conference that the bans on the Clay Cross Eleven be lifted. I'll never forgive the traitors in our parliamentary ranks who opposed justice.

David wrote a very good book about the struggle, *The Story of Clay Cross*, with Julia Langdon who was a journalist on the *Guardian* before she moved to the *Daily Mirror*. On the 40th anniversary of the battle, Graham penned a great piece in the *Morning Star*. He captured better than I ever could the significance of the fight and the personal cost to the councillors involved.

I don't want to embarrass anybody, but an immense pride in all of the councillors swelled up in me when I read Graham's account. They paid a high price for refusing to take the easy way out. Not for them rolling over, using the law as an excuse to capitulate. This is Graham's story:

Eleven councillors met for the monthly council meeting. They were Charlie Bunting (chairman), Terry Asher, Roy Booker, George Goodfellow, David Nuttall, David Percival, David Skinner, Graham Smith, Arthur Wellon, Eileen Wholey and myself – soon to be known as the Clay Cross 11.

The Reverend WH Barratt opened the meeting with prayers. The meeting progressed through the agenda and at item nine, titled: 'Housing Finance Act.' The following resolution was proposed by councillor Arthur Wellon. 'That this council will not operate any of the provisions contained in the Housing Finance Act 1972, and that the electorate shall be informed of this decision together with all the reasons for coming to this decision, and the officers of the council be instructed not to make any preparation for implementation of any of the provisions of the Act, nor to act on behalf of the Conservative government as a commissioner.'

The proposition was seconded by councillor Graham Skinner. On being put, the proposition was carried unanimously.

That was the start of a conflict between the Clay Cross councillors and Ted Heath's government, although Clay Cross councillors had had previous run-ins with the district auditor over the level of council house rents. This started in the '60s when Clay Cross Labour Party reformed itself and took on the task of a slum clearance and house-building programme led by Dennis Skinner, Bunting and a few other determined socialists. Clay Cross was built after the famous civil engineer George Stephenson put the Sheffield to London railway line under Clay Cross. He didn't build it – hundreds of workers did, drafted in from all over the country and billeted in huts. Several workers died during its construction. Coal was found and Stephenson, who was no different from any other venture capitalist, sought to exploit it.

Coal shafts were sunk and hundreds of hurriedly built houses were put up for the workers – the miners who predominantly formed Clay Cross. They were long terraced houses, up to 50 in each row without any gaps between them. These houses quickly became slums. There were only piece-meal efforts to knock them down before Clay Cross Labour Party told the electorate that it would flatten the lot and build houses fit to live in at a rent workers could afford – the first affordable housing policy.And it happened. If the rest of the country had done the same, there wouldn't be a housing shortage. Bungalows built for the aged and disabled with warden control systems were built, and Clay Cross had more of them per head of population than anywhere in the country.

Yes, we were proud of the achievements of Clay Cross Council and its councillors, who didn't back off when the district auditor threatened them over their rent policy. Some fell by the wayside, but there were plenty of others to take their place.

The district auditor was concerned about the seemingly low rents, but the councillors stated time and time again that you couldn't expect people who have moved from a slum to be forced to pay through the nose for a decent council house. He was also reminded that the area was suffering from high unemployment. The local pit had closed and the council was encouraging other industry to the area, which they did successfully. The auditor went away for another year.

The Housing Finance Act enabled the government to directly involve itself in the level of rents that councils charged the council tenants. It had to be opposed – and many councils throughout registered their opposition to the Act. However, with the threat of being kicked off the council, surcharged or made bankrupt – as we were – they all caved in. Even the threat of jail was forever bandied about, in the main by right-wing newspapers which would have enjoyed seeing us behind bars.

The Act, of course, had been long opposed when it was in the Bill stage by the Labour Party and other organisations. Large councils such as Sheffield, under the leadership of Ron Ironmonger, opposed it when it was in the Bill stage. 'Over my dead body,' he said. As soon it became an Act they voted for it. Clay Cross Labour Party had made it clear that the thing had to be stopped and that the extension of central powers would not stop at council house rents. At council elections up to September 1972, Clay Cross Labour candidates made pledges to fight the Bill and the Act.

Indeed I stood for election in May 1972 and made it clear that levels of rent should be made by local councillors not government ministers. We had other issues to contend with during our last two years in office. Thatcher, flexing her muscles, stopped the provision of school milk. We used a penny rate for the benefit of the community and used it to provide free school milk for our primary school kids. But when it came to the February council meeting, the treasurer, unable to contain himself, announced that there would be a shortfall for about a month until the new financial year during which time the kids would be without milk. We took the smile off his face when we announced that the chairman's allowance, which was £25 and was spent on the annual wreath on Armistice Day, be raised to £300 pounds. Bunting promptly declared that he was donating it to the milk fund.

Then we had the wage freeze for council workers imposed by the supposedly 'independent' Pay Board. The council, in its wisdom, was concerned about the level of cover for emergencies – snow, ice, high winds etc. – and negotiated a stand-by payment with the local branch of the National Union of Public Employees (Nupe). It was finally agreed that all the workforce should be on stand-by and paid the going rate. Officers said we couldn't do it. But we did! The threats came thick and fast. We were getting a bit of publicity and support from people all over the country. We were eventually surcharged by the district auditor for not collecting the increased rent. It then sought to recover the money by sending in bailiffs and making us bankrupt. That meant we could be barred from holding any public office for life – unlike the surcharge which lasted five years.

I had my Ford Escort seized and other councillors suffered similar losses. Poor George Goodfellow, a school caretaker, had booked his first holiday abroad – a trip to the Black Forest for him and his wife, a school cleaner. The holiday firm went bust and Goodfellow lost his money. But then the government bailed the losers out and Goodfellow got the cheque, only to find that the receivers took it off him. None of us had anything in the bank. We did challenge the government through the courts and were represented by the excellent Mike Seifert and Tony Gifford.

It was always a futile gesture, but it had to be done in order to stop our opponents and the Labour Party from saying we should have done. At the Appeal Court Lord Denning, who was clearly acting in an independent manner, said that we weren't fit to be councillors and the sooner we were disqualified the better. I got the impression he was missing his black cap. He stated that there must be 11 others who could take our places. Ironically, he was right. Clay Cross Labour Party had over 120 members and four weeks before Clay Cross Urban District Council disappeared under the local government changes, a new council was formed – North East Derbyshire District Council.

The Labour Party fielded the second 11 candidates to Clay Cross council. Ten were elected, the 11th missing out by just two votes. The turnout was a massive 71.5 per cent – for a local election!

During this period of trying to beat the government in the courts, it appointed a housing commissioner to collect the unpaid £1 increase in rent. This was a bloke called Patrick Skillington, a retired civil servant from Henley-on-Thames, who'd probably never seen a council house. He came in October 1973. He left in March 1974 without collecting a single penny.

The thing about bankruptcy is that it could be for life. It meant that we couldn't obtain goods and services – gas, electricity and so on had to be turned over into someone else's name. We couldn't get hire purchase, even in our wives' names, unless they were in full-time employment, apart from one store and that was the Co-op.

The government stripped us from every office it could – school governors, social security appeals tribunals, even Darby and Joan clubs. We had an incredible amount of support in Clay Cross and throughout the country. The town was full of press and TV reporters, some welcome, some not. One of my favourites was Sid Waddell, who sadly has recently died. This was before he took over the darts presentation. He was a very funny man. And, of course, we had to suffer the panto chanters of the revolutionary whatever.

When Harold Wilson came back to power in 1974, the Finance Act was repealed, but the question of retrospective legislation was scuppered by some traitors on the Labour benches. The damage had been done and since then the government has been continually putting its fingers into local government coffers.

Things would have been different if Clay Cross had been supported by other councils to defeat Heath's raid on councils' independence. But we at Clay Cross never gave in and we never collected one penny piece of Heath's rent increase. I have never regretted doing what we did. Would it happen again? I very much doubt it – councils are much larger and councillors now get paid.

The new district council was given the task of collecting the arrears of rent in Clay Cross, although the six remaining councillors from the Clay Cross struggle opposed this. They spread the collection over a number of years. The six members from Clay Cross were outvoted.

In 1987, after we had had the bankruptcy lifted, I was elected to the North East Derbyshire District Council for Clay Cross. I was looking forward to resuming where I left off in 1974. Within six months I was removed from all committees, and again from all outside bodies that I had been appointed to – again, even from the Darby and Joan clubs. My removal was down to a Clay Cross (so-called) colleague of mine, one of the first 11, who was now leader of the council. The reason? Supporting a bin men's strike in that authority. I was, after all, the Nupe branch secretary.

So after four years of watching my back, I was not nominated to stand again. But I had other things on my mind. My wife Eileen, who had been by my side and supported me throughout, was dying with breast cancer. I spent my time after that with the trade union movement and I have just completed 51 years with Nupe/Unison – which has not been without its problems, I might add. I am currently the retired members' secretary for Derbyshire Unison, trying to make sure all are getting the benefits to which they are entitled.

I reckon that, together with Thompson's Solicitors, I have helped to get members close on a million pounds in compensation for injuries caused by Derbyshire County Council alone. I also grow trees and make rocking horses. Sadly four of the comrades of Clay Cross 11 have died. They are George Goodfellow (school caretaker), Eileen Wholey (school cook), Charlie Bunting (ex-miner) and Roy Booker (coking plant worker).

Since Graham's account appeared at the back end of 2012, another of the Labour councillors, Arthur Wellon, the youngest of the 11, has passed away. I still feel that sense of betrayal strongly and when Labour won power nationally in 1974, Harold Wilson leading a minority Government from the Feburary before securing a majority of four in October, the bar on standing for office should've been lifted.

Every year the Labour conference called for the removal of the disqualifications and a specific motion was passed in 1977. Nothing happened. I went back to the rostrum in 1978 to castigate furiously the inaction of the party's National Executive Committee and the Labour Government. We all felt let down by the party we believed in.

In Clay Cross we didn't just talk about socialism – we put it into practice. We were way ahead of the Labour Governments of Tony Blair and Gordon Brown after 1997. By 1970, the elderly of Clay Cross had free TV licences, bus passes and warden-controlled bungalows. We'd demolished 95% of slums in record time and saved every council tenant £80 apiece. No other council of comparable size provided a wider range of amenities. Thinking about it, I see why Heath's Conservatives had to get shot of us.

Clay Cross was a colossal battle and I learned a hard early lesson on the value of trusting your own instincts, and making up your own mind, during the 1972 national pit strike. It was February 1972 and Tommy Swain said he was going back to Derbyshire and offered me a lift in his car. Lord Wilberforce's inquiry was due to give miners a big pay increase to end a seven-week strike that had blacked out Britain. I thought he, like me, an ex-miner and member of the Derbyshire NUM, would stay in London to hear the offer. 'You're working too much,' said Tommy. 'We can't make any difference, so let's go home.' He lived in Chesterfield and dropped me off in Clay Cross. Rather than going home, he turned around and drove back to London. When Wilberforce's recommendation was made, Tommy got up in Parliament on a point of order while I was marooned in Derbyshire. It never happened again.

How I worked didn't endear me to the Conservatives. Travelling south to London on the train, Tommy and a Tory MP he was sitting with hailed me to join them in the First Class carriage. The Tory, Gainsborough's Marcus Kimball, fumed:

'It's the fault of people like you that Parliament is changing.'

I snapped back: 'What do you mean?'

'We used to finish in May and return in October,' he spat, 'and now these Labour people like you want to work every day.'

What's wrong with putting in a decent shift?

There was one other personal pledge when I arrived in Parliament. I consciously decided to avoid being trapped by the spell of patronage. I'm a democrat, preferring elections to appointments.

It's why I was one of the minority of Labour MPs who voted against Ed Miliband axing elections for the Shadow Cabinet and chief whip in opposition.

I never wanted to get my hands on the despatch box, yearning to be a minister. You can achieve much in politics and for a constituency if you stick to your guns. And if you accept a ministerial post, you're swallowing patronage. I recall when Jim Callaghan, who succeeded Wilson as Labour prime minister in 1976, invited me into the Aye lobby for a quiet chat. The long and the short of it is Callaghan offered me a job. I wasn't tempted. I suspected he wanted to buy me off, to get me on side under the cloak of collective responsibility. I valued speaking up for what I believed in. I wasn't for sale. 'Jim,' I told Callaghan, 'you have the power to hire me but you also have the power to fire me.' The conversation was cordial and he asked me who I considered might make a good minister. 'Bob' Cryer. He'd be a good 'un,' I suggested. Bob was to be a minister in the Department of Trade and Industry between 1976 and 1978.

My view of patronage didn't blind me to a recognition that Parliament, in its current system, needs people who want or are prepared to sit on the front bench. Bob had his own political principles but I knew he'd accept the job. I'd heard him and others say countless times 'If I was at that despatch box I'd say...' Bob resigned on principle when the government dropped support for the Trident motorcycle co-operative in Meriden.

I'd first met Bob at Labour conferences in the 1950s. Both left-wingers, we'd challenged the order of business, demanding what is known as a reference back to change the agenda. Bob was a delegate that first time we bumped into each other. We'd rushed to the podium at the same time. I was a visitor and not allowed to speak, but the stewards weren't so hot on checking credentials as they are now.

He was elected for Keighley in 1974 and we'd sit together on the front bench under the gangway. When Bob lost his seat in 1983, he went off to Brussels before returning as MP for Bradford South in 1987. He knew Parliament like the back of his hand. He was a dedicated anti-European, a great speaker who could perform brilliantly off the cuff. He was a committed socialist both in and out of Parliament, and an expert on procedure. During the eleven years of Thatcher we used to keep Parliament up, in session, to harry the Tories. He was on the Statutory Instruments Committee and knew which orders enacting legislation we could pick to debate for one and a half hours. Bob would identify up to four to prolong a sitting by as much as six hours. Capable of talking the hind legs off a donkey, Bob could keep going on the most obscure issues. Thatcher and the Tories were furious, their beauty sleep ruined by a couple of troublemakers. We played the game until the Tory-dominated Jopling committee chaired by Michael Jopling, a former chief whip, introduced fundamental reform of proceedings to tip the balance in favour of the government of the day and away from backbenchers.

So I remember the day I heard the news he'd died as if it was yesterday. It was in April 1994. I was in for Questions and wondering where Bob was, thinking he must have been held up in traffic. Don Dixon, the deputy chief whip, came in and whispered he wanted a word with me in the No lobby. I told him I was lining up a question and would see him later. Don said no, it was urgent and he needed to speak to me immediately. Tell me here and now, I answered. Don persisted and I realised something must be up. We left the chamber and he said I had better sit down.

'What is it?' I asked.

Don replied: 'Bob Cryer has been killed on the motorway.'

'What do you mean?' I said, struggling to take it in.

Don explained Bob had been driving from Bradford to London when his car flipped over on the M1. Bob died. His wife, Ann, who later became an MP, survived with minor injuries.

I couldn't take in what had happened. It was as if I was watching a film, really. I was hearing Don and thinking there must be a different ending, that what he was saying couldn't be true. Then I saw Don's grave face and realised it had actually happened, that Bob was dead. I was in a daze. I wandered back into the chamber and sat on the bench. Terry Lewis, a left-winger representing Worsley, asked what was the matter and I explained Bob was dead. 'I just don't know what to do, Terry,' I said. 'What do you think?' Terry said I shouldn't be asking a question in my state. I can't remember anything else about that day. I was stunned.

I lost a political soulmate as well as the closest friend I had in the place. Bob Cryer was a true socialist. He kept the faith. I too have never wavered.

CHAPTER SEVEN

Socialist till I die

Mike Ashley, the billionaire operator of sports shops on many high streets and the Newcastle United football club in the premiership, owns a huge Sports Direct warehouse in Shirebrook in the Bolsover constituency. I secured £21 million from Gordon Brown when he was chancellor of the exchequer to flatten Shirebrook's pit tips and Ashley's buildings sit on the reclaimed site. So Ashley's plant was subsidised out of the public purse.

Sadly, MPs such as myself have no control over planning matters and East Midlands regional development agency didn't heed advice to demand that trade unions be recognised. As a result, if all the workers I've seen from the place are representative of the whole workforce there, the warehouse is filled with hundreds of workers on insecure zero-hours agency contracts at little more than the minimum wage. So taxpayers subsidise Ashley a second time by topping up the low pay with benefits to enable his workforce to survive.

No trade union is recognised at Sports Direct in Shirebrook and I know from conversations with countless nervous workers that they're terrified of speaking out of turn because they fear they'll be sacked. Almost everybody I've come across was recruited through an agency, on poor conditions, rather than through Jobcentres. I know of very few workers there who are on full-time permanent contracts paying a living wage. I wrote to Ashley asking why at Newcastle United, the football club he owns, a trade union is recognised for the players but he doesn't recognise a trade union for the workers at Sports Direct. Ashley never replied. What's more, I, as the local MP, have never, on principle, set foot in the warehouse.

Greedy bosses such as Ashley are why I shall be a socialist as long as I breathe. He's rich beyond the dreams of avarice by exploiting workers. Worth an estimated £3.75 billion, his loot increased by £1.45 billion last year according to the latest Rich List. He's amassed a fortune even bigger than that grinning tax dodger Richard Branson. The helicopter Ashley flies in, to and from that Shirebrook plant, is paid for by the sweat of men and women who struggle to afford a bus fare home.

The truth is the Professional Footballers' Association (PFA) force Ashley to recognise a union at Newcastle United. Footballers are a tightly knit small group with a transfer value on the market. At Sports Direct, Ashley holds all the cards – the company hiring and firing at will. He dips into a large pool of vulnerable unemployed labour.

Ashley, of course, is not alone. He and many other bosses like him now routinely hire workers from outside Britain, including Poland, who are especially susceptible to the demands of voracious firms driving down wages and conditions. The exploitation at work of East Europeans is why there's friction between the newcomers and families who've lived here for generations. Bad bosses are setting worker against worker.

In the pits after the war, we saw a surge of Polish and Ukrainian miners yet there was rarely any trouble because we ensured they were paid the same as us, and they joined the union. Employers today push workers into a race to the bottom. The key to improving community relations is to guarantee everybody is on a good wage and nobody is undercut. If trade unions were stronger, the friction would be reduced and the gains enormous in terms of harmony between people from various countries. Strengthening employment rights is central to the battle for fairness and decency at work. Inequality soaring, with pay at the top shooting ahead when millions at the bottom are forced to scratch a living, is Britain going back to the tough conditions of the 1930s when I was born.

The next Labour government must come up with answers in its early days. New employment and trade union rights are badly needed so people can stand up against the Mike Ashleys of this world. The Jobcentre network should be revived so reasonable conditions are part and parcel of advertised jobs. And the exploitative employment agencies are a major part of the problem and must be banned.

The so-called free movement of labour in Europe is a myth. The desperate men in camps at Calais, living in squalor and hoping to stow away in a truck to find safe haven in Britain, might be classed under free movement if any label can be attached to their misery. But many of the workers from East Europe are brought to Britain by employment agencies. The agencies only have to pick up a telephone and there'll be another 300 or 400.

Shut the agencies and value the trade union ethic and we'll eradicate the tensions between communities.

The Tories shoulder a major share of the blame for the friction with Poles and others by stripping away employment rights and creating an economy in which abuse is encouraged by weak laws. UKIP, a party of Turbo Tories, would be even worse. I would vote in a referendum to leave the European Union to improve conditions in Britain. UKIP would do so to give bosses a green light to cut rights, including paid holidays.

I am a socialist from experience. My politics are homespun rather than from the adoption of a creed, and are based on what I saw from an early age. I don't use the s-word in public often but I know in my heart it pushes me to reach conclusions. The environment I was brought up in taught us that capitalism fails the working class. There is a better way of organising society by controlling the economy. It involves public ownership, assertive trade unions, redistribution of income and wealth, regulations and democratic control. There have been Mike Ashleys as long as capitalism has existed. It was only too evident that the reason my father was out of work was because there were millions of unemployed so the bosses could pick and choose for a pittance.

There have been many governments since that have practised those economics. The Tories and Liberals try to camouflage what they're doing but unemployment is a capitalist weapon. They invent slogans such as 'We're all in this together' as if everybody is pulling their weight. We know the weight is on the many at the bottom who are supporting the Mike Ashleys at the top. Nobody is filthy rich on their own. They've climbed on the backs of others to amass fortunes.

You can't be pessimistic if you want to change the world. Optimism is central to left-wing politics. You're asking all the others to believe in the ideal of attaining equality for all and it's a big task. So you've got to be upbeat or you'd be crushed by disappointments along the way. But you must never, ever give up. I've never been a romantic. I'm a realist. And as a realist I've recognised we'll not build a Nirvana without people struggling.

I've seen good people pay a high price for that struggle. In the miners' strike people lost their homes. After the 1972 national building workers' strike, Des Warren and Ricky Tomlinson were victims of an establishment conspiracy and jailed on trumped-up charges. I visited Des in Lincoln jail. He was in a bad way. I tried to persuade him to do a deal to shorten his sentence, that none of us would think any less of him if he did. Des would have none of it. He'd been imprisoned unfairly and wouldn't compromise. What happened to Des, and Ricky, was a crime. Des was never the same again when he came out. But you couldn't be other than inspired by his sacrifice. To aim to create a society for the greatest happiness for the greatest number and nobody is left behind sounds a bit Jeremy Bentham, but fighting for what we believe is the only way a fundamental shift will be achieved. They give the idea you can have it all and you can have it now if only you work hard enough. It's a myth, of course, a myth to keep the masses quiet or blaming themselves when they don't get to the top.

Life isn't fair and we can make it fairer both in terms of opportunities and results. If we think of life as a 100-metre race, some people are born on the starting line with the concrete boots of poverty, while a wealthy few are born wearing the latest trainers only a step from the finish. Or compare how some families are crushed by the bedroom tax while a few lucky kids are bought homes by their wealthy parents. Life isn't fair for most people when we could collectively make it fairer.

Standing up in Parliament, voting for what I believe, means rubbing up the Labour leadership the wrong way and I regard that as an occupational hazard. I can't help it. I am who I am. I don't believe in perfection. It doesn't exist. The Labour Party is the only political vehicle representing the best interests of the working class. But politics isn't empirical. It isn't 2×2 always $= 4$. Politics is a matter of judgements and if my conscience will not allow me to vote the line decreed by the party hierarchy, I must follow the conscience.

I joked once on Radio 4's *Today* programme that an announcement by a party leader or approved bigwig on their morning programme wasn't party policy until it survived the 1 p.m., 6 p.m. and 10 p.m. news bulletins, and then was all over the following day's newspapers. I was joking, but when you stop and think about it that feels how policy is sometimes formulated.

Towards the back end of 2012 I received a letter from the Labour whips. They demanded to know why I had voted in Parliament against the Conservative–Liberal Democrat coalition government's savage welfare cuts when the party leadership had decided in its ultimate wisdom that we should abstain. The answer was wanted in writing. So I sent a Christmas card with the message: 'Just to let you know my principles conform with the way I vote on all issues.'

My politics are practical and rooted in a confirmed belief from experience that working together beats fighting like rats in a sack. I never discovered it in a book or pamphlet by a Marxist theoretician.

The discovery was in the poverty I was born into, down the pit with the men I worked alongside and at Clay Cross where Labour councillors made a real difference to people's lives. I voted against those Tory welfare cuts because my conscience wouldn't let me do otherwise.

Proud as I am to be a socialist, I don't regard socialism as a dirty word, even if I don't repeat it as a mantra. Those in the higher reaches of the Labour Party who get the jitters when the term's used should have a look at the membership card. I fought against the removal by Tony Blair of the old 'common ownership' Clause IV not because I was attached to the wording, but because of what I feared the move signified. We lost that fight but by way of compensation I point to the opening sentence of the new Clause IV: 'The Labour Party is a democratic socialist party . . .' Every Labour MP should keep the card with those words in a wallet in a breast pocket near their heart.

Siding with the underdog isn't a conscious choice but a natural reaction. Taking a stroll in a London park I heard a feller with a drinks stall ripping off a French tourist.

'Don't buy that – he's fleecing you,' I told the tourist.

'What are you going to do about it?' squeaked the seller, knowing they were guilty. The Frenchman had opened the can but he handed it back.

It was a tiny incident in the grand scheme of things, yet it's as difficult to ignore the minor wrongs as the huge injustices.

For every tycoon there is a dealing room of speculators in the City of London or a Mayfair office of hedge-fund managers spinning that roulette wheel, gambling with the incomes and jobs of millions of people who work hard for a miserly reward. The wealthy look after their own, a self-perpetuating elite. There are always going to be Alan Sugars, the exceptions from humble beginnings who earn a fortune. The question is: how many necks did they tread on to get up the ladder?

Irreversible advances will be achieved together or not at all. The idea that an individual can embark on their own and deliver a brave new world is a load of crap. Work in the pit was all about solidarity and struggle. Trade unionism is people banding together for the collective good. The parable of the Good Samaritan stopping to help someone in need is a socialist story. We weren't greatly influenced by Marx in Derbyshire and far more NUM leaders had been Methodist lay preachers in their time! We would help someone over a stile without blinking an eye. The Tories and Liberal Democrats are incapable of representing working people, as they are proving with their squalid ConDem coalition. Capitalism must be confronted because, if you try to compromise with capitalism, capitalism will compromise you. So yes, I favour the radical transformation of Britain in the interests of working people and their families.

The case for public ownership is stronger than ever with gas and electricity companies, nearly all foreign owned, ripping off customers. Rail is ripe for renationalisation to restore sense and end rocketing fares which steal more from passengers than the Great Train Robbers got away with. Inviting profit-hungry firms to cherry-pick parts of the National Health Service will drain the life blood from a public service which cares for us, keeping us alive instead of checking our credit status before agreeing treatment.

The banking collapse of 2008 exposed the myth that the private sector is more efficient than the public sector. The tens of billions of pounds of public money poured into the banks to stop them taking down the entire British economy, the country coming within hours of the cash machines running dry, made the case for a new order. In the end all the talk of the private sector taking risks was shown to be baloney when, after the banks had made years of profits on the backs of firms and customers charged extortionate lending rates, the British government was forced to shoulder unimaginable losses. The biggest market failure of them all made an unanswerable case for an economic alternative anchored in public ownership and state intervention.

If the Tories were so confident in the intrinsic value of the private sector, they'd privatise the armed forces. We'd have the G4S Fusiliers and the JCB Armoured Corp supported by the Virgin RAF and P&O Navy. That we don't, that the Conservatives are afraid to go there, betrays how even the Right doesn't fully trust the private sector. If they are worried about privatising defence, why are they not also worried about privatising the NHS, which is a matter of life or death for many of us?

I'm not an angry man and I have more patience than may appear. But I do get angry at the Establishment. The working class are taken for a ride. They create all the wealth. I acknowledge there are some people who come up with ideas but the people who create things and build things are on the shop floor and floors in shops. When I show people around the Houses of Parliament, they say it's beautiful and ask who was the architect. I say, think of the craftsmen who carved the stone and built the towers. Politics isn't just about elections and Parliament. It stares you in the face every day. It's about your kids' education, finding jobs and about money. There's no doubt that the distribution of income and creating work for everybody are the most important issues. When I left school and went into the pit, I can't recall ever going into the Labour Exchange – which would be a Jobcentre today. Working underground creates a desire that might be greater than in other jobs to fight for what you believe to be right, accentuating your determination to secure safe conditions and a living wage. That drive has never left me.

We need to rekindle the optimism of Clement Attlee's Labour government. We didn't have two ha'pennies to rub together. Look at the massive social, industrial and economic change he delivered after the Second World War. It was one of the most remarkable periods in peacetime history. Attlee rebuilt a ravaged country on grounds fairer than those of the nation in the grinding pre-war poverty of the 1930s. It took a Herculean effort but the Labour Party had the political will. In education, health, welfare, employment, energy and housing. Demobilised soldiers coming out of the war were found jobs when today the much smaller numbers coming out of the forces are given a redundancy notice by the defence secretary, then a dole card by the work and pensions secretary. My generation witnessed the power of change, the unlocking of the potential to transform Britain for the better.

The official history of post-war Britain is wrong, written by a wealthy overclass to promote their self-interest. Britain was a happier country in the 1970s, at its most equal in 1978. Public ownership, strong trade unions and a welfare state were central to the creation of a country much more equal than today. The greed unleashed by Margaret Thatcher, the destructive Big Bang in the City, privatisations and anti-trade union shackles, widened the gulfs in wages and wealth to the point where there are Two Britains.

I admired Harold Wilson with his four election victories in 1964, 1966 and two in '74 when I was an MP. The first was on the back of a miners' strike and the second on a manifesto promising to extend public ownership. He pledged to nationalise shipbuilding and aerospace and he did so without a majority to speak of. Wilson was a skilful operator and we ambushed the Tories, Michael Heseltine a bad loser who picked up the mace – the symbol of power – in the chamber then didn't know what to do with it. We sang 'The Red Flag' to wind them up even more. It was exhilarating. We'd proved how much you could achieve with commitment. He was no great orator, Wilson, but he made a decent fist of it and was terrific at putting people down on TV, which was an increasingly important attribute in politics.

I've championed organising and regulating the economy with strong public ownership for as long as I've delivered political speeches. I proposed a socialist budget in the House of Commons back in 1972 as an antidote to the early Thatcherism of Ted Heath, unemployment topping one million when he was in Downing Street for the first time since the 1930s. The same policies applied with added vigour under Margaret Thatcher, sent it soaring above three million before John Major matched her miserable feat. I look across the chamber now in the House of Commons and see the Tories are more right-wing than at any time in the last 40 years. David Cameron described himself as a 'child of Thatcher' and she'd be proud of what her little posh boy is doing to Britain, impoverishing millions of people and destroying education and the National Health Service.

During 13 years the most recent Labour governments, headed by Tony Blair and Gordon Brown, achieved much but nowhere near enough. If only the 1997 Labour manifesto had been more radical. I tried and failed to paint a red vision before the May election at a meeting of the Shadow Cabinet and the National Executive Committee. The gathering was the Clause V meeting which, under the Labour constitution, agrees the manifesto. I secured a guarantee that BBC television and radio would remain in public hands. In a febrile period when too many at the top of Labour were frightened of Tory zombies, implausibly fearing Conservatives would rise from the grave and snatch victory from our grasp, the BBC assurance wasn't to be sniffed at. I failed to find a seconder on the NEC for other attempts. Brown made it crystal clear he wouldn't buy a majority stake in Railtrack, which ran the lines and stations on the privatised network. Rail renationalistion is popular, as is restoring gas, electricity, water and mail to public ownership. The Railtrack plan would have cost £2 billion. In due course the Labour government was forced to rescue Railtrack when it was collapsing, transforming it into Network Rail. The annual subsidy by taxpayers into the industry tops £4 billion. We missed a golden opportunity.

Building a new economy must be accompanied by the decency of valuing individuals, families and communities with everybody treated with respect and consideration.

I've marched on more demonstrations than I care to remember. I've backed every left-wing cause going from public ownership and trade union rights to CND and abortion. I marched from London to Aldermarston for nuclear disarmament with Michael Foot. I was on crutches when I joined the students protesting against the tripling of tuition fees by the ConDems, another Nick Clegg broken promise. I hobbled to Millbank with the students, then hobbled back. Probably just as well. I switched on the TV and saw there was fun and games outside the Conservative Party head office.

I voted for equal marriage because who am I to deny two men or two women the opportunity to marry? I was called at the Commons office by a teacher in Derbyshire who said she wanted to talk to me about gay marriage. I said: 'Well, let's start now.' She thought it should be a free vote and she was worried about churches and what would be taught in schools. I told her it was a free vote and even if it wasn't, I'd have treated it as such. As for churches, they wouldn't be forced to marry gays. Nor would it result, as bigots suggested, in pupils being taught to be gay. I allayed her worries. We believe in treating everybody equally. And we believe in the power of argument, engaging the other side instead of running away.

I sit in the elected House of Commons to pass laws but the vestiges of feudalism sustain anti-democratic institutions. I vote to abolish the House of Lords and do away with the barons and dukes who either through patronage or birthright are granted powers to block and frustrate the Commons. Unelected peers are on the front line of the Establishment's resistance to fundamental change. As is the monarchy. Debate is central to politics and I don't buy that people aren't interested. They are. I only have to be in a marketplace or high street for a few minutes and people are raising political issues. They don't always regard them as political – pay, jobs, housing, schools, health, transport – but the answers are.

The debates on the floor of the Labour conference are managed in this era but the discussions on the fringe and in the bars are healthy. I've attended every Labour conference since 1957 and would like to return to the days when debates in the hall mattered and the conference made policy. This was before Neil Kinnock and Roy Hattersley introduced changes which ultimately resulted in the formation of the National Policy Forum. What's more I have always tried to keep away from the lobbyists who hang around the main hotel at the conference. One year the *Daily Express* tailed me in Blackpool in the hope of catching me out and ended up in a nice little place in Coronation Street. By coincidence the Al Jolson Appreciation Society was meeting in the hotel and I popped in to sing a few hits. The *Express* pictured me next to a photograph of Roy Hattersley in the much grander Imperial on the seafront. We both laughed.

Nor will I accept payment for writing for newspapers. It's wrong for MPs to moonlight on Fleet Street. The *Sunday People* offered me to do a weekly column in the early 1990s to succeed Peter Mandelson. I told them no. I speak to journalists who stop or ring me for a quote, after checking first if they are in the National Union of Journalists.

To broaden Labour's popular appeal I understand the involvement of celebrities as long as the politics isn't diluted. I watch *Coronation Street*, so it's no chore meeting the cast at Labour conferences or taking them round Parliament. David Neilson, the actor who plays the awkward but engaging Roy Cropper in the Roy's Rolls cafe, is a solid Labour man, as are a number of others on the cobbles.

Ridding the world of weapons of mass destruction has to be high on any political agenda. I'm a long-term supporter of CND. Frank Allaun, a Salford MP, was chair of Labour Action for Peace. He sidled up in 1972 to ask:

'Dennis, do you know Jane Fonda?'

'I've seen her films if that's what you mean,' I replied.

'Well,' he said, 'I need somebody to meet her at St Stephen's Entrance and bring her into a committee room.'

Frank had persuaded one of Hollywood's biggest stars to speak about the Vietnam War to MPs in the Commons. She was taking terrible flak from the military and the Republicans in the US for visiting Vietnam, the Right denouncing Fonda as 'Hanoi Jane' and lobbying for her to be blacklisted in Tinseltown.

I popped down to St Stephen's and there were a lot of people coming through. It was an era when anybody could wander in unchecked. I'm looking at all these heads, expecting to see somebody glamorous with perfect hair and make-up. I asked the police officer on sentry duty if he'd seen Jane Fonda. He hadn't, so I'm thinking I've failed Frank and wander along to the Central Lobby. There, sitting on her own, looking very ordinary, was Fonda. I took her up to the room and she went over the familiar arguments, and I remember Labour Action for Peace had a turnout much bigger than usual.

Avoiding the nuclear destruction of the world is important but it needn't crowd out other issues such as, for example, cruelty to animals. Fox hunting is cruel. I didn't vote to ban hunting with hounds on class grounds. I did so because I have considered it barbaric since as a kid I saw hounds and mounted horses pursing one of the animals. The idea that these grown men and women want to chase this little red fox is repugnant to me. The truth is you rarely see foxes in rural areas, although I know they're more likely to come in the night. You've more chance of seeing them in cities where takeaway food is chucked away and there are a lot of bins.

*

Most of the people I meet deserve a hand better than the one dealt them. Over the years I've acted as a sort of unofficial shop steward for some of the staff in the House of Commons who can be mistreated. In early 2013 a Tory grandee, Christopher Chope, called staff in the dining room 'servants', which was a very telling phrase and betrayed how some MPs, despite his own explanation, look down their noses at workers in Parliament. The men and women in the Tea Room and the Strangers' cafe are shrewd and know what's going on, but there was this disabled lass who used to forget to clock on. She had trouble remembering things and would turn up for work early but forget to put the card in the clock punch to record when she'd arrived and knocked off. One Christmas they stopped her money, despite the fact she'd worked every day, and put her in this little cubbyhole to wash pots. 'Have you heard what's happened?' asked one of her colleagues. Well, I hadn't until then. I realised I needed a witness, so I asked Dale Campbell-Savours, then the MP for Workington, to come with me and I played merry hell with the manager responsible, threatening them with the press and everything. Taking away her money before Christmas was cruel, as was sticking her in a tiny little alcove all day long. I got her money reinstated and her out of the cupboard.

The desire to improve the lives of working people in Britain is why I remain resolutely against the Common Market, the ultimate capitalist club. I was against it well before Nigel Farage and that mob started UKIP. Ted Heath took us in without a referendum and it was a band of 44 rebel Labour MPs, the likes of Roy Jenkins and John Smith, Roy Hattersley and David Owen, who defied the Labour whip at the end of 1971 to pass the Tory bill. Without them, Heath wouldn't have been able to get Britain into the Common Market. Labour rebels defeated a Tory rebellion!

My objection in principle to the European project is about its implementation of the free movement of capital and labour, the undiluted capitalism at the heart of the Common Market project. Employers undermine wages and employment conditions, shifting production to lowest cost countries. I believe in intervening in the market and the regions. The movement of capital drags labour with it. You could see that from the very beginning. Schuman's European Coal and Steel Community in 1951, which set the whole charabanc rolling, operated in the interests of producers. Miners and steel workers were to lose their jobs in the six countries.

I was part of the No campaign for the 1975 referendum called by Harold Wilson. The Labour Party conference voted against, but he as prime minister, and most of the Cabinet, declared in favour. Margaret Thatcher, the Tory leader, was in favour too. A greater proportion of Conservative MPs were in favour than Labour. The newspapers backed a Yes vote. The Yes camp was financed by industrialists and bankers in favour of the free movement of capital and labour, as you would expect them to be, so we were outspent by their £10 for our every £1. When the question 'Do you think the UK should stay in the European Community (Common Market)?' was put, it was no massive surprise when we lost 33 per cent to 67 per cent.

I wasn't accepting that that was the end of it. My main leaflet at the May 1979 election, when I was returned with a thumping majority in Bolsover but, tragically for the working class,

Margaret Thatcher's Conservatives defeated Jim Callaghan's Labour to unleash eighteen years of hell, was headlined: Stop the Common Market Crippling Britain. I've never given up the fight against a capitalist club. I've voted against all the major pieces of European legislation. The idea that's taken hold recently, painting Mrs Thatcher as some great anti-European, is wrong. She signed the Single European Act in 1986, a massive shift towards political union. Her swinging the handbag was a load of European spin to cover what she was really up to. Thatcher championed enlargement, ensnaring more countries in a system she supported. Going on about rebates and a speech in Bruges were smokescreens.

I opposed Maastricht when John Major was the tenant in No. 10 and the Treaties of Nice, Amsterdam and Lisbon when Tony Blair and Gordon Brown had their feet under the table in Downing Street. I support a referendum now and I'd vote to quit.

The best bit of political advice I ever heard was from Joe Rysdale at Clay Cross council. Joe had letters behind his name and had worked for the authority since he was a young lad, getting to the top the hard way – graft. We were discussing what it meant being a councillor, how suddenly people recognised you and came to you with their problems. People were forever stopping me in the street or at work. It was a new experience. 'You get worried when they don't stop you,' growled Joe, 'because that's when they have lost faith.' The wise old owl was spot on, absolutely right. I've never forgotten his pearl of wisdom. When you put yourself forward for election you are asking people to put their confidence in you. To be Labour is to deliver for people, to be on their side, to fight their corner and to improve their lot.

I've never shared this eagerness of prime ministers to take us to war. I've voted against them all: Falklands, Serbia, Afghanistan, Iraq, Libya and the one we stopped, Syria. I'm an internationalist. I'm proud the last Labour government set a target of spending 0.7 per cent of our Gross Domestic Product (GDP) on eradicating poverty and developing the emerging countries. I cheered the anti-colonialist movements in Africa and India. But I don't support imperial adventures.

Anti-apartheid in South Africa was one of the great international movements. From the 1970s on I'd join pickets outside South Africa House in Trafalgar Square. We demanded the end of white supremacy, championing black majority rule and the release of Nelson Mandela. Over the years I stood with Labour MPs such as Bob Cryer, Dick Caborn, Bob Hughes, Jo Richardson, Martin Flannery, Ian Mikardo, the Joans Lestor and Maynard, Jeremy Corbyn and many more who supported the dismantling of apartheid. So I was delighted when Mandela was finally freed in 1990 on 11 February, coincidentally my birthday. Those of us who'd campaigned for that day were so happy. And those, particularly in the Tory Party, who with Thatcher had supported the apartheid regime should have dug holes and sat in them for ever. We were happy. They were brazen.

Mandela, displaying a remarkable lack of bitterness, was pivotal in the peaceful progression of South Africa. Lauded on the international stage, he was invited to London and asked to address both Houses of Parliament in Westminster Hall. I gave my seat to an elderly man who knew Daksha Masrani, a Westminster Labour friend of my partner Lois. The elderly man was a young lawyer in South Africa during Mandela's early days and desperately wanted to be there. I slipped in at the back anyway to hear Mandela. But an hour before it kicked off I took a peek from the top of Westminster Hall near St Stephen's entrance. Sitting near the front were a row of Conservatives, including Nicholas Winterton and Ivan Lawrence, who for years gave succour to the apartheid regime. It was too much. 'What a gang of hypocrites,' I taunted. 'You're nothing but hypocrites. The lot of you.' Either through shame or a lack of guts, the Tory appeasers of apartheid uttered not a word back.

What I really can't stand is political hypocrisy. As an MP, you have to state your positions to persuade people to vote for you. Nobody can keep all their promises because of the pressures of deciding priorities. But you mustn't tell the electorate a pack of lies. Everybody makes errors, commits mistakes, including me. What you must do is strive to be true to yourself and to those who put their faith in you. That's what I do. I will be a socialist till I die.

CHAPTER EIGHT

Bend it like Beckham

Nothing, absolutely nothing, would've changed for the better in our country if people hadn't, over the centuries, taken a stand on issues small and large. I admire hugely the trade unionists and socialists, suffragettes and a host of other campaigners for social justice who fought hard for the great causes they believed in deeply. We don't know the vast majority by name and they, if not their deeds and movements, were swallowed by history but we may honour their memory by continuing the struggle. In politics, you need your head as well as your heart. One is no good without the other. Answers are found in thinking through a problem, not solely in an emotional response – however angry we feel.

From an early age I was taught to challenge and not just accept things because, supposedly, that was how they'd always been and would remain for evermore. Dad was prepared to challenge authority, often at considerable personal cost as I've explained, when he thought a cause was right, a grievance was justified. Tony Skinner knew the miners before him who had fought to create a union didn't give up even when defeated. They regrouped and came back stronger. He taught me to challenge authority too, and it was a lesson I took to school, where I wasn't afraid to defy the teacher if I believed the rules were wrong. Refusing to conform meekly earned me many a detention. I wasn't consciously causing trouble, going into a classroom seeking a confrontation. Speaking up was my automatic response whenever I saw or heard something that I felt was unfair. The behaviour was part of me and my confidence grew at the pit and on the council. But there's no point banging a head against a brick wall if it isn't going to fall. Picking the right battles to fight is crucial. Nobody wants a show pony, causing trouble for the sake of it. But nor should the power of protest be underestimated.

The Byzantine procedures of the House of Commons were completely alien to me when I arrived in the place. In 1970 the Palace of Westminster reeked of deference. It had the feel of what I imagine it's like in a posh gentlemen's club. The rules, atmosphere and hierarchies were intended to intimidate outsiders. Rough boys from outside were expected to conform, to behave like the others and perpetuate what was an unwritten conspiracy against working people. The choice was clear: conform or challenge. I took the second option out of temperament and belief. Rules in Parliament are made to be bent the way David Beckham could swerve a ball around a wall and into the net.

I go to Parliament to work, yet some of the practices would be found in no other workplace I can think of. On the death of Anthony Eden, the former Tory foreign secretary and prime minister, I discovered the House of Commons gave itself the day off. Eden died in January 1977 some twenty years – yes, twenty years – after he'd abandoned the House of Commons. He'd put on ermine as the Earl of Avon to live a cushy life on the plush burgundy benches of the House of Lords. Eden was a colossal failure during his short spell in Downing Street. He was up to his neck in deceit over the imperial folly that was Suez, yet the Establishment always looks after its own and his reward was a grand title.

Unbelievably, a motion was tabled to adjourn the House of Commons for the day when he died. I was sitting in the chamber, listening to the Labour prime minister, Jim Callaghan, and Maggie Thatcher, then leading the Conservatives in opposition, competing between themselves to see who could ladle the most nauseous plaudits on a politician who had been publicly discredited.

Callaghan praised Eden as a 'most distinguished man' and asserted he was a victim rather than the villain of a period when British imperialism was in retreat, presenting Eden as a spectator rather than a player. Thatcher lauded Eden as a 'distinguished statesman' and all the rest of the great and the good, including sailor Ted Heath and that smuggest of Liberals, David Steel, were on their hind legs to bury Eden in sugary phrases. After nearly an hour of this charade, a Tory MP by the name of Dudley Smith, who represented Eden's old seat of Warwick and Leamington, got up to pay what was intended to be the final tribute before the Speaker adjourned the House so everybody could troop into the bars or go home early.

I'm not one to go out of my way to speak ill of the dead. I see the good in everybody. Or nearly everybody. I've been honoured to deliver the tribute at many a funeral. I'm not religious but I stand in the pulpit of churches to pay tribute to good people, recalling the best of them in orations. But the bosses don't give workers a day off when somebody passes away, particularly when that somebody left the workplace long ago. Sitting in the chamber, listening to the platitudes garlanded around Eden's neck, it would've been dishonest to remain silent. I would've regretted taking the easy route and conforming, when it is inappropriate for a democratically elected chamber, in which the members are supposed to represent the interests of the people of Britain, behaves like the worst of cosiest clubs.

Steeled by the advice of my dad always to treat Parliament as another workplace, I rose to my feet to object to the adjournment and sought to force a division. There was an audible rumble of objections from the club members on the Conservative benches. Most of the thirsty Tories headed for the exits and brandy regardless, led by Thatcher with her handbag. But I wasn't making a gesture, staging a pointless stunt. I felt very strongly that what we were doing was wrong. So I told the House that MPs didn't only speak and act as 'members of a club' but as legislators, making the laws by which others lived. They didn't get the day off when an old boy departed, so why should we?

'MPs should understand that the people outside, whom they represent, very rarely have the opportunity to down their tools and pack in,' I argued. The chamber emptying fast was no deterrent. I went on: 'People will never understand the way in which the Commons adopts these double standards . . . To pack up and go, to abandon the ship at this time after only three hours is a total and utter disgrace.' I told how in the pit if a miner died in an accident the only men to be granted the rest of the day off were the four who carried his body out on the stretcher. The widow was paid a £250 lump sum as part of an agreement to keep the hundreds of other miners hewing coal.

There was uproar among the remaining Tories. Eric Heffer, the Labour MP for Walton in Liverpool who was on the left of the party, also thought I'd gone too far. His cloak of defence hid criticism. Eric said: 'It took a lot of courage and guts for Mr Skinner to do what he has done,' before suggesting I shouldn't have. Eric's conclusion – 'I think he has got to be recognised as having done it honestly' – was hardly a ringing endorsement.

Where I didn't lack support was in the real world. Newspapers, ready to side with an Establishment they're part of, didn't appreciate the intervention and were hostile. It was water off a duck's back. I was heartened by the chord I'd struck with the public. The people who paid our wages, the voters looking in from the outside, were appalled by the cosy little games played in Westminster.

One woman sent me a copy of a long letter she'd written to the *New Statesman* condemning a piece by James Fenton, the poet who was then the magazine's political correspondent, who'd apparently attacked me as a misguided romantic. She quoted Fenton, who had asked: 'Is it likely that, in housing estates up and down the country, tongues are clicking because the Commons adjourned early?' I never bothered to discover how often Fenton visited housing estates but the sheer weight of letters, dozens and dozens of them, proved a nerve had been touched. I read them all and although, alas, I didn't have time to send back long, personal replies to everyone, I replied to each and asked that they forgive my brevity.

One letter was from nine women, eight signing as Mrs with a single Miss, from the Torquay Labour Women's Section. The group wrote:

We the undersigned heartily endorse your action in objecting to the adjournment of Parliament in the paying of homage to the late Lord Avon. There is no precedent for this sheer wasteful form of elitism, furthermore we feel that all Labour Members should have made the same objections.

They weren't all from Labour and left-wing people. I had one on the notepaper of the Liberal association of a Greater Manchester constituency! The lady said:

Dear Mr Skinner,

I never thought the day would come . . . but may I congratulate you [she underlined 'congratulate' to emphasise her point] on your attempt yesterday to get the House to get on with the job. I was appalled to learn that they adjourned in such circumstances, and am only sorry you had such a hopeless reception. Thank you for trying, anyway.

I received a congratulatory note from Harry Fletcher at the National Council for One Parent Families and another from a vicar in Bury St Edmunds who wrote: 'The only thing that shocks me is that no one had the courage to second your effort to divide the House.' I wasn't shocked about that, only saddened. One woman sent a postcard. It read simply: 'UP DENNIS SKINNER!' OK, the message was penned in actual green ink. But she'd included her name and address in London W6, so I marked her down as a supporter.

I genuinely felt strongly that we shouldn't clock off early. I can't recall them trying to pull the same stunt when Heath,

Wilson and Callaghan passed away, so despite the fuss and palaver the protest may have left a slight mark. Thatcher went during a recess and I didn't attend when Parliament was recalled unnecessarily.

My most spectacular bending of the rules was also my best day in Parliament. I've a layman's interest in science and am excited about the possibilities, regularly reading what's in the papers and following scientific debates in the chamber. Researchers have developed cures for all sorts of illnesses that were fatal when I was young. At the heart of the progress for the past thirty-odd years is stem cell research. This is one of the greatest advances in human biology. It has the potential to unlock cures for terrible diseases such as diabetes, leukaemia, Parkinson's and, I hope, the dementia which took my mother.

The Warnock Report in 1984, published by the Committee of Inquiry into Human Fertilisation and Embryology chaired by Baroness Mary Warnock, shone the way forward. Here was a way of experimenting medically on stem cells – taken from the placenta of an embryo – which wouldn't hurt anybody yet held out a genuine prospect of wonderful breakthroughs. But science will never solve all our problems. Politics and economics are absolutely crucial. And politics, as I was poised to discover, can mould scientific research.

Not everybody agreed on the value of blossoming stem cell research. The reactionaries were determined to nip it in the bud. There was a sizeable, well-organised, vocal group who wanted to halt experimentation. They accused scientists of 'playing God' and were determined to prevent what was to be a great leap forward.

In Parliament Fridays are different from Mondays to Thursdays. On Fridays when the House is sitting the MPs take back control for what's known as backbench business, proposing legislation rather than being instructed by whips to support or oppose this or that bill. It's the fag end of the week and the MP behind a Private Member's Bill may have trouble persuading sufficient MPs to stay away from their constituencies to give them a chance of enacting a law. Few of the successful bills are controversial, but there have been some huge exceptions to the rule. Election manifestos tend to promise free votes on conscience issues rather than firm commitments, to avoid splitting parties. So the death penalty was abolished in 1965 via Sydney Silverman's bill and abortion legalised in 1967 by David Steel's. More recently the Labour MP for Worcester, Michael Foster, introduced a bill outlawing the savaging and killing of animals with hounds in England and Wales. After that was defeated the government eventually came up with the 2004 Hunting Act because so many of us were against blood sports. Bob Cryer and I regularly fought Private Member's Bills we objected to in the 1970s and 1980s. These days there is a group of Tories who hate most legislation, the likes of Philip Davies and Christopher Chope, who stop many of the bills on principle. But back in the 1980s a cabal of right-wingers plotted to exploit a Private Member's Bill to kibosh stem cell research.

Step forward Enoch Powell. He'd fallen out with the Conservative Party, if not conservatism, and was sitting in Parliament as the Ulster Unionist MP for South Down in Northern Ireland. We were on opposite ends of the political spectrum. His Rivers of Blood racist incitement confirmed we'd never see eye to eye on much, if anything. Powell fancied himself as a great

Parliamentarian. He was comfortable in the Westminster club. He knew the procedures and how to use the rules. And in 1985 Powell came perilously close to putting on the statute book his Private Member's Bill, the Unborn Children (Protection) Bill, to outlaw the research. It was a terrible threat when people are suffering and dying from incurable diseases and, rather than halting research, we should be doing everything possible to unearth cures.

Powell thought he'd pulled a parliamentary masterstroke to kill stem cell research in Britain. There's an annual ballot to decide which twenty MPs may table a bill. To have any chance you must be near the top or there'll be no time for you on the Fridays allotted. Powell was drawn number five and the vast majority of Tory MPs in those grim Thatcher years were keen to get his bill on the statute book and help him to get it into a committee for detailed scrutiny. Opponents were holding it up so Powell needed to pull a trick out of the hat.

Powell, to gain extra time for his bill, persuaded Brighton Tory Andrew Bowden to give him a day he'd secured for a debate of his own. Backbenchers in that era could put their names down for a Friday debate and if they were selected hold a discussion on whatever they wanted. I was lucky my name came out of the hat soon after I first entered Parliament in 1970. I proposed an alternative socialist Budget. The main thrust of the argument was this was the moment to change, not rearrange, Britain. The list of measures advocated included higher wages, stronger trade unions, investment in schools and hospitals and nationalisation of the banks – a policy implemented by Gordon Brown's government in very different circumstances. I was denounced by Tories as a Marxist. Powell's revolutionary idea was to borrow Bowden's big day.

The smug South Down MP was lauded in the press as a great constitutionalist. He'd read every page of *Erskine May*, the weighty tome known as the parliamentary bible that dictates who can do what, when and where. He was convinced he'd engineered the biggest coup in history. His cunning plan took everybody by surprise. It was unusual, and very clever. By taking Bowden's place and packing the chamber with enough MPs to keep the Commons sitting over the weekend, he thought he'd be home and dry. Powell needed 100 MPs to keep a debate going. We reckoned he had 150, perhaps 200.

Powell's ploy was scheduled for Friday, 7 June in 1985. In the run-up doctors, scientists and groups representing victims of diseases and disabilities were in uproar. There was what you'd call a right panic on. We could see Powell had the numbers. Thatcher's Tories had won a 144-seat majority at the 1983 general election. Although a minority backed stem cell research, there was no shortage of flat-earthers prepared to produce voodoo objections.

On the Labour side frantic meetings were held as people tried to think of ways of stopping the Powellites. Jo Richardson and Ian Mikardo, London Labour MPs on the left with me, came up with a plan to present petition after petition from electors to eat up Powell's time. It was worth a try. We all recognised it wouldn't do the trick on its own. In the pit I'd read the Mines and Quarries Act from cover to cover until I knew some of the law underground like the back of my hand. Seeking a means to stop Powell, I went into the Commons library a fortnight before the show-down to study *Erskine May* as closely as my foe had.

The Conservative MP for Brecon and Radnor in Wales, Tom Hooson, had died a couple of weeks before. By-election writs were moved by the chief whip of the dead member's party. That was the convention. But it set me wondering: is it custom and practice or a firm procedure detailed in *Erskine May*? The moving of a by-election writ takes precedence over all other business. If there is one, it must be the first business of the day after prayers. *Erskine May*, I discovered, didn't stipulate that only the chief whip could move a writ. Which meant on the killer Friday I could initiate a debate on the Brecon and Radnor by-election by moving the writ. If I played my cards right, I could seize the battleground and occupy the field with a filibuster to save the medical break-through and wreck Powell's own wrecking.

I read, re-read and then read again the wording to ensure I hadn't misinterpreted the rules. I hadn't. I was tingling with excitement. I realised I needed to keep my trap shut: if word got out somebody might move the writ before me and hold a brief debate to scupper the filibuster. Another fear was the Tory chief whip might call the by-election, inadvertently sinking my plan. With secrecy paramount, I couldn't utter a word for two weeks. That prevented me consulting others to check I wasn't barking up the wrong tree. Richardson and Mikardo both suspected I was up to something. I told them not to worry. But I wouldn't tell. I felt guilty because they were trusted colleagues. The risk was if I shared it with them, they might share it with others in good faith. A secret shared is often a secret spilled. Jo, a terrific feminist and champion of women's rights, had set up a group of MPs to discuss how to derail Powell. She had a few Tories on it so I didn't join them. Jo would say: 'You're up to something, aren't you, Dennis?' I'd reply: 'You do your thing and I'll do mine. Don't worry.' Of course I was worried myself. I suffered from self-doubt, wondering during those two weeks if I was pissing in the wind; that I'd misinterpreted what looked clear to me.

Aware the chair and clerks might be unaware of *Erskine May*'s wording and afraid I could be shot down immediately, I had agreed on the eve of Powell's big day to go and see the Speaker, Bernard Weatherill, at 7 p.m. In all my years in Parliament, Weatherill has been the best Speaker. He's championed the rights of MPs in difficult circumstances. He was a Tory, and Tory governments ruled with large majorities during most of his spell in the chair, but Weatherill did what he thought was right. Once challenged by a Tory why he called me to ask questions, Weatherill replied: 'Because he's always here.'

I'd phoned the Speaker's Office as late as I could that Thursday afternoon to give them notice that I was entitled to move the writ first thing the following morning. I informed them I needed to discuss an urgent matter of parliamentary procedure and off I went to his apartment in Speaker's House, the country's grandest tied cottage.

I said to Weatherill: 'Do you really want to stay here all this weekend?'

He responded: 'Dennis, does anybody?

I replied: 'There are some in your party who do. Think of the staff, think of the cost. This is no way to behave.'

The Speaker mumbled something about there was nothing he could do.

'I have a plan to stop it,' I said.

'What is it?' he asked immediately.

I explained *Erskine May* didn't specify who could move a by-election writ so I, an MP, would do it tomorrow and as the motion took precedence over other business I'd open the debate. Weatherill was doubtful.

'Get the chief clerk in here and he'll tell you different,' I urged him. The clerk came in and I explained my case.

'That's very unusual,' he said.

'It might be very unusual but it's in order,' I barked.

Weatherill snapped: 'Don't you talk to him like that.'

The Speaker and the clerk left the room to consult. I strained to eavesdrop but couldn't quite hear what they were saying. They checked *Erskine May* and, lo and behold, it stated in black and white that the writ was moved 'normally, but not necessarily, by the Chief Whip' of the party defending the seat. That 'normally, but not necessarily' was my bullseye.

Weatherill, reluctantly I felt, approved my attempt. I was handed the wording on blue paper to initiate a debate on the writ. Almost as soon as I'd got back to the Tea Room, one of our whips marched in and said Peter Shore, Labour's shadow leader of the House, and Michael Cocks, the party's chief whip, wanted to see me. The pair pleaded with me not to do it, that it wasn't the convention. Shore argued that if I moved the writ it would be defeated, and under the rules a second by-election writ couldn't be moved for another three months.

'I don't intend to vote on it,' I said. 'I'll hold a debate on moving it and withdraw at the end of the debate.'

Both continued to urge me to desist but I had a good case in a great cause. I was lighting the blue touch paper the following day.

Friday sessions for backbench business ran from 9.30 a.m. to 2.30 p.m., so if I occupied most of the day I'd defeat Powell and his mob and the weekend extension would be as dead as his bill. My priority was controlling the chamber, sustaining the debate on an issue of national importance, otherwise known as the Brecon and Radnor by-election. Speaking in pit canteens and on street corners were the best debating societies you could attend, far more testing than the Oxford or Cambridge Unions. If you could hold your own and sustain a disciplined argument in front of a shift of sceptical miners, the chamber was a picnic. I wasn't nervous on the Friday morning. Slightly excited, yes, and also wary that if I got it wrong I'd fluff a golden opportunity to save stem cell research.

In many parliamentary confrontations, parties line up like opposing armies. The ground and numbers are in favour of the Government. Private Member's Bills can be fought over on more equal terms. So at 9.36 a.m. on Friday, 7 June, immediately after prayers, order was called and a Labour MP – me – moved the writ for a by-election in the country constituency of Brecon and Radnor to succeed Tom Ellis Hooson, Esq, deceased. In Parliament this was a small earthquake. The traffic didn't halt in Parliament Square. London Underground tubes didn't stop running on the District Line. But the 'Whats?', mumbles and puzzled faces, especially on the Conservative benches but on the Labour side too, were heartening. The Tories had turned up for Powell but were watching me seize his limelight. I suspect they thought the ruse would run out of steam, fizzle out in a few moments. They waited for the chair to slap me down, to rule I was out of order. If that's what they expected, they were satisfyingly disappointed. I knew within a few minutes that we'd pulled off a great escape for stem cell research.

The chair ruled I was in order and to remain within the rules I had to be careful to address the question of the by-election itself.

I paid tribute to Hooson's six years' service to the House. The Tory had taken the seat from Labour in 1979, Hooson dying at the early age of 52. I said I thought Brecon and Radnor was synonymous with Caerwyn Roderick, Hooson's Labour predecessor who was parliamentary private secretary to Michael Foot when he was Labour leader.

> Therefore, when I heard that there was the possibility of the writ for Brecon and Radnor being delayed, and I read the usual outpourings in the press – it must have been about a fortnight ago – I thought that it would be a good idea to get the thing hurried along. It so happened that at that time there was the suggestion that other matters would be moved this Friday. I am not sure whether I was thinking of moving the writ early, before the shock waves of the suggestion of the right hononourable Member for South Down hit the House of Commons, or whether it came after that, but it was about that time. I must make that point, because I am trying to show that it is purely a coincidence that my application falls on the day when other matters might have been discussed.

That 'coincidence' was stretching a point for a higher purpose and is part of the cut and thrust of debate. I was, to use a modern phrase, in it to win it.

Tam Dalyell, a Labour MP who knew how to operate skilfully in Parliament, jumped in and, sticking to Brecon and Radnor, said that before I left the question of Caerwyn Roderick, he wanted to mention Tudor Watkins, who had been the seat's

Labour MP between 1945 and 1970. Why, Tam informed us, only three days earlier he'd visited the widowed Lady Watkins in Brecon and the memory of Tudor Watkins should be respected by anyone interested in agriculture and hill farming, which were his specialist subjects.

That was exactly the kind of intervention needed to keep my filibuster on the road. It presented me with an opportunity to reply that, although Tudor Watkins left the Commons at the election when I arrived, in 1970, I used to see him at Labour Party conferences. All this was eating into Powell's time and we had to stick to the script or we'd be ruled out of order and the game would be over. The beauty of a by-election rather than, say, discussing a hospital closure is that absolutely anything could crop up in the contest. As long as we kept coming back to the by-election, anything and everything could be aired. It was like remembering to address the question when writing an essay in a history exam.

I told Tam that I presumed he'd visit Lady Watkins on his tour of the country to uncover the truth of the sinking of the Argentine cruiser, the *General Belgrano*, during the Falklands war and that the torpedoing 'will become an issue in the by-election'.

The art of a filibuster requires opponents to unwittingly play their role too, helping run down the clock with interventions. When your only aim is to keep a debate going, criticism is music to your ears. Dale Campbell-Savours, the Labour MP for Workington until he took ermine in the Lords, rose to his feet to ask if I knew Hooson was a great advocate of what my party opponent termed 'life issues':

'He voted in all divisions in favour of life issues,' stated Campbell-Savours. 'Does not my honourable friend believe that the use of this procedure in this way does a great disservice to his memory?'

Here was a triple irony. Stem cell research offers the potential of life to those who otherwise might die. The by-election created by the death of an MP, who for all I know might have voted to block that research, gave us an opportunity to save the research. And Campbell-Savours had nudged the clock a minute or so closer to the finish time by objecting. He'd opened the door for me to climb the moral high ground and again assure the Speaker that I was determined to stay in order, however others behaved. I told Campbell-Savours he had:

a bit of a cheek, because he is part of a small group in the House which proposed to change the business of the day in a way which many people – not me – thought was an abuse of the procedures. Now he is trying to chide me for doing something to which I plead not guilty. In any case, Mr. Speaker, I think you would agree with me – I know you would – that we should talk about the issues that will be discussed during the by-election campaign, and not become involved in genetic engineering and other matters. I should say in passing that it is a bit rich that there is all this complaint about genetic engineering, yet the right honourable Member for South Down is acting as the master scientist and pottering about with that young embryo, the honourable Member for Brighton, Kemptown.

The young embryo remark earned a rebuke from the Speaker: 'I am not sure that that has much to do with the writ.' Resuming the thread, I said:

> No, but I think that you would agree, Mr. Speaker that that might become an issue in the by-election. It is fair to say that anything that can be discussed in the House of Commons will become an issue in the Brecon and Radnor by-election. The Labour party candidate, Richard Willey, is only too anxious to get on with the job of raising those issues.

You never know who is going to say what but Campbell-Savours again inadvertently helped out with a sarcastic 'What solidarity' grumble, another scrap that wasn't allowed to go to waste. I responded:

> My honourable friend suggests that Mr Willey may not be the greatest left-winger of all time, but I shall be down there campaigning for him because he is the Labour candidate. I rest in the knowledge that our standard bearer in Brecon and Radnor will do a first-class job in raising all the issues that I may mention later, including the economy, the welfare state, and the countless other matters that may affect that rural area. It is between 30 and 40 miles wide—'

Just as I was working up a head of steam, a Tory railway enthusiast, Robert Adley, rose and in the spirit of a good Parliamentarian, one anxious for as many interventions as possible, I gave way.

It is perhaps nothing more than a coincidence, but I had a premonition that this might be a suitable day to raise the subject that the honourable gentleman has raised, and I happened to come in armed with several books about the railway history of central Wales. Will the honourable gentleman refer during his speech to this vital consideration in the forthcoming by-election? If he does not, I hope that he will not consider it wrong of me to take up the point later in the morning.

Powell sat stony-faced across the floor. Elaine Kellett-Bowman wasn't the sharpest Tory on the green benches and shared many of Powell's prejudices. She raised a point of order complaining I'd mentioned the name of the Labour candidate, eating a few moments extra of her lot's time.

And so we went on from 9.30 a.m. to nearly 1 p.m. The sympathetic interventions became lengthier, to the point where others took over, and I remained seated, letting the debate take its course. And the Powell mob got shirtier, powerless to regain the initiative.

If we set a date that Friday for the by-election it couldn't subsequently be altered. Grumbling Powell gave me another opportunity to stress I'd read *Erskine May* and was following the parliamentary bible. To irk Powell while remaining in order, I praised my rival as an expert on procedure, which Powell undoubtedly was, and added that whatever happened, a sovereign House of Commons could, within the next few days, overturn the decision.

I noticed a little exchange between the Speaker and a clerk while Paisley's Norman Buchan was raising the question of

European vetoes. That was a danger sign. The Speaker was calculating, I realised, if we were addressing issues around the Brecon by-election or wandering off into a free-for-all. Seeking to keep up the initiative, I said:

> I kept my eye firmly on you, Mr Speaker, while my honourable friend made that point, and I saw a little bit of a nod, which suggested that we should not travel down that road. There are areas where we should not tread today. We should keep to the straight and narrow. One thing is certain – the Common Market is not straight and narrow. It has gravy trains, but it is not straight and narrow.

On we carried. Dave Nellist, a Labour MP for Coventry whose expulsion from the party I later opposed, asked for the issue of the young unemployed in Wales to be raised during the by-election campaign. Doug Hoyle returned to Caerwyn Roderick who, said the Warrington MP, had a 'robust knowledge' of the education needs of the Welsh people. 'Does he', meaning me, 'believe that, together with the problem of youth unemployment, education will figure largely in the by-election campaign? Does he agree that that needs to be brought to the fore?' Indeed I did, and I had some figures to prove it.

The Powellites were growing restless, but they couldn't stop us as long as we kept coming back to Brecon and Radnor.

Jack Straw, well versed in the workings of Parliament and a future leader of the House, as well as a home and a foreign secretary, got up to ask if the SDP–Liberal candidate would be supported by the leader of the SDP in Wales or by the leader of the SDP in the United Kingdom. The Speaker described me, tongue firmly in cheek no doubt, as a 'new-found establishment figure' for remaining in order when there were challenges to my interpretation of *Erskine May*. I brought Robinson Crusoe into it, his reliance on a Man Friday evidence that the Tory advice to stand on your own two feet would be torn apart in the by-election. Others, all opposed to Powell's attempt to halt stem cell research, raised unemployment, nurses' pay. The death of Jimmy Inskip, a leader of the Durham Miners, was raised. Yes, I believed, that might crop up in the Brecon and Radnor by-election.

I'd lie if I pretended I didn't enjoy myself. I'd been around long enough to know that on the day you mustn't get cocky. Carelessness could snatch defeat from the jaws of victory. But demoralising your opponents, rubbing in what's happening, is a useful tactic in political battle. If they despaired, lost heart, we were closer to our triumph. A flash of swagger in a speech also heightens the morale of your own side. I said:

The House of Commons is an unusual place. There are many heartaches and few blessings, but one thing is certain. This place, like life generally, is full of surprises. One comes here one morning and the unexpected happens. In a way, that is reinvigorating. Just as one is beginning to lose faith a little, something new happens. This Friday has been one of those unusual days. It was started by the right honourable Member for South Down, who put the cat among the pigeons. I know that the motion is in the name of the honourable Member for Kemptown, but I think that the right honourable Member for South Down will agree with me that there are days when we win and days when we lose and I have a sneaking feeling that this day will belong to those of us who are arguing for this writ and for an early by-election.

Alan Beith, a Liberal with a high opinion of himself, bit instantly and asked if I'd 'ascertained' if the Labour and Conservative chief whips had arranged to come up with a motion to stop MPs deciding on whether or not to hold an early by-election. A Cardiff Tory, Gwilym Jones, accused me angrily of 'indecent haste' when Hooson had died only four weeks earlier. He was sucked into an exchange with Andrew Bennett who argued it was better to have the by-election before the summer, otherwise September would be the earliest date. I do firmly believe by-elections should be held soon after an MP has died or quit for whatever reason, wanting people to be represented instead of left without a voice.

Welsh Nationalist Dafydd Wigley jumped in, favouring a by-election in July before voters went on their holidays. Robert Adley raised votes for holidaymakers! The Tory in Thatcher's hometown of Grantham, Douglas Hogg, received stick from fellow Conservatives for welcoming a challenge to the 'cosy relationship' between the Conservative and Labour whips. Cyril Smith, squealed to the Speaker he'd heard Hogg talking to Labour MPs about talking until 11a.m. and that it was a misuse of parliamentary time. The Speaker wasn't interested and Hogg continued until he'd been round the houses and decided he thought chief whips should move by-election writs.

The clock ticked on with each and John Biffen, the Tory leader of the Commons sitting on the government front bench, answered a couple of the points of order despite the Speaker dismissing them because, said Biffen, he wanted to get on to the embryology debate.

Another Tory, Stephen Dorrell, argued helpfully that debating how and when by-elections should take place wasn't an abuse of parliamentary time, but at the very heart of what the House of Commons should be.

Just before 11.30 a.m., after nearly two hours, the Speaker announced one more backbencher would be called before front-benchers would give us the benefit of their wisdom. It was Ann Clwyd. The Labour MP for Cynon Valley was in favour of stem cell research. Ann took half a dozen interventions. She pronounced Llanfairpwllgwyngyllgogerychwyrndrobwllllantysiliogogogoch, the village with the longest name in Britain, to make a point that it wouldn't be important in Brecon and Radnor to be able to pronounce Llanfairpwllgwyngyllgogerychwyrndrobwllllantysiliogo-gogoch during the by-election. It was marvellous!

The Speaker got into a tangle when Ann was discussing Welsh whisky, mistakenly claiming the motion was about a writ for an English by-election not alcohol. The laughter and shouted protests alerted the Speaker who quickly corrected that to a Welsh by-election. In its way, though, the slip of the tongue eased the tension and everybody involved in the filibuster felt happier.

Next up was Peter Shore who, as shadow leader of the House, went over ground we'd covered and made the obvious point it had been the convention of whips to move by-election writs without waiting too long.

We were getting on for noon and I knew it was now impossible for Powell to succeed. We had petitions lined up to talk into his remaining time. We were close to the winning post. I now played the part of the MP seeking to curtail the debate, arguing my intention had been to test opinion. I said I'd withdraw the motion yet I knew, should other MPs wish to continue the debate, I'd fail. 'Mostly it is revolution, but today it is roses,' I declared.

MPs opposed to Powell duly shouted 'No' and we carried on, with John Biffen, as leader of the House, called to the despatch box at high noon. Biffen, with great theatricality, expressed sorrow that my withdrawal of the motion had been thwarted before adding that he hoped, on further reflection, the Commons would move on. The Tory hierarchy, like the Labour command, didn't want MPs deciding when by-elections are held. Party leaderships love to keep these powers to themselves.

Two votes were held, including the vote on holding a vote, which took about half an hour. I was on the losing side, as I wanted, to win the day. It was 1 p.m. and MPs were lined up to read out and present petitions to Parliament before putting them in the bag behind the Speaker's chair. It's where the phrase 'in the bag' is reported to have originated and it was in the bag for us, more than an hour spent as MPs in our camp read, slowly, their petitions.

There were a dozen, differently worded, against Powell's bill alone. Labour MPs including Joan Maynard, Clare Short, Ann Clwyd, Bob Clay, Jo Richardson, Alf Dubs and Ian Mikardo took turns to walk at a snail's pace to the chair and produce the petition. Harry Cohen's urged a vote against the bill. The strain was telling on Powell who realised he was hopelessly outmanoeuvred, snapping 'Get on with it'. We were – getting on with saving scientific research and lives.

A few Tory MPs presented petitions against the Unborn Children (Protection) Bill on the grounds it would hinder IVF which allowed women to have babies. There were petitions on other issues, too. Jack Straw delivered one on a brewery. Dafydd Wigley, the Welsh nationalist, on ambulances. Frank Cook raised a point of order on scaffolding on the terrace of the House of Commons.

When Andrew Bowden, who intended to donate his debating time to Powell immediately, was finally called it was 2.15 p.m. and his heart didn't sound like it was in a hopeless plea for extra time. Michael Foot was busy arguing why he didn't deserve an extension when Big Ben chimed 2.30 p.m. and that was that. The bid to hold back scientific discovery, to ban stem cell research, was defeated.

Afterwards, Powell came up and said to me: 'It's been a very interesting day. Only you could have done that.' Our politics were worlds apart, him on the right, me on the left. We both knew how Parliament worked and he accepted he was beaten. That he, a Parliamentarian, was outmanoeuvred comprehensively must have hurt. He hadn't seen it coming. Powell's was a clever ruse. Ours was cleverer.

I received a huge number of telephone calls and letters. Doctors and scientists wrote, as did parents of children with incurable diseases who were praying for a scientific breakthrough. Professor Robert Winston, now a lord, sent a nice note. The letters which confirmed to me that I had acted properly, that we were absolutely right to bend the rules, were those from desperate mothers and anguished fathers of sickly kids. I fail to understand how people can come up with moral objections to the harmless use of stem cells to save and improve lives.

I used the same parliamentary manoeuvre on a second occasion in January 1989 to stop Ann Widdecombe eroding the right of women to choose to have an abortion. She looked gobsmacked, absolutely sickened, when I moved the writ for a by-election in Richmond in North Yorkshire. The *Catholic Herald* described Widdecombe as 'Skinnered alive' when we blocked her bid to roll back the 1967 Abortion Act. I've always found it contradictory that Tory MPs such as Widdecombe preach personal responsibility and freedom, then seek to force women to have unwanted babies. It must be difficult to decide to have an abortion and we, as MPs, shouldn't make the decision any harder.

Tony Banks was lined up to move the Richmond writ but he got cold feet so I was asked by those opposing Widdecombe. The fact is I didn't want to go round that track again. It's not easy. I opposed Widdecombe's Private Member's Bill and would have intervened and, of course, voted, but I was hoping somebody else would take the floor. They wouldn't, so I performed the same trick.

Again I had the benefit of surprise, with Widdecombe caught on the hop. She looked as if she'd swallowed a wasp. Andrew MacKay, a saturnine Tory who spent a lot of time on golf courses and was to be forced to quit Parliament with his wife, another Tory MP called Julie Kirkbride, after they were dubbed Mr and Mrs Expenses, claiming for a home each, immediately raised a point of order to accuse me of breaching parliamentary privilege.

Betty Boothroyd, in the chair, knew the score and told him to write to her.

The content of my speech was mundane. That didn't matter. The intention was to reoccupy the floor so Widdecombe would sit fuming impotently. I wouldn't have been surprised if she'd self-combusted. She was livid. Four times she raised points of order, each absorbing a few more of her precious seconds. As if reading a road map, I said:

> When the writ is agreed, I am looking forward to going up there and revisiting Richmond, Northallerton, Catterick camp and Leeming Bar, I and Peter Heathfield were held up there on our way to a meeting during the miners' strike. That is a real diversion, but I just remembered that when I looked at the map. I remember those two hours at Leeming Bar service station because it looked as if we would not get to Northumberland for the meeting. The constituency is, in many ways, part of old England and there it is, stuck up in the north, surrounded by several Labour constituencies.

Andrew Bennett, Tam Dalyell and a few old allies were joined by the likes of Bob Cryer, Jeremy Corbyn, Dawn Primarolo, Alice Mahon and Tony Banks himself to keep the Richmond debate going with questions, interventions and speeches. During the debate I announced that I'd lived just off the Pennines. The former Liberal leader, David Steel, sitting on the bench behind me, mumbled: 'The honourable Member is off the edge of most things.' Maybe so, but sometimes it pays to be 'off the edge', as he so charmingly put it.

The trick worked a treat that second time. The Richmond speech, just like the Brecon and Radnor filibuster before it, wasn't a great one. The two didn't set pulses rating, sending people to the barricades. But both did an important parliamentary job. There'll never be a third. The House changed the rules and rewrote *Erskine May* to prevent backbench MPs like me moving by-election writs.

The Richmond by-election proved to be interesting when it took place in February 1989. Tory Boy William Hague, who'd wowed a Conservative conference aged 16, won and when he grew up was a disastrous leader before landing the job of foreign secretary in the Cameron–Clegg coalition. In the by-election the disarray between the SDP and Liberals saw on the ballot paper a Social Democrat, a Social and Liberal Democrat and a Liberal. Leon Brittan, the constituency's MP, had abandoned Parliament for a commissioner's seat on the Brussels gravy train.

A few years back the editor of *Hansard*, Ian Church, rang me and said he wanted to include Brecon and Radnor in a *Hansard* collection of the greatest parliamentary speeches of the past hundred years. We met for a cup of coffee on the terrace of the House of Commons. I wasn't sure. I told him: 'I don't think it was a great speech.' Church replied: 'I know it wasn't but it was a great parliamentary event.'

The long and short of it is I agreed to nominate the speech based on the impact it made. It duly appeared in a 2009 *Hansard* centenary volume alongside 45 others nominated by MPs and peers including Liberal Chancellor David Lloyd George fighting for his People's Budget, Winston Churchill in 1940 and Nye Bevan's championing of a National Health Service blueprint in 1946.

Bob Cryer, Willie Hamilton, Max Madden and I became quite expert at bending the rules. We adopted guerrilla tactics to stop an Eastbourne Harbour Bill in 1975 which would've made a killing for the then Duke of Devonshire who, despite the title, owned estates centred in Derbyshire. The Chatsworth Estates also owned the port of Eastbourne and a lot of land in East Sussex. The duke's plan was to use Parliament to earn himself another fortune by building 2,500 houses, shops and this and that as well as a marina for mooring boats. He'd persuaded Ian Gow, the Eastbourne Tory MP who was Thatcher's friend and was later assassinated by the IRA with a car bomb, to be a willing helper in this enterprise.

The Conservatives were prepared to keep the place up all night to pass the Eastbourne bill through, so we changed our tactics. Instead of keeping the place up, we'd put it to bed early. The debate began just after 7 p.m. and I and a few others were in the chamber while other Labour MPs made themselves scarce, scattering about the place or wandering outside so it looked as if there were few of us. As we predicted, the Tories drifted off to dinner in London's restaurants, believing there wouldn't be a vote until 10 p.m. at the earliest. Gow and a few Conservatives were on their side and I could see the feudal Duke of Devonshire sitting above in the gallery, watching and listening that June evening. He was entitled to expect it would be plain sailing for the Eastbourne Harbour Bill.

But we weren't playing a parliamentary game. I objected to the Thatcherite Establishment demanding the working class tighten its belt, making cuts in public spending, while at the same time proposing a great big development on the south coast to enrich further an already fabulously wealthy son of privilege who possessed substantial land in Derbyshire, Yorkshire, County Limerick and Sussex. I called it not a land-grab but a sea-grab by a duke who wanted to bring a Bill of Parliament to take part of the sea. I quoted from a Tribune Group statement which pointed out that 750,000 jobs had been lost in manufacturing to be replaced by only 250,000 in services. The British economy was changing, and not in favour of the working class. The 1,000 extra jobs in leisure services that would purportedly be created by the duke were a drop in the ocean. If we gave the green light to Eastbourne, another 29 marinas would be developed on the south coast and none of them would help ordinary people. Eastbourne had 5,000 on its housing waiting list but they couldn't afford what was then an expensive £50,000 house with a private mooring.

Elaine Kellett-Bowman, a Tory with a grand opinion of herself, sat muttering during my speech and after one intervention I inadvertently called her, sarcastically, 'darling' instead of the honourable or right honourable Member for Lancaster. The Deputy Speaker must have been distracted because I wasn't pulled up. I don't think Gow had a clue about what was going to hit him. He jumped up on a point of order when I called the Duke of Devonshire a 'benevolent despot'.

The Deputy Speaker ruled I'd gone too far and requested I amend the expression. 'I am prepared to withdraw the "benevolent" bit,' I told him. The chair instructed me to withdraw both parts and carry on my speech.

'On the basis that one of the Duke of Devonshire's antecedents – I think it was the second Cavendish – was the man responsible for putting down Wat Tyler, just after the Peasants' Revolt, and he got £40 a year for doing it from the then King,' I replied, 'I am prepared to rephrase it and to say "a descendant of a benevolent despot' – I beg pardon, I mean "despot". That took some working out, Mr Deputy Speaker.'

I wanted a radical transformation of the economy in favour of the working class, not a marina in Eastbourne in the interests of the Devonshires. I've always believed in setting out an alternative when opposing any measure, so explained what I believed was needed.

'If there is a desire to do something for the social good of the area, why not build a gigantic workers' convalescent home? It need not be just for miners. It could be for pneumoconiosis, rail-waymen and others. Perhaps the duke could be reminded of the many different types of workers in his home county of Derbyshire. Many of those could well spend a month on the Eastbourne coast. If this area is to be developed and something is to be done for the nation, that kind of proposal might be acceptable.'

I was accused of 'fanning the flames of class warfare' by Jonathan Aitken, a Tory MP who was to go on to be a Cabinet minister, but then received a prison sentence of 18 months for perjury after his 'simple sword of truth and the trusty shield of British fair play' turned into a twisted sword and rusty shield. He lied about an arms scam involving the Saudis and on this occasion in the House of Commons he was promoting the interests of a hereditary peer.

Some people from our side did a tour of the Strangers' Bar and the Dining Room but couldn't find many Tories. We received a nod in the chamber from one of the Labour MPs and called a division at about 9 p.m. We won without a vote, Gow realising we'd completely outmaneuvered him. Everybody headed off into the night. I stayed around for a while before going to the cloakroom at a quarter to ten to pick up my coat. Tories were starting to flood into Parliament. Most of the lights had been turned off.

'Where is everybody?' asked one the Conservative MPs.

'Didn't you hear,' I said, trying not to sound gleeful. 'We packed up an hour ago. Everybody's gone – you're too late.'

And with that I left, leaving bemused Tories. Thatcher made it a personal mission to ram it through the Commons. But we'd made a point, winning a battle if not the war in Eastbourne.

We had, however, won the war on stem cell research. Delaying it by even a few years would've stayed progress and cost lives. Britain stole a lead on the US where the Bible thumpers and Republican backwoodsmen fought against the future in even greater numbers.

So Fridays can be important in Parliament. Mike White in the *Guardian* wrote that I'd snookered Powell. I'm a competitive man, I admit. Part of me wanted to defend and promote stem cell research for the very best of motives. Another bit of me just wanted to beat Powell.

CHAPTER NINE

Never be dull

Rhythm. Public speaking is all about rhythm. Just as singing is about rhythm. Or cross-country running when I was a kid at school. The comparison with slogging over fields may sound odd but when I was 12 and 13 I discovered that if I could control my legs, arms and breathing, I'd stay in the race. I'd think 'rhythm, rhythm, you must keep the rhythm', to maintain a steady pace and save enough for a sprint to the finish. Speaking in public requires an equally strong pattern.

I prefer public speaking to reminiscing on a page and I readily admit some of my speeches have been better than others. You sense immediately whether it's going down well, coming together nicely, or going awry. I've never delivered a perfect speech. I'm a tough judge and always think afterwards that I should have said this or I should have said that, dwelling on what was missed rather than what worked. But I'm fortunate to be able to think on my feet and draw on a keen memory, and that sustains the confidence to get up in front of a crowd and seek that rhythm. The goal of a speech is to persuade the audience to listen, engaging their emotions. You want them to be excited by what they hear. To make them laugh, make them cry, make them think and send them home happy.

Like much in life, I learned how to speak in the pit and on the council. Including the bottom line – never be dull. It's rare to hear someone wishing a speaker had gone on for longer. Alas it is more common to hear complaints that the speaker droned on too long. In the pit, faced with a group of men in the canteen at six in the morning, you went straight to the point and put the argument succinctly and persuasively or they were off. It wasn't a bad lesson to learn.

Tony Blair threw a backhanded compliment in my direction when he wrote I was a 'genius at a particular type of left-wing rally speech'. Decoded, he meant a speech he'd never dream of making and, presumably, he thought should never be given. I remember the occasion that triggered the comment. We were both invited to speak in Spennymoor Town Hall in County Durham. Blair was the new Labour MP for Sedgefield, elected in 1983 after winning a selection tussle with Les Huckfield, a left-wing former MP who'd given up Nuneaton in the hope of landing a safer constituency. Thatcher had won her second general election, the Falklands and the Gang of Four in the Social Democratic Party together gifting her a 144-seat Conservative majority.

I'd accepted the invitation to speak at the 'Lessons from Defeat' rally. The fresh-faced local MP was, I was assured, a nice, intelligent young man but his lessons from defeat weren't my lessons. Nor were his Labour politics. Blair came from a very different background. That much was obvious from the start: Fettes, a private school in Scotland, then Oxford University, gave him a healthy head start over everybody else in that hall.

Blair was very polite when he introduced himself. I'd jotted down a few notes for a speech condemning Thatcher, attacking the SDP and calling for a united response from the labour movement. Until Tony spoke. He went first and his starting point was that Labour had lost touch with people and needed to change. The working-class audience was in many ways similar to those found in Bolsover and Blair wasn't in tune with them. He had this bizarre notion that we as a party were happy watching black-and-white telly when voters wanted colour TVs. Then he delivered a riff about what he'd learned at his grandmother's knee. It was a world apart from what I'd been taught at my grandmother's knee. I thought: Right, two can play this game. So I ditched the original plan and jotted down a few fresh notes.

He'd misjudged that audience completely, Blair. He shouldn't have lectured folk who were suffering under the stilettos of Thatcher. When I speak, especially when I'm the last speaker, I tie up all the ends by referring to who has spoken and what was said before. That evening I devoted a fair chunk to parodying Blair.

Blair gives an account in his memoirs. His version is, I believe, largely accurate, although I recall I spoke about our mothers instead of grandmothers. Modernising, as he might describe it, the familial reference because I thought I'd touch a rawer nerve if I conjured pictures of mothers instead of grannies. Blair's account of the speech, published with his own running commentary in his autobiography *A Journey*, reads like this:

'So,' he began, 'your new MP, supposed to be a Labour MP (particular emphasis on word 'Labour'), whose experience in Labour politics (again much emphasis on 'Labour') up to now includes (here reading from a piece of paper with extraordinary thespian timing and skill) Durham Choir School (private school hated by the local proletariat); Fettes College, Edinburgh – the Eton of Scotland I'm told, (in an aside) not that I'd know (much laughter and applause); St John's College, Oxford (said with an especial sneer); and the Bar (here applause) – and that's not one you buy a pint in (uproarious outburst of laughter) but one full of lawyers (pantomime hisses); your new Labour MP thinks our grandparents didn't know what they were talking about; that it's time we disowned them; that now's the moment when we tell them – many of whom never owned so much as a wireless, never mind a black-and-white TV – that they don't belong in Thatcher's Britain (looks of horror on faces of audience). Well, let me tell you, Anthony Charles Lynton Blair (my full name, rather unfortunately printed several times in the course of the Beaconsfield by-election), my grandparents were poor, it's true; were humble folk, I admit it; were, I dare say, a little old-fashioned in their principles of loyalty and solidarity, but THEY WERE DECENT PEOPLE AND PROUD OF BEING WORKING CLASS.' The last words rose to a crescendo accompanied by an eruption of applause, cheers and general favour to a degree that fairly lifted the roof off the place.

Blair admitted staggering out, dazed. He was sharp enough to recognise he hadn't gone down as well as he might have hoped.

I'll readily admit I subsequently gave him, when asked, a few tips on speaking in the House of Commons, when he was prime minister. I advised him to push up the microphone instead of lowering it, avoiding the appearance of a bowed head on TV. That makes you look as if you've something to hide. I told him to keep his head still instead of moving it about. And to sing from the diaphragm instead of speaking from the throat. The voice carries further if you use the chest. Opera singers finish with their arms out to improve the breathing. Good speakers do something similar.

Other tips I give to Labour MPs include thinking of a speech as a tree with the main ideas the trunk, asides and jokes branches growing off the central body. I've never believed in writing or typing a full speech in advance, let alone using an autocue. My method is to grab a sheet of paper and jot down two or three words for each idea. I'll add a few extra if they later come into my head. Speakers who set it in concrete are trapped. Far better to be on your toes, adapting, as I did with Blair, when thoughts pop up. Most speeches read out word for word lack the passion, the vigour of quick thoughts. No matter how often they're rehearsed, or how many gag writers are employed to insert the jokey rehearsed spontaneity, written speeches lack life. The fear of stumbling when script-free, of suddenly drying up, keeps the adrenalin flowing and the words coming.

My final tip is to locate an object or a face to focus on. In the House of Commons I'll look at a wooden panel on the wall diagonally opposite to the right. It beats scanning Tory MPs. At a rally or a meeting, I'll select a person who I'll return to again and again. It assists if they're brightly dressed or wearing a hat, so easily identifiable. If you go back and they've gone, don't worry. Find someone else.

Michael Foot used the same ingredients as me in his speeches. He could hold an audience spellbound. Foot sank Thatcher in a special Saturday debate after the Falklands invasion. His speech when Labour lost a parliamentary vote of no confidence in 1979, an election called a few months ahead of schedule, Scottish National Party turkeys voting for their own early Christmas by fluttering off with Tories, was one of the best I heard him deliver: clever, funny and intensely political.

Outside the House of Commons I heard Foot electrify a rally at a Labour conference in Scarborough during the late 1950s. Foot's theme was the Red Flame of Courage. He set the place alight. Foot was learned and hilarious, compassionate until it came to the Tories, when he was ruthless. It was a pleasure as well as an education to listen to Foot.

Tony Benn possessed superb pronunciation and delivery. He selected his words carefully and in my opinion was at his best in the House of Commons. His winding-up speeches at the end of debates in the late 1970s, when Labour had lost its majority, were wonderful. Tony could be relied upon to rally the troops. Conservatives would come in early before the vote to listen to his forensic arguments. It is a pity they weren't on TV. Our vote might have gone up at the election.

Robin Cook had a decent delivery and his resignation speech over Iraq earned headlines. Overlooked were his performances at Business Questions when he was leader of the House. MPs could ask anything and Cook batted away Tory barbs effortlessly. He was very amusing and never got into a ruck he couldn't win.

Harold Wilson's total command of his brief enabled him to sound clever at the despatch box. MPs feared him, worrying what Harold would reply in response. I wasn't in Parliament for his golden years in the 1960s but he remained impressive in the first half of the 1970s before his resignation in '76. I had a little chat with his wife, Mary, in 2003. I was recovering from a heart operation and would sit on a bench in St James's Park, then try to walk slowly to the next seat about 10 yards away. She told me the story of how they realised he was forgetting things. It sounded as if they knew he had Alzheimer's by 1975, the year before he quit. It must have been terrible for a man with his brilliant brain to know it was coming. I was especially empathetic because of my mother.

Wilson's predecessor, Hugh Gaitskell, didn't set the world on fire when he spoke but I heard his 'Fight and Fight Again' speech against unilateral nuclear disarmament and, while I disagreed with him, the sheer passion left a lasting impression.

I'd never forget Nye Bevan who was a great speaker with that quaint, halting delivery. Bevan was controlling his stammer and it inadvertently became a plus. I heard his 'Naked into the conference chamber' appeal for Labour to ditch unilateralism. As with Gaitskell's, I wouldn't fault the performance. And once again I didn't buy the content, remaining to this day a supporter of CND.

One of the best trade union orators was without doubt Lawrence Daly, general secretary of the NUM. It was a joy to listen and at the end you'd have followed him anywhere. Of the Tories I've heard, John Biffen was the best performer in the Commons. He could think on his feet, just like Wilson.

Over the years I must have spoken in every constituency in England, most in Wales and many in Scotland. I've been called a mini-Ashcroft, drawing a crowd to raise funds for the party to counter the millions of pounds poured into Conservative coffers by a wealthy peer who didn't pay his fair taxes in Britain as a non-dom.

This year, 2014, was the eighteenth invitation to speak at a Durham Miners' Gala since my debut at the Big Meeting on the old racecourse in the City of Durham – the country's biggest annual expression of working-class solidarity, pit communities continuing to march behind brass bands and banners despite the extinction of coal mining. In 1978, my first time, I spoke alongside Tony Benn and Lawrence Daly. I'd go on to share the platform with Arthur Scargill, Peter Heathfield, Neil Kinnock, John Prescott, Ian Lavery, Ron Todd, Paul Kenny, Bob Crow, Tony Woodley, Dave Prentis, Rodney Bickerstaffe, Len McCluskey, Frances O'Grady and many more.

The Northumberland miners called their gathering a picnic to bypass legal restrictions on demonstrations in the nineteenth century. The lustre of speaking at gatherings of pitmen has never faded. I made a little piece of history by addressing the South Wales miners for a fourth time in 1983. I'll admit I was proud of that, not even the great Aneurin Bevan himself achieving the distinction of a quartet of invitations.

Class injustice is a recurring theme of my speeches, working people denied a fair crack of the whip. David Cameron's million-aire's row treating working people as whipping boys, imposing the bedroom tax and flogging public services, are doing what is natural for Conservatives and if I'd written down my speeches it wouldn't take much adaptation to apply those delivered during the governments of Heath, Thatcher and Major to Dodgy Dave and his chums.

I've found my way to the pulpit, giving the tribute for departed friends at many a funeral. I was invited to open a Christmas fete to raise funds to repair the roof of Wessington church in the Bolsover constituency. It's a nice-looking building between Matlock and Clay Cross. They thought getting me along would be unusual and they'd pull in a few extra. It was a successful afternoon and afterwards a woman, interested rather than hostile, said she hadn't expected to see me because she knew I wasn't religious. 'What's that got to do with anything?' I answered. 'Churches are works of art built by working people and I'll always help save them.' She seemed satisfied.

Speaking in the Commons is very different to in a hall or at a rally in the open air. Parliament is empty, only twenty or thirty MPs in the chamber during most of the day. TV pictures showing it full for Prime Minister's Questions give a false impression. MPs are required also to speak through the chair, remembering to say 'Mr Speaker' now and again. I learned how to do that as a councillor so it wasn't hard, but you do see some people struggle. I advise them to read *The ABC of Chairmanship* by Walter Citrine, general secretary of the TUC from 1926 and through the war to 1946. The advice is as relevant today as it was then. Whether you're chairing the meeting or participating, Citrine's worth digesting for the understanding.

Rosie Winterton, Labour's Chief Whip, asked me to give a few lessons to new MPs in 2010. I challenged the conventional view that MPs should wait to make a formal maiden speech before asking questions. My advice was to note down a few lines and learn them before asking a short, sharp question. The likes of Catherine McKinnell, Ian Mearns and Pat Glass have never looked back.

The wood panel trick allows an MP to concentrate on what they're saying instead of being distracted by the expression on the face of the minister or prime minister. It doesn't always work. Everybody will be diverted now and again when an opponent shouts abuse. The rule remains – never respond to heckles. The last thing you want is to be thinking about what somebody else is saying to you. It's hardly likely to be favourable.

I advised Ed Miliband early on to memorise his speeches and his 'One Nation Labour' performance at the party's conference in Manchester in 2012 went down a storm. He was impressive in repeating the act in 2013 in Brighton. I've been in a few times to talk to him about handling the Commons. During the early days of Prime Minister's Questions he allowed himself to be distracted by hecklers, responding with answers that made no sense to viewers watching on TV because they didn't hear the jibe. I gave the same advice to Jim Callaghan when Parliament began to be broadcast regularly on the radio.

David Miliband asked for a bit of help before he made his first big speech to the Labour conference.

'You've been doing this for years. What should I do?' he asked.

I enquired: 'How long have you got?'

'Ten to fifteen minutes,' he said.

'Then learn your lines,' I told him. 'If you can avoid that autocue, do so.'

The trap many politicians fall into is speaking a language unfamiliar to millions of people. The danger is Beltway jargon, spouting terms and acronyms that are meaningless outside the political class. I speak the language of people that I was born and bred with. Politics is about their lives as well as mine. There's a dangerous risk in Parliament of being sucked into exchanges which appeal to other people in the Commons chamber and the media. I imagine what the men and women in Bolsover would think. Will it interest them? Will they know what I'm trying to say, and sometimes saying?

The best reception for one of my speeches was probably at the 1992 Labour conference in Blackpool. In the *Guardian* Patrick Wintour, who is now the paper's Political Editor, wrote I 'brought down the house with a bravura performance'. I wish I had brought John Major's Tory government down and saved what remained of the coal industry. Andrew Rawnsley, who in those days wasn't a bad sketch writer on the *Guardian*, contrasted my rousing reception with the 'smattering of polite applause which you might expect at the end of an academic seminar' for another Labour figure. The recipient of that polite applause? Tony Blair, who two years later would be leader. According to Rawnsley: 'The casual visitor from outer space, dropping in to the Labour conference for the morning, would have been in no doubt who was who in the Winter Gardens. The way they whooped and whistled for him, the leader of the Labour Party could only be Dennis Skinner.'

Scargill enjoyed a terrific reception at the same conference and we both used it to expose the vindictive, expensive idiocy of Major and Michael Heseltine's plan to close 31 pits and shut down most of what was left of the coal industry. I accused the Government of 'seeking total revenge on the NUM: they want to close the lot down. This could be the mopping-up operation'. The pits were profitable, British coal was more than £50 a ton cheaper than the foreign and apartheid coal being imported from South Africa, but Major and Heseltine had cooked up a politically motivated plan to make men redundant and chuck communities on the scrap heap. No speech could save them. Major knew nothing about miners because there weren't any collieries near Chelsea or the Oval or Lord's cricket grounds.

I was speaking from the platform as a member of the party's National Executive Committee (NEC) so had longer, seizing the opportunity to extend the attack. I'd never rated Norman Lamont as a chancellor of the exchequer. His humiliation had come a fortnight earlier on Black Wednesday. Lamont, a Little Lord Fauntleroy called David Cameron at his side, put up interest rates from 10 per cent to 12 per cent then 15 per cent to save the pound in the currency-fixing European Exchange Rate Mechanism before surrendering to reality. The Lamont who sang 'Je ne regrette rien' in his bath was the type of out-of-touch Tory who probably thought miners still kept coal in a tin bath. I gave him and the Conservatives what was coming to them. I told the conference:

Norman Lamont borrowed money to put a side bet on the Stock Exchange. The media said it was a great victory, but a fortnight later, it all went down the pan. Ten billion pounds went just like that. We could have saved a hundred thousand miners' jobs for the next ten years with that kind of money. Those yuppies made him a laughing stock. They voted Tory on General Election day, then ripped the Government apart on Black Wednesday. They know where their morality lies. If Lamont had been a Labour councillor, he would have been surcharged.

The applause in defence of the mining industry was thunderous and there was a standing ovation. I got up and some people mischievously claimed I was clapping myself. Funny but non-sense. I was applauding the miners in the hall and the public gallery.

I've stood for and won eleven Westminster elections in Bolsover and must have spoken in every patch of the constituency. I tried something different in May 1979. 'Dear Electors,' began the leaflet. 'This year I thought you might be getting a little tired of the usual and numerous election pamphlets ... so I have taken a little gamble and tried to woo you with a few rhyming verses ... here I go.'

I'd later write and sing parodies of the traitorous Social Democratic Party and Conservatives to entertain Labour Party members and trade unionists, but I cringed when I re-read the 'Dear Elector' verse for the first time in decades. I'll admit it isn't brilliant. I didn't spend long on it, yet what followed wasn't 'a few' verses but nineteen of four lines each. My efforts were spread over two pages. I appreciate it sounds eccentric and probably is. It smacks of self-indulgence. But the verse was a genuine attempt to engage voters. And you know what? I enjoyed a more enthusiastic response to that ode than any election leaflet I've put out before or since. People would stop me in Bolsover marketplace to tell me they'd read and enjoyed it. OK, some may have been polite to save my feelings. In other cases once voters started they had to finish, for good or bad. I've not tried the same trick again. Maybe I struck lucky the first time and don't want to risk putting voters off. Anyway, here is the unexpurgated 'To the Electors of Bolsover Constituency':

The election is here again, nine years since my first try.
How strange that the issues haven't changed by and by.

The Tory leader then was Ted Heath who promised less tax,
Lower prices, and civil servants removed from your backs.

The voters gave him a chance but the cuts never came,
Instead of lower taxes for workers . . . they carried the blame
For putting up prices; wages were tied to a norm
And Mrs Thatcher, who helped Ted then, will run true to form.

Tax cuts for the wealthy, but VAT will rise high
On the goods that the low-paid and the pensioners buy.
She'll make prices rise and council rents will soar
Together with fees for doctors, hospitals and more.

Her magic cure for solving the ills of the state
By cutting social spending will suffer the fate
That she will recall, as part of Ted's team,
When the policy was tried and became just a dream.

The unions she says should be shackled and tied.
That was tried once before and the workers replied
By voting against sanctions in a free and fair vote
They stood up to the Tories and kept freedom afloat.

Waste, Mrs Thatcher says, is the Tory target today.
She has got a 'cheek' to say that when you examine her way.
Tories reorganised Councils, Water and Health in two years
With the result that bureaucracy grew out of its ears

Like most mining families we didn't have a camera when I was young. This was taken during the Clay Cross rent strike in the early 1970s: me, brothers Graham and David who were councillors, Mam pouring the tea, Dad in his cap and the second-youngest brother, Gary.

The Star Walk in Sheffield, 1956. I finished second and could've won it. I would be up to 7.5 miles per hour when I was really shifting.

Opening Clay Cross Council's new offices as chairman, without a chain hanging from my neck. The group includes Joe Rysdale (third from left) and Bill Lander (on the right of the group), who worked with me at Parkhouse and Glapwell collieries and was deputy editor of the *Clay Cross Clarion*, which we produced to get Labour's message across.

Some of Labour's Key Policies...

- Back to full employment just as the Labour Government achieved after the war.
- 35 hour week and retirement for those who choose at 60.
- Rebuild N.H.S., scrap prescription charges, fair deal for nurses and health workers.
- Restore education cuts, grants for 16-19 year olds, nursery education in all areas.
- Scrap Serpell report and instead invest in British Rail.
- Freeze rents, provide 50% more for new dwellings and repairs.
- Cut VAT and introduce wealth tax.
- Get out of EEC and join the world again.
- Stop money flowing abroad by exchange controls.
- Pensions up to a third of average earnings, free TV licences, £20 Christmas bonus, death grant up to £200.
- Equal rights for women and minority groups.
- Ban 245T, lead in petrol, control toxic substances, scrap Sizewell and PWR programme.
- Repeal Tory Employment laws.
- Ban export of live animals and extreme livestock systems. Royal Commission on animal protection.
- Increase greater participation in sport and leisure by providing better facilities.

Vote Labour ☒

Published by P. Trickett, 85 Coronation Drive, South Normanton, Derby
Printed by Duffin & Son (Printers) Ltd., 81 Market Street, South Normanton, Derby

DENNIS SKINNER:

WHAT THEY SAY ABOUT HIM

"One who remembers his roots"

"A True Socialist"

Observer, 8.10.78:
"Mr. Skinner has some claim to be regarded as the finest Parliamentarian of our time"

New Statesman, 21.1.77:
"Skinner's speech was one of the best I have so far heard in Parliament—partly because of it being made at all, partly because of the passion with which it was delivered"

Birmingham Post, 23.11.78:
"Conservatives may fear and loathe him and Labour M.P.'s are wary too, but in time Mr. Skinner may be seen as one of the great Parliamentary performers of the second half of this century"

Punch, 5.1.77:
"If I were asked to nominate a backbencher who does qualify for the title of sea-green incorruptible, I would nominate Mr. Skinner"

- A full-time MP who believes that all MP's should, especially with four million unemployed, be satisfied with one job only.
- Youngest ever President of Derbyshire's miners.
- Educated at Tupton Hall and Ruskin College, Oxford.
- National speaker for disabled, pensioners, people's march for jobs, nurses, health workers and other groups under Tory attack.

BOLSOVER CONSTITUENCY

Thursday, 9th June, 1983
Polling 7 a.m. to 10 p.m.

DENNIS SKINNER

SACK THE TORIES BEFORE THEY SACK ANYONE ELSE

- Worst level of unemployment
- Biggest slump for 60 years
- Record bankruptcies and failures
- Heaviest tax burden ever

I've always written my own election leaflets. This was for the 1983 General Election. I won Bolsover but Labour lost nationally to the Tories and Margaret Thatcher.

Speaking at a fundraiser for Colin Burgon in Elmet after the pit strike. He was to win the Yorkshire seat for the first time in 1997.

I was sent anonymously this photo on a picket line with a note saying: 'You'll like this.' I think it was during the *TV-am* dispute when I was to be arrested and thrown in a cell.

Speaking at the Durham Miners' Gala with Neil Kinnock looking on.

Above: With friends on a visit to Barlborough old people's centre.

Right: With a couple of St John's Ambulance Brigade volunteers while opening a fete in Bolsover town.

Below: Waiting to speak in Trafalgar Square after a march for jobs in the 1980s.

The Albert Hall in 1986: 'I hear Thatcher and there's no one there . . .'

If you can, it's better to speak from notes and memory than reading out a script.

The room without a window off an upstairs corridor in the House of Commons from which I worked for many years.

With Tony Blair. I might have been telling him that Bush was as thick as two short planks.

At a Labour fundraiser, one of the many over the years I've spoken at to raise money for the party.

The Common Market we suffered, and are still suffering now
From that big Tory sell-out and to which I won't bow.
The British housewife is raped by the prices from the EEC
And eight hundred million pounds is paid as a membership fee.

The Germans pay much less and France nothing this year
Little wonder the British people shout, hear, hear
To those MPs, like me, who refuse to yield on this point
And say if you want to save money, let's 'get out of the joint'.

They lured Britain in to get their hands on our oil supplies
And if the Tories succeed . . . they will take another big prize
Without British safeguards and with Common Market control
The oil tap will be opened fully, and for more miners . . . the
    dole.

So Labour must win this election and take power again
From the Common Market Commission and its beloved
    'gravy train'.
The Tories and Liberals have no answer you know
They sold out to Euro-big business a long time ago.

But what about Labour you ask, what will they do?
It's a fair question to put and must be answered for you
We shall increase pensions in line with both prices and wages
Five pounds more than the Tories would give, in their
    proposed stages.

Television licences will be free for all our old folk
It's time it was done . . . and I'm pleased that I spoke
At the NEC meeting way back in December
When the decision was made . . . how well I remember!

Health service charges will be removed . . . about time too
The payment for teeth, specs and medicine will then be
  taboo.
Waiting lists must fall and cash will be used
On hospitals, nurses and workers who have been much
  abused.

Education is another area that needs all our backing
Unlike the Top Tory who says 18,000 teachers 'want'
  sacking
Money for nurseries, school and leisure is an absolute
  must
That way some of the vandalism and crime will then 'bite
  the dust'.

The environment too, is another big issue that has now taken
  hold
So as technology develops, fumes and toxic waste must be
  controlled
And animal welfare is catered for in Labour's mandate
So live animals being exported should not suffer that fate.

The railways need helping and not running down
More traffic on rail will reduce chaos in town

Bungalows and houses, to rent and to buy, must be built with
   more speed
So that young married couples and elderly can have a place
   that they need.

But, most of all, we must shorten the dole queue
Schemes of earlier retirement and shorter hours are long
   overdue.
School grants for over-16s must be paid as of right
Instead of hanging around street corners by day and by night.

My story is ending . . . the kids have switched on the 'telly'
It's not been pure Shakespeare or Milton nor Shelley.
I thought I would do it like this to lighten your day
Better than reading pamphlets printed all the same way.

Good luck on the third . . . I hope you all vote
Your forefathers fought for that right . . . so please note
Give Labour a victory that you know it deserves
And make it a big one . . . thus soothing my nerves!'

I secured a 17,379 majority over the Tories in that contest but in
Britain, alas, the Tories beat Labour. Looking back over the rest of
that election leaflet, I cringe at some of the language commonly
used back then. I would never say now that a British housewife was
'raped' by EEC prices. Other lines were perspicacious, including
grants for 16-year-olds staying on at school, a measure enacted
by Labour after 1997 with the introduction of the £30 a week
Education Maintenance Allowance until Tory public schoolboy
Michael Gove axed it.

The lazy conventional notion that people aren't interested in politics is exploded by the invitations I continue to receive to speak at public as well as Labour Party meetings. People still want to listen to speakers, to argue, to join debates. They want to laugh, cry, think then go home happy.

To remind myself of the value of communicating effectively I recall a Yorkshire miners' rally. I was on my way to speak when I bumped into the late actor Roger Lloyd Pack on Doncaster station with his children. Roger was on the left and was a friend of the unions, active in Equity and happy to attend gatherings to add a touch of show-business glamour. Anyway, Roger said he was speaking to the rally. I still remember the shocked look on his face as I told him: 'The only thing you'll be doing is judging the fancy dress.' But he did get to sit on the platform during the speeches.

He was best known as Trigger, the dopey road sweeper in *Only Fools and Horses* who said he'd won a prize for having the same broom for 20 years, then revealed it had 17 new heads and 14 new handles, yet he still thought it was the same brush. When the chair introduced him as Roger Lloyd Pack the crowd didn't move a muscle. Nobody knew him by his real name. I thought: Right, I'm going to sort this out. When my turn at the microphone came round, I announced we had Trigger up on the stage with us. Then everyone knew who he was and they clapped and cheered. Roger was happier too.

CHAPTER TEN

I wah in Derbyshire

I wah telling m'duck I'm from Derbyshire. Wah isn't 'were' but 'was', and the people of the county can be irritated when grammatically incorrect translation is applied.

The Derbyshire dialect is mine, it's how I speak. I'm one of those people irritated when it's misquoted in the newspapers and readers are told I thought 'I were' doing this, that or the other when I actually said, correctly, that 'I was' doing it. I'm not trying to make a big deal out of it. The intention is to give a flavour of how people of my generation in Derbyshire talk.

To the ear outside Derbyshire we're regularly mistaken for Yorkshiremen and women. Not a huge crime in itself and, as one from North Derbyshire, I understand how the confusion occurs. I was brought up and live close to the border with South Yorkshire and we both say 'thee' for 'you', which is, I imagine, a twist on the biblical thou. The dialect's stronger in the north of the county than the south, although it's softening as we are all bombarded with identikit BBC standard accents on TV and radio. People are far more mobile than when I was a boy and swap counties, and indeed countries, in numbers and with a speed that was once unimaginable. In Derbyshire it remains relatively common to hear words such as clonk for hit, eh for he and nowt for nothing. We've also our own phrases such as 'strong int arm an quick in t'ead', which is a compliment, used to describe somebody with a physical presence who thinks swiftly on their feet.

The county's probably best known for the Peak District, the county cricket team and football clubs, Derby County and Chesterfield. Clay Cross is just outside the Bolsover constituency. My seat in Parliament is a big area geographically. At its longest it stretches 25 miles and is another 25 miles at its broadest, including towns such as Creswell, Shirebrook, Whitwell, Clowne, Barlborough, Bolsover itself and South Normanton, where I live, as well as some of the nicest villages you'll find anywhere in England. The M1 slices through it and many drivers enjoy the view of Bolsover Castle on the hill to the left when heading south and the right going northwards.

I've always held advice surgeries around the constituency and you can't beat standing in Shirebrook marketplace to keep your finger on the pulse, talking to men and women about pay or jobs or the NHS or whatever else is on their minds. The feedback is also useful for other reasons. It was in Bolsover that I was diagnosed by a woman, a pensioner, as needing a new hip. 'Eeh, Dennis,' she shouted, 'thee need t'get that hip of yours sorted.' I'd put it down to old age. She spotted I was shifting the weight to the good side and knew what was wrong because she'd had the same trouble a few years earlier. It was good free advice and I had the hip replacement in 2011.

In our area we've lost not only the pits but the textile factories too. There used to be ten, and big employers they were. Companies such as Courtauld, who supplied Marks & Spencer until that high-street chain stopped buying British and started trawling the globe for the cheapest goods. The impact of the twin closures, coal and textile, were devastating on jobs and incomes.

Tibshelf Community School is evidence of why I believe you can't be solely local to be an effective MP, and must be in Parliament to win the best deal for the people you represent. Under Labour's Building Schools for the Future programme we saw our schools modernised, with the secondary in Shirebrook, Heritage in Clowne and Frederick Gent in South Normanton replaced with new and refurbished classrooms. The guillotine came down in May 2010 when the Tories and Liberal Democrats formed their coalition. I had a fight on my hands to argue that Tibshelf should be an exception when hundreds of rebuilding schemes were scrapped. I took the head, deputy head and Tory chair of Derbyshire education committee to see Lord Howe, a minister in the Department for Education. Another school in the constituency, Bolsover Church of England, used to hold up the gym roof with a hydraulic pit prop. I argued hard that Tibshelf was in a similarly bad way and deserved to be rebuilt urgently. Pit props holding up a roof, I said during the discussion of Tibshelf, was a disgrace.

Well, one thing led to another and Howe accepted we'd put an 'exemplary case'. The Education Secretary at the time, Michael Gove, cited pit props when he announced Tibshelf was to be an exception and would be saved from the axe. The head and deputy head were delighted, as were the pupils, parents and teachers, because they were getting a new school. I never claimed there was a pit prop holding up Tibshelf, although I may have sailed close to the wind. The confusion was theirs and I felt it would've been inappropriate on this occasion to correct Gove in the House of Commons. The episode, however, underlined how an MP needs to be in the constituency and London to get results. If you box clever locally and nationally you can win some great battles. We secured everybody a brand new house in Arkwright Town, between Bolsover and Chesterfield. They'd shut the pit in a hurry and in 1988 there was a flare-up when somebody was lighting a fire in one of the several terrace rows of colliery houses. Methane, an explosive gas, was escaping from underground.

British Coal was to blame, and we organized what was to be a very successful campaign by Arkwright and Calow Labour Party, including Norma Dolby and Pat Kerry, a couple of local councillors, and Reg Race, who'd been a London Labour MP and was Chair of the Parish Council. We brought in a firm of environmental lawyers, Leigh Day, who reckoned we had a good case.

We had British Coal by the short-and-curlies and they agreed to build everybody a new house on the other side of the main road. Bungalows and semi-detached houses replaced the old terraces. It paid resettlement allowances of £2,500. The chip shop, village pub, school and miners' Welfare were all replaced, and we acquired a new community centre. British Coal wanted to open cast the old site. I was against that, but others approved. The whole town marched across the road to their new homes when they were ready. It reminded me of the return to work after the 1984-5 strike. This time we'd won.

To get around the whole of Bolsover in one go I came up with a bike ride of 40-odd miles to tour the constituency every late July or August, when the sun would be shining. It was a mixture of business and pleasure, seeing people and calling in pit canteens along the way for my dinner. I did it annually for years. I bought a Raleigh 10 speed with an aluminium frame. I'm not into possessions in a big way but that was a great bike, very light and I could pick it up with two fingers. You cover a lot of miles on two wheels and I still enjoy a Sunday ride in Hyde Park when in London.

Cycling isn't, as any rider will tell you, without its risks. My single semi-serious accident was on New Year's Day in 1980, the start of the first calendar year of Thatcher's reign of terror. I fancied a breath of fresh air and jumped on the bike to head for Matlock, the county town. There and back would be about 20 miles. It was cold and the road glinted under a light frost but it wasn't thick enough to cause problems. I was climbing Beeley Moor hill and remember noticing a father and son playing with a model aeroplane. I recall thinking as I passed them: He's bought it for the lad but really it's his own Christmas present. The next thing I remember is feeling groggy and not knowing where I was.

The bloke who found me, sprawled unconscious on the Tarmac, reckoned I'd been hit by a car because I was on one side of the road and the bike was on the other. He and his wife picked me up and put me and the bike in the back of their car to take me to Chesterfield hospital. I spent a week on the ward, the room spinning every time I opened my eyes. I had a hairline fracture of the skull. I couldn't remember a thing about it happening. The police thought it may have been a hit and run but they never caught anybody. I needed another four weeks' convalescence at home before I was fit to return to work. The one upside was I did receive a medical certificate after the treatment was completed to confirm that the Skinner brain was in perfect working order.

In Derbyshire they say the Labour Party owes more to Methodism than Marxism and I reckon that's true, Harold Wilson once using a similar line. I've never called people 'comrade' because that wasn't a term we used in the pits. On Derbyshire County Council we did have a Labour councillor from Shirebrook called Ron Lewis. Ron was a Methodist lay preacher. He stood for Parliament in West Derbyshire and lost before going on to be elected MP for Carlisle between 1964 and 1983. It's ironic really but Ron did say that if he hadn't been a Methodist he might have become a Marxist.

The Bolsover area is full of great socialists. One of the most striking examples was Graham Parkin, Chair of Bolsover Constituency Labour Party for more than 25 years and a good friend of mind for 40-plus years. I first encountered Graham, who died last year, in 1972. He sent me a letter about how miners were losing their jobs in the village of Doe Lea, where he lived, as pits were shut.

Graham was a clever man who read two non-fiction library books a week and knew an enormous amount about subjects such as astrology and astronomy. He worked on building sites until his epilepsy made it unsafe and he had to give up his job. Today Atos would strip him of his benefits, but Graham would have fought them to the bitter end. On one occasion he took a benefit case all the way to London and won an appeal on a legal point, so he would've stood up to the new benefit bullies.

Graham missed out on higher education in his younger years so, as I got to know him, I suggested he go to the Co-op College in Leicester, where he passed a diploma with flying colours. I then suggested Graham go to Hull University, where he went on to gain a BSc in Economics. He was a councillor and deputy leader of the Labour group until ill health took its toll. When he ran initially for the council, I asked to see his election address. I knew it: he hadn't mentioned the degree. I told him to remind voters that a Doe Lea lad with epilepsy had gone to university. He strolled home in the election.

Graham was an active campaigner, too. When I pass the Belisha crossing near the entrance to the old Glapwell pit, I still think of it as Graham's crossing. He lay on the road during protests to have it installed.

During the 1984–5 pit strike, Graham was on the picket line every morning at Bolsover colliery until he fell seriously ill. He was admitted to Walton Hospital in Chesterfield and was in a confused state when I saw him. His condition worsened and he fell into a coma. Graham was transferred to the bigger Chesterfield Royal Hospital. He had a beard and straggly hair and when I visited him on a Friday evening, the nurse asked when he'd stopped drinking. Graham, I told them, had epilepsy and never drank. I saw an immediate change in the staff's demeanour. Graham hadn't been taking his tablets, and the hospital didn't know about the epilepsy.

When the bell went at the end of visiting hours, I refused to leave and staged a sit-in until I saw a doctor. I was fed up with the way he was being treated and wanted to explain his medical history. The following morning, a Saturday, the phone rang.

Overnight he'd been transferred to the Hallamshire in Sheffield. The hospital said they knew I was his friend and was unhappy with his care. They were going to pump him full of steroids to try and bring him round. The member of staff calling from the Hallamshire admitted it was risky but said they'd run out of ideas.

I went to Parliament on the Monday and received a message to contact Pete Darby, a mutual friend. Fearing the worst, I rang back. Pete told me Graham had opened his eyes on gaining consciousness and, noticing he was in a hospital single room, his first words after days in a coma were: 'Hey up, Pete, I hope this isn't private'.

CHAPTER ELEVEN

The front bench below the gangway

Political satire is worth a guinea a box. I don't believe in banal humour, cracking a silly joke just to make people laugh. But satire as a weapon is devastating, ridicule capable of destroying an enemy. I acknowledge, too, that it may backfire. Quips are capable of rebounding. And if you dish it out, never whine when you're the one stung.

Prime Minister's Questions was like a repertory company when I entered the House of Commons. The same small cast of players was called to perform for fifteen minutes on a Tuesday and Thursday after lunch before Tony Blair used Labour's landslide majority in 1997 to amalgamate them into a single half an hour at high noon on Wednesdays so he had to swot only once.

In the 1970s the cast was tiny, most MPs sitting as an audience rather than participants. A Conservative MP called Neil Marten was billed as a suave star performer. I watched and wasn't impressed. Eric Heffer, the Labour MP for Liverpool Walton since 1964, told me so few MPs bobbed up that he'd been called twice in a single quarter-hour session. Eric saw I was sceptical so he took me into the Library and showed me in *Hansard*. I thought: Right, I'm going to get into this act. Eric cautioned me to go slowly, to play myself in. I got stuck in straight away. The likes of Gavin Strang and Gerald Kaufman followed suit and we bust open the show.

Ted Heath, the Tory premier, was a sailor and the party's friends in the City and industry would chip in to help him sail a succession of ever-grander yachts, all called *Morning Cloud*. The financial relationships stank to high heaven and it's hard to imagine nowadays a prime minister surviving if rich benefactors were bankrolling him to sail the ocean seas. Sailor Ted seemed to spend much of his time in Cowes on the Isle of Wight. It was the tradition in that parliamentary era to ask the PM on the order paper when he intended to visit a place before putting to him what you really wanted. I decided to ask Heath if he was intending to visit Cowes in the near future.

The clerks informed me that I couldn't because it was satirical and they were going to block the question but I stood my ground, arguing that Cowes was a town in Britain like all the others they allowed to be mentioned. The clerks backed off reluctantly and the question duly appeared.

Eric warned me: 'You have to be in here a long time to do that and pull it off, Dennis.'

'No, you don't,' I answered. 'You've just got to do it.'

Haughty Heath was visibly annoyed. Our lot laughed at him, his face turning red. His side either shouted 'Shame' at me or sniggered behind their order papers. The question took him down a fraction of a notch and carved out an opening to criticise his Conservative government more generally.

I work on the basis that stirring up trouble within the opposition is worthwhile. Heath's fanatical Europeanism, taking Britain into the Common Market without a referendum, wasn't universally approved by Tories and, I readily concede, split the Labour Party with me firmly in the anti-camp. Heath bought the full Common Market package and would snuggle up to Georges Pompidou, the French president. My asking a question in the French I'd learned at Tupton Hall about Monsieur le President had me pulled up immediately by the Speaker. Norman French is permitted for bills. MPs must speak English when winding up Tories. The use of Franglais emphasised Heath's subservience to Pompidou better than many a technical question.

I've sat on what is known as the front bench below the gang way from the beginning of my forty-plus years in Parliament. The long green row, divided by a walkway from the stretch directly in front of the despatch box where ministers or shadow ministers crowd, is traditionally occupied on our side by Labour left-wingers. I naturally joined Frank Allaun, Sydney Silverman, Russ Kerr and sometimes Ian Mikardo and all the rest. The seat in the corner I occupy is at the very heart of the action and quickly became my regular spot, except in the early years when it would be filled at Prime Minister's Questions by Russ. He suffered a medical condition which caused him to nod off. It was the job of whoever sat in the chamber next to him to nudge Russ awake.

Operating on the front line lets you hear what the Tories and their allies are saying and, equally importantly, they can hear you when you want them to. David Cameron's yellow Tories, the Liberal Democrats, are directly opposite in the coalition. When they get up to speak we'll shout 'Here comes another Tory Boy' to put them off their stride. They hate it. You see the pain on their faces. That's why we continue. The truth hurts the Liberal Democrats. The ability on the front line to pick up what's said over there also has unintended consequences.

Norman Tebbit was an uppity backbencher before Thatcher stuck him in the Cabinet. Tommy Swain, a fellow ex-miner from Derbyshire, was sitting opposite Tebbit who was muttering away. I didn't catch precisely what Tebbit said but, looking at Tommy, he'd said something like 'The old man's turned up for once' in a clear dig.

'What did he say?' asked Tommy.

'He called you a bastard,' I answered to wind up Tommy. He cursed Tebbit, then a few moments later I heard:

'Tebbit's said something else – what was it?'

'He's called you a bastard again, Tommy.'

Tommy wasn't happy. Tommy shouted at Tebbit that he wanted a word and Tebbit, the silly sod, got up to speak to him. I was thinking what a fool Tebbit was when Tommy pounced at the back of the chamber. I can see the pair now: Tommy holding Tebbit by the tie with one hand, Tommy's other hand screwed into a menacing fist in Tebbit's face. The two of them were near the heavy double doors into the Members' Lobby so beyond what's known as the bar of the house and officially out of the chamber. The Speaker was unable to save Tebbit from a pasting if Tommy wasn't appeased. Bernard Weatherill, then a Tory whip and later himself a Speaker, saw what was going on and rushed over. Tommy complained that Tebbit was bad-mouthing him and Weatherill told Tebbit to apologise. I saw Tommy later with a piece of paper in his hand. It was a letter of apology from Tebbit!

I don't know what Tebbit said exactly but I must have been nearer the truth than I imagined.

Tebbit had a revenge of sorts much later when I was chucked out of the chamber for accusing him of lining his pockets by privatising British Telecom as trade and industry secretary then, when he'd left Thatcher's government, taking a job as a non-executive director of BT. I was ordered to withdraw it. I couldn't – it was true that Tebbit sold off BT and then, just three or so years later, joined the board.

I've never kept a count of the times I've been thrown out, notching them up on the spine of a leather-bound collection of *Hansard*. It must be about a dozen. The remarks were largely spontaneous, not pre-planned. The last suspension was when we were in power and George Osborne was the Tory Shadow Chancellor. Gordon Brown was the Chancellor of the Exchequer and we were discussing growth rates during Treasury Questions in 2005. Des Browne, chief secretary to the treasury, was defending a 1.75 per cent growth rate by arguing the average growth rate was 2.7 per cent a year under Labour compared with 2.2 per cent before we'd ousted the Tories in 1997. George Osborne, Gideon, was chuntering away in his usual aloof manner.

Osborne had been in the Sunday newspapers. There was a photograph of him in his younger days with an arm draped around dominatrix Natalie Rowe. The table in front of them was cluttered with wine bottles and all the signs of a party in full swing. I said in the 1970s and a lot of the 1980s, we'd have thanked our lucky stars in the coalfield areas for growth of 1.75 per cent. Then I added: 'The only thing growing then were the lines of coke in front of boy George and the rest of them.'

There was pandemonium. The Speaker, Michael Martin, demanded instantly that I withdraw the remark.

'It was in the *News of the World*,' I said. 'No, I will not withdraw it. It is true.'

'I order you to leave the chamber,' ruled Martin. I knew that was that, he wasn't going to change his mind.

'It's true!' I shouted as I left, adding: 'That was in the *News of the World* and you know it.' The picture was also in the *Sunday Mirror* but using one of their own newspapers against them hurt the Tories more.

I was excluded from the chamber for the rest of that day's sitting. A badge messenger came to my office and said: 'You're alright, Dennis, as long as you don't go in the chamber.' They were worried about what to print in *Hansard*. At a subsequent fundraiser in the Pontefract and Castleford constituency of Cabinet minister Yvette Cooper, her husband Ed Balls, himself a Cabinet minister, joked: 'I don't know why they kicked you out, Dennis. You were only talking about piles of coke and not lines of coke, weren't you?' The happiest person was the real Boy George, singer George O'Dowd. He sent a letter to the House of Commons thanking me for getting a reference to him on the front page of London's *Evening Standard* newspaper on the night of my suspension.

When in my head I go through most of the suspensions, they include punishments that should never have been imposed. In 1980, for instance, it was pathetic that I was shown a red card for calling Jim Prior, the Secretary of State for Employment, the Minister of Unemployment. Dole queues were lengthening rapidly under Maggie Thatcher and on their way to three million, yet the Tories howled. Speaker George Thomas called: 'Order, order,' and demanded I withdraw. Minister of Unemployment was deemed unparliamentary language. Today nobody would bat an eyelid. I thought: I'm going to stand my ground here. I refused to leave. Prior jumped up and down. The Speaker ordered the Serjeant at Arms in his tights, with sword dangling at his side, to remove me. As he approached, I snarled: 'Geroff, I don't need you to escort me. What do you know about unemployment?' The Serjeant looked startled. I don't think he knew what had hit him. Wisely, he didn't make a grab for my arm. Rather he took a step back. I knew I was on my way. I got to my feet and walked out under my own steam.

On another occasion I was ordered out for calling agriculture minister John Gummer a 'little squirt' and a 'wart on Thatcher's nose'. He bloody well was. Gummer was supposed to be this European wet, yet he did whatever she wanted when he was climbing that greasy ministerial pole.

I was out for a day in 1995 for accusing ministers of a 'crooked deal' to sell off what was left of the coal industry, reversing the nationalisation of 1947. In truth there wasn't a lot left to flog off after the closure programme. The principle, however, was important.

George Thomas sent me out for complaining that, as Speaker, he shouldn't have gone to Christchurch to open a garden party for the local Tory, Robert Adley. The money raised went into Conservative coffers. That intervention was planned. I was warned by a couple of MPs not to do it but felt strongly so there was no alternative.

Alan Haselhurst, a Tory Deputy Speaker, ordered me out for accusing him of political bias towards his own party when he let

Theresa May get away with saying Tony Blair had 'misled' the House – lied – about the NHS when she was the Shadow Leader of the Commons. Geoff Hoon was asking her to withdraw it when Haselhurst jumped up and declared he'd have intervened if he thought she'd made an 'entirely improper' accusation. In a stage whisper I said: 'She was let off because she's a Tory.' Haselhurst heard, as intended, and demanded I withdraw what he deemed 'a grossly offensive and misleading remark'. I, thinking silence might be the best option, didn't respond. He banned me for the rest of the day.

I was picked up for calling that traitor David Owen a 'pompous sod' in 1985. Labour and Tory MPs burst out laughing. The pompous sod, unsurprisingly, didn't see the funny side. Nor did Jack Weatherill in the chair. He asked me to withdraw the remark. I said I was in a benevolent mood so I'd withdraw pompous. Weatherill said that wasn't the description he was looking to erase. I said I wasn't going any further and that was that – I was off again.

I couldn't stomach the elitism and betrayal of Owen and the rest of the traitors who stabbed Labour in the back. The Social Democratic Party, and the alliance it struck with the Liberals, helped sustain Thatcher and the Conservatives in power until the scab party collapsed in on itself and they merged into the Liberal Democrats. History is repeating itself with the Liberal Democrats now sustaining Cameron's Conservatives. The SDP Gang of Four – Roy Jenkins, Shirley Williams, the member that everybody forgets who is Bill Rodgers and Owen himself – wanted to destroy the Labour Party. Woy Jenkins, who'd enjoyed a good living out of Labour to fund his claret, quit Westminster for Brussels, then quit Brussels for Westminster after he'd licked the cream dry in Europe.

After he won the Glasgow Hillhead by-election in 1982, word reached me that he thought the corner place where I sat on the front bench below the gangway should be his by right as the leader of a political party. He was wrong. Jenkins sauntered back into the chamber as if he owned the place and stood in front of me, his backside too close to my face for comfort.

I said: 'What do you want?'

Woy replied: 'Traditionally, that seat is for the leader of a party.' The response wasn't to his liking:

'Traditionally, you used to have your hand on the despatch box when you were representing the Labour Party and taking money from the Transport and General Workers' Union. You can stand there as long as you like because I'm not budging. So bugger off.'

An added reason Jenkins wanted the spot was so he'd be within whispering distance of David Steel in the row behind. We were to force Jenkins to snuggle up with Cyril Smith, a fate worse than I imagined given what was revealed about the Rochdale Liberal after his death.

Owen, when he succeeded Jenkins as leader of the SDP, tried to occupy the corner seat himself. We would not be moved. Owen started putting cards in the little brass holder on the seat to book it for prayers at the start of the daily session. The convention was if you nabbed a spot for prayers you stayed in it. Owen would have to do better than that. With two other Labour MPs, Dennis Canavan and Bob Cryer, we started putting in cards before him. We'd arrive at 8 a.m. when the doors into the chamber opened. I had no intention of going to prayers and regarded it as a clocking-on card. In the pit we'd hang a metal tag on a hook when we took down our lamps and the manager would know who was underground. In factories millions of workers clocked in and out with a card. One morning we found an SDP kid sneaking in to place the cards for those too grand to be up early. That wasn't allowed and we lodged a complaint.

There were several scuffles with SDP MPs trying to muscle in on our bench. On one occasion Owen accidentally bumped into Clare Short, who'd decided to come on to our bench. We raised a point of order about kicking a woman, suggesting the incident was more than it was to embarrass Owen.

Steel, a very pompous man now in the House of Lords, would've loved the SDP in front of him. The Liberal envisaged the microphone above his head dangling from the ceiling as his gateway to the nation, permitting his words to be heard in homes across the land. The mic also picked up the Derbyshire vowels of a critical running commentary whenever he spoke.

There was a childish side to the spat over who sat where, but it was serious too. We didn't want to be pushed around by the upstarts. Refusing to budge symbolised a disgust at the betrayal and their ultimate impotence. And sitting on the front line means Tories at the despatch box cannot ignore whatever you say.

One Tory MP, Peter Fry, threatened to sue me. It was about 25 years ago after a meeting in his Wellingborough constituency. I'd read out details of his entries in the Register of Members' Interests and those of Norman Tebbit. The reporter on a local newspaper jumbled them up and Fry went up the wall. The paper had made a mistake and caved in. I consulted a lawyer who said the paper's admission undermined me and I should settle too.

No way. I could prove everything I'd said. So I decided to represent myself and started contacting pensioners who'd been in the audience to call as witnesses. I heard nothing else from Fry.

The moniker 'Beast of Bolsover' was conferred not by a Conservative enemy but another Labour MP, Andrew Faulds. He had this booming voice from his time as an actor and his pronouncements would fill the entire chamber. An MP in the West Midlands for many years to 1997, Faulds was a good heckler himself. Very quick on his feet, his background as a thespian ensured he was heard when he opened his mouth.

Faulds was a passionate supporter of Palestinian and Arab causes, a voice for OPEC oil when I was championing the miners who produced Britain's coal. During a Faulds speech on the Middle East, he started mentioning some of the countries he'd visited. I knew he'd gone on freebies and not dipped into his own pocket, so I shouted something like: 'Aye, and who paid for all your trips?' Faulds was outraged. He pleaded to the Speaker: 'Can't you control this bloody beast of Bolsover?' The title stuck. It is alliterative, geographically accurate and I did have a fiery reputation. I wasn't bothered in the slightest from the moment he said it. The name's done me no harm over the years. It may even have done me some good. Anyway, I've never worried too much about people calling me names.

During Jim Callaghan's time as prime minister, 1978 I think it was, we had a row in the House of Commons about a stoppage by NHS hospital telephonists. The Tories had put down questions to bash the unions, adopting the usual anti-working-class stance you'd expect from Conservatives. I made the reasonable point that in any strike, official and unofficial, two sides were involved in the action and the single biggest cause of disruption in the NHS was the massive cuts in public expenditure.

Tebbit was pulled up by George Thomas for calling me a fossil-ised dragonfly, the Speaker ruling it was unparliamentary. It might have been, according to the rules, but I didn't care. Tebbit protested and I told him he could say what he liked as far as I was concerned. Thomas said that was a terrible invitation and ordered Tebbit to withdraw the phrase, which he meekly did.

The trick to conferring a name on somebody is to be obvious. Thus I called Thatcher's diminutive sports minister Colin Moyni-han 'Subbuteo' because he wasn't much taller than a plastic player we flicked with our fingers. Moynihan didn't like the name nearly as much as I hated a bill he was bringing in to stop people going to football matches, treating them like foreigners in Britain by making identity cards compulsory at grounds.

Timing is always crucial in delivering a jibe. John Major thought he'd won the football pools when he succeeded Thatcher. At his first Prime Minister's Questions, the Tories cheered wildly. He rose to his feet and in the split-second hush between his MPs falling silent and Major uttering his first words I yelled: 'Resign!' There was utter pandemonium. Our lot roared and the Tories protested. Major looked crestfallen. By the end of his spell in Downing Street, a lot of Tories agreed with me. Grey Major resembled one of his dad's garden gnomes that had been left in the garden too long, all peeling paint and no colour. He called the right-wing anti-Europeans who made his life hell and tried to dump him 'bastards'. History remembers Major only for his cones hotline and perhaps Edwina Currie. He should've resigned when I invited him.

Mockery is a deadly weapon. When Jeremy Hunt's special adviser Adam Smith carried the can over close ties with Rupert Murdoch, the then Culture Secretary winced when I said posh boys always sacked the servants. It hurt because it was true. I killed two birds with one stone in telling Cameron he should send Murdoch packing and as a final humiliation ask Chris Huhne, the Lib Dem former Energy Secretary who was to be jailed for getting his then wife to take his penalty points for speeding, to drive him to the airport.

Michael Heseltine finishing off what Thatcher had started by announcing in 1992 that 31 of the 50 remaining coal mines would shut sparked national outrage against the industrial vandalism and political spite. Heseltine, President of the Board of Trade – his fancy name for the job of Trade and Industry Secretary – wanted to wipe out the industry. In Derbyshire he was to shut Shirebrook, Bolsover and Markham pits to kill mining in the county.

The public was with us, wealthy shoppers and office workers cheering when we marched down Kensington High Street with our banners and yellow 'Coal not Dole' stickers for a big rally in Hyde Park. Perhaps those who'd sided with the Tories in the 1984–5 strike felt guilty after realising we were telling the truth and the Conservatives were liars. At a rally in Chesterfield I chatted with a group from Cheltenham who'd come to give us support. Workers in factories making hydraulic pit props and equipment came to the meetings because they realised they'd also be thrown on the scrap heap if Heseltine got his way.

There are occasions when a member of the public will come up to you and make an unusual request. The wife of a pitman stopped me after I'd spoken in Chesterfield. 'Here, throw these at Heseltine,' she said, trying to hand me a pair of pit boots and kneepads. I told her I didn't want the steel-toe-capped boots because they were heavy, but I'd take the kneepads.

In the past I'd tossed a few books in the direction of Geoffrey Rippon when he was Environment Secretary during Heath's period. I didn't hit him. I never intended to. It was frustration that made me do it, frustration at Tory ministers blithely indifferent to the terrible damage they do to working-class communities when they close this or that.

I took the kneepads with me into the chamber when Heseltine was on his hind legs. I contrasted how he could shut pits at the stroke of a pen while miners were forced by law to hold a lengthy, expensive ballot to fight to keep them open. I tossed the kneepads, dirty with coal dust, at Heseltine and they landed at his feet. The Tories were in uproar and shouting this, that and the other. Heseltine didn't know what was going on. The kneepads on the floor confused him. It would've been a different matter if I'd taken the boots from her and hit him with a steel toe-cap.

I've also had things thrown at me, reminders of what a dirty business politics can be. It was during Jim Callaghan's spell as Prime Minister. I was listening to Labour backbencher Tam Dalyell who was three rows behind. There weren't many of us in the chamber that evening in 1978. A kerfuffle up in the Strangers' Gallery caught my attention. I looked up and saw something coming our way. In that split second I thought: Christ Almighty –

what is this? It was flying fast through the air. Whatever it was narrowly missed me and splattered all over the place.

The stink was the first clue. It was horse manure. I'd walked in enough of the stuff in my boots in Derbyshire to know immediately. The plastic bag dirty bomb was one of three hurled by Yana Mintoff, daughter of Malta's socialist premier Dom Mintoff, and a male accomplice, to protest against the British armed forces in Northern Ireland. She was a schoolteacher in London as well as a member of the Trotskyist Socialist Workers Party (SWP). He, I think, supported the Troops Out movement. The stench was terrible indoors. The papers reported that my face and sports jacket were covered with the stuff. They weren't. I had a narrow escape. Tam carried on speaking about Scottish devolution, blissfully lost in his West Lothian question. A few of the other MPs had dived to the floor, trying to shelter under the green benches. The Speaker, George Thomas, called: 'Order, order.' It should've been odure, odure. The pair upstairs were dragged, kicking and screaming, from the gallery. There was chaos.

Thomas announced an adjournment for twenty minutes so cleaners could wipe up the mess. By this stage I saw the funnier side. Nobody was dead. It was manure not explosives. So I raised a point of odure. I began: 'Mr Speaker, there is a new motion before the House . . .' Thomas cut me dead, declaring solemnly that this was no time for hilarity. Yet there was room for irony. The manure had come my way when, in fact, I supported the civil rights demonstrators in Northern Ireland.

I'd opposed the Labour government's draconian Prevention of Terrorism Act, with its power to detain suspects for up to seven days without charge, after the terrible Birmingham pub bombings that killed 21 drinkers in the Mulberry Bush and the Tavern in the Town in 1974. It was obvious, and so it proved, that a political settlement not military action would resolve the Troubles in Northern Ireland. Giving the police carte blanche to do what they liked would inflame the situation and lead to further injustices, as the Birmingham Six found to their awful cost. But the Speaker didn't appreciate the quip about a new motion.

We've had a few public interruptions over the years though nothing too serious. A handful of hunt supporters ran on the floor from behind the Speaker's chair in September 2004 while we were debating the fox-hunting ban. I suspected immediately they must have had help on the inside to find their way about in the warren of corridors. I've been against blood sports ever since as a kid I saw a hunt's dogs chasing a fox. That's not a sport. It's animal cruelty, barbarism.

In the May of the same year, Prime Minister's Questions was disrupted by condoms full of purple powder, catching Tony Blair on the back and landing in front of John Prescott and Gordon Brown. A glass security screen had recently been fitted in front of the public gallery. The flour bombs were thrown from one of the galleries running above the length of the chamber. A couple of Fathers4Justice campaigners obtained tickets from unsuspecting Labour peer Baroness Golding, an ex-MP. Golding was clueless about their intentions and was forced to give a grovelling apology.

Me? I thought: Only purple powder? I had horse shit thrown my way. Blair, you're lucky. Nobody really cared when Dom

Mintoff's daughter threw horse shit because it wasn't on TV. This will be all over the news. And it was.

The one time I was comprehensively beaten at my own game in Parliament was by an artist of the name of Graham Jones. Tony Banks, who then chaired a committee putting pictures up all over Parliament, sidled up in the lobby and said he wanted me to have my portrait done so I'd be the first MP painted who'd never had his hands on the despatch box.

'Tony, I'm not interested,' I answered. 'It's not me.'

'Oh, go on, Dennis,' said Banks. 'Have a think about it. I've got this artist who did Michael Foot.' I went away, thinking no more of it. Some time after the phone rings and this voice says:

'Mr Skinner?'

'Yes.'

'You're interested in helping unemployed people, aren't you?'

'Yes, of course. Who is this?'

'Well, I'm one of them. I'm an unemployed artist and I want work painting your picture.'

The approach was straight out of my book. He caught me napping by playing a blinder. I agreed and the picture was in Portcullis House for a while. I don't know where it is now. Probably in some dungeon. I won't be trying to find out. I go to Parliament to work, not look at the pictures.

From the front bench below the gangway we put the socialist case for a Labour alternative to austerity, exposing the fundamental failures of a Conservative Party incapable of representing working people because it doesn't value their interests. And we harry the enemy to weaken its morale.

I've continued putting a name card in the holder behind the corner seat ever since that tussle with David Owen. I don't attend prayers in the chamber but a number of Labour MPs, one of them Glasgow's Tom Harris, take the printed cards to their constituency fundraisers. I'm told they are raffled for as much as £40. What is the world coming to?

CHAPTER TWELVE

The agony and the ecstasy

We've lived long enough to be proved publicly right in the year-long miners' Strike for Jobs of 1984–5. The release of Thatcher's personal papers and Cabinet minutes confirm what we argued at the time: she and her Conservative government had a secret plan to butcher the coal industry; total war was declared on pitmen and the National Union of Mineworkers as the precursor of a broader attack on all workers; and entire communities were to be devastated in the ethnic cleansing of coalfields, an unprecedented act of industrial and political spite.

This was the most honourable strike I have ever taken part in. Most disputes about money and wages are important. But this strike was honourable precisely because it wasn't about wages. Put simply, it was about a 55-year-old miner in one part of Britain being prepared to sacrifice the roof over his head and lose his house in a year-long strike to save a job for a 16-year-old kid in another part of the country. Somebody he didn't even know.

We knew we were right. We had no doubt that the National Coal Board's plan to close 20 pits was politically motivated, that it was the start of the systematic destruction of coal mining in Britain. We argued at the time that she and her lot had 70 pits on a secret hit list. Thatcher and her acolytes denied it. And thirty years on we got to read the proof in black and white. The official documents vindicate miners, their families and their supporters. Thatcher was nailed as the greatest liar in the history of twentieth-century Britain.

At a May Day rally this year (2014), in Aylesham, in the Kent coalfield she abandoned, I told the crowd of 300 that we meet on anniversaries of the strike because we believed in what we fought for and we knew then, and know now, that we were right. The cheers nearly took the roof off the hall. It was the same in Chesterfield. Worksop as well. Markham Main too in the Doncaster constituency of Ed Miliband, who after I'd spoken told the retired and redundant miners that he'd backed the strike in 1984–5. That Neil Kinnock did not when he was Labour leader remains an enduring pity. Kinnock never helped us get on to the front foot, working against rather than with us.

Miners never marked the milestones after the 1926 General Strike when they were let down by the TUC, as they were to be in 1984–5, and starved back to work, forced in '26 to swallow lower wages and longer hours. I talked to Dad about 1926 after the miners won the 1972 national dispute with Ted Heath, blackouts securing a sizeable pay rise after a inquiry headed by Lord Wilberforce agreed we were badly paid relative to other workers. The NUM executive had extracted a deal from Heath and were leaving Downing Street when somebody said: 'What about the Durham widows?' The wives of dead miners in the coalfield lost concessionary coal allow-ances when their husbands were killed or passed away. Everywhere else the deliveries continued. Lawrence Daly, the union's general secretary, went back into No. 10 and secured their fuel.

Dad was blacklisted after the '26 strike and was a veteran of the earlier and similarly unsuccessful 1921 strike. 'Dennis,' he said to me, 'I have waited nearly 50 years for this. We lost in 1921. We lost in 1926. I never thought I'd live long enough to see a victory like this.' He died, alas, a few years after witnessing the triumph.

The miners beat Heath again in 1974 when the Tory lost a 'Who governs Britain?' general election he called. Voters decided it shouldn't be him, and Harold Wilson entered Downing Street in the February at the head of a minority Labour government before securing a tiny majority of three in October of that year. The Conservatives never forgave the miners and were determined to wreak revenge on the National Union of Mineworkers.

After a false start in 1981, when Thatcher threatened a confrontation before backing off, she mobilised the full powers of the state to crush the miners. She lied to the people and Parliament for a year. She deceived the country for the full 12 months of the dispute, pretending the closures announced were the work of the NCB and axeman Ian MacGregor, hired at great expense from America as chairman to do her dirty work. They weren't. She was the evil puppet master, pulling the strings in the shadows. She lied in denying there were considerably more than the 20 named pits on the list. The reports confirm there were 70. We were right, she was wrong.

A minister caught lying once to Parliament is required to apologise and be admonished. Thatcher lied and lied then lied again to Parliament throughout the strike. After the records confirmed the mendacity, on a point of order I asked the Speaker, John

Bercow, what he was going to do about it. He promised to consider it but no answer came. Thatcher's lies were so continuous, so heinous, the parliamentary system is unable to comprehend, let alone correct, such sustained duplicity.

I've spoken often about the agony and the ecstasy of that strike. There were a lot of highs and a lot of lows. But we always believed we could win. We very nearly did. The support and generosity of trade unionists, socialists and the general public was inspiring. The tragedy is we didn't win. We lost.

It would've made sense for the strike not to have started in March 1984. The Tories picked Cortonwood in Yorkshire for closure, to lure the miners out ahead of the summer. There was a good argument for continuing an overtime ban started in November the previous year, to reduce coal stocks, and strike in the following autumn or winter, when the cold weather and dark nights would increase demand for electricity. Mick McGahey – Scargill's deputy, who Joe Gormley had prevented from getting the union's presidency by extending his own term until McGahey was too old to run, Scargill strolling into the job – was a very wise man. McGahey was leader of the Scottish miners. Firmly on the left, he was a Communist. Mick felt the overtime ban should be kept going into autumn '84, reducing coal stocks by half a million tons a month, before a strike.

Cortonwood was a trap, of course, intended to infuriate miners in Yorkshire, the biggest coalfield. It was a receiving pit, taking miners from other pits that had shut. It had lots of years of work ahead. Shutting Cortonwood was planned to be a red rag to a bull. Yorkshire made the call but within days several coalfields were out. The walkouts spread and a national strike was becoming a fait accompli. The media and the Tories and, to his shame, Neil

Kinnock clamoured for a national ballot. They didn't understand the federal structure of the NUM or want to accept that areas already had mandates, from their own ballots, to strike to save pits.

We had some support in Nottinghamshire but sections of the union wanted to work on. It was a repeat of 1926 and Spencerism when George Spencer, leader of the Nottinghamshire Miners' Association, broke away to form a bosses' union and keep open pits. NUM men such as Henry Richardson, a good friend of mine, and Ray Chadburn stuck with us but lesser men, the likes of Roy Lynk and Neil Greatrex, worked hand in glove with the coal board and Tory government. They fuelled Thatcher by refusing to strike and ultimately dug their own graves. They formed the scab Union of Democratic Mineworkers (UDM). Their reward from the Tories? Notts pits shut. The last in the county, Thoresby, is scheduled to finish next year. You can judge the character of Greatrex from his subsequent imprisonment for stealing from a charity caring for elderly miners.

With the miners divided, working in Notts, it made victory harder. But despite everything Thatcher threw at us we came tantalisingly close, twice, to winning.

The first was in early July. The second front we'd been seeking opened when the dockers went on strike. The prospect of ports grinding to a halt, ships stranded unloaded, imports and exports going nowhere, terrified Thatcher. She knew the Government would be brought to its knees. The national docks committee of the Transport and General Workers' Union called the stoppage to protect jobs after British Steel used workers who weren't registered dockers to unload iron ore at Immingham on the Humber.

Dockers stopped working around the country. It was an exciting moment.

I was speaking at the Durham Miners' Gala on that city's old racecourse. The weather was gorgeous. You could feel the anticipation, the belief that after four months we were on the verge of a breakthrough. I stood up and told the mass of people: 'The sun's out, the miners are out and now the dockers are out.' I should have sat down and left it at that. The roar from the field deafening, the shouts of hope from pitmen scenting a victory. I can still hear it. The wall of sound must have shaken the Norman cathedral on the hill.

Tragically it was a false dawn, the employers scrambling to settle the dispute and snuff out the hope. Individual unions were brilliant but the TUC let us down. Time after time I urged it to encourage trade unions to dust down big pay demands and whatever else they wanted to increase the pressure on the Government. Instead the TUC hierarchy put obstacles in our way, as did Kinnock, when support could've tipped it our way.

Defeat was snatched from the jaws of victory when a triumph was there for the winning a second time in the late summer. In law, pits require deputies to be on duty to operate. These men are foremen, or middle managers, responsible for safety. Worried about their own jobs and their own union, the National Association of Colliery Overmen, Deputies and Shotfirers (NACODS), six months into the dispute they voted overwhelmingly to strike. Without deputies, Nottinghamshire would cease working. Not an ounce of coal would be produced underground. Thatcher would have to do a deal with the NUM.

The second front we craved appeared to reopen. Once again our hopes were cruelly dashed. NACODS was never a militant union. Thatcher chucked them a bone in the shape of a review structure, so the future of pits would be assessed before they were shut. NACODS swallowed it. The bone has stuck in the throat ever since. Not a single pit was saved.

The police state imposed by Thatcher abused miners as the enemy within. Striking miners were stripped of civil rights, victims of summary justice. The courts were a tool of her oppression. Strikers were barred from picket lines and jailed on the uncorroborated testimony of police officers who made it up as they went along. It broke my heart to see miners trickle back to work towards the end, starved and beaten.

We suffered a strategic defeat in the June at the British Steel coking plant in South Yorkshire at the Battle of Orgreave. In hindsight, the field wasn't an easy place for us to make a stand with a mass picket. The ground was too open, and there were few choke points where we could stop the convoys of lorries. The police in riot gear, with their dogs and mounted cavalry, lined up in their thousands. It was as if they wanted us there, coppers shouting mockingly 'See you tomorrow' when they went off at night. We were well and truly battered by the police. Some of the coppers were out of control, bashing anybody in reach. Mounted officers rode their horses at miners and used batons as swords. To escape being trampled under the hooves I climbed up a young tree, the sapling's thin branches straining and threatening to drop me into the path of the cavalry. It was like a scene from a massacre in a Wild West film.

Orgreave confirmed the BBC was part of the campaign against the miners because the film broadcast on TV was reversed and it was forced to apologise after the strike, which was too late. The

BBC showed first the miners throwing sods of earth at the police and then the police retaliating but it had happened – and was filmed – the other way round. The BBC lied just like the Tory government.

The police would boast about overtime and taunt workers who'd not been paid a penny for months by waving £10 notes in front of them. I gave all my wages to the NUM, every penny in that year. I'd done the same in the 1972 dispute. I was seen as a miners' MP and had been elected to Parliament only a couple of years before. In '84 I was talking to NUM officials who'd said they wouldn't be paid. 'What about you, Dennis?' they asked. My answer was: 'I'm going to do what I did in 1972.' I didn't want to do anything else.

It's true I went around Parliament switching on lights to eat up electricity during pit strikes. I've been asked the question a few times and yes, I did it. On a few occasions I was followed by a policeman who'd switch them off again.

I must have spoken at upwards of 200 rallies in every bit of England, Scotland and Wales. I regularly joined picket lines, driven much of the time by Pete Darby, a Derbyshire miner friend of mine. Peter would be at the wheel, me in the passenger seat reading the map and looking for ways around police roadblocks. He'd spent a night in a police cell for calling a scab a scab and as a consequence was banned from going on picket lines. So he'd drive and I'd protest.

The hostility of the police was frightening, officers breaking the laws they were sworn to uphold. They were emboldened by immunity. Heads of miners were cracked and men wrongly arrested in their thousands. Thatcher turned Britain into a police state. Kent miners were turned back at the Dartford tunnel when they drove north. On my way to join a picket at Shirebrook pit in the Bolsover constituency, I was threatened with arrest by a copper. He insisted I wasn't allowed to walk past a police line and along the pavement because the crowd ahead was judged too big.

'I am the Member of Parliament for this constituency,' I told him.

He snarled back: 'We don't care who you are – you're not getting past this line.'

Thatcher had created a national police force and you never saw coppers you knew. In Shirebrook that day we had, I think, the Met and Devon and Cornwall. There was a woman standing in her front garden near to us, watching and listening. I climbed on to the wall in front of the house and said to her:

'Is this your wall? Can I use it?'

'Walk across it, Dennis. Bugger 'em,' she answered. So I balanced on it to detour on private property and go down the side of the cops blocking the pavement.

We enjoyed fantastic solidarity, nationally and internationally, from places and groups you wouldn't automatically have expected to be on our side. Support groups sprung up outside mining areas, collecting money for families, including unlikely places in the south such as Worthing and Stroud, Torquay and Swanage. Money was raised in buckets and raffles. Food donated by the ton. And soup kitchens opened to feed the hungry.

It's interesting which rallies stick in your mind. I remember a mass meeting in Cowdenbeath in the football stadium. Mick McGahey rang to invite me.

'Will it be you, me and Scargill?' I asked. Mick replied:

'I'll tell you when you get up but I've asked Gordon Brown, who is a product of the trade union and labour movement in Scotland. In any case he'll only have five minutes.' The future Labour PM had been elected an MP only the year before. He spoke well, if briefly. Scargill liked to do his own thing, address his own rallies, so he wasn't there.

The strike was a catalyst for social change. Miners' wives came to the fore for the first time, invited on to platforms to speak instead of sitting at the back. Macho mining areas embraced feminism and we experienced the empowerment of women. I saw it myself in Wimbledon.

The Wimbledon miners' support group was twinned with Creswell Colliery, which is geographically in Derbyshire yet part of the Notts coalfield as a legacy of past ownership of the pit. I was sitting on the platform at a Wimbledon meeting and next to me was a woman from Creswell.

'I'm scared stiff, Dennis, I don't know what to say. I've never done this before,' she whispered.

'Don't worry,' I said, 'you'll be fine.' I whispered she should talk about what she'd been up to today and the past week.

'I helped in the kitchen to feed the families,' she answered, 'but there was a fire.'

'How did that happen?' I asked.

'Scabs set it alight,' came her reply.

'I think you've got a story,' was my reply.

She stood up and tearfully told the good people of Wimbledon how hard it was to survive and scabs burning down the kitchen had made it harder. When she finished half the audience was in tears. I hissed to the chair:

'Hold the collection now.'

'We're going to do it after you,' he said.

'Do it immediately,' I hissed a little louder. They raised a small fortune.

On another occasion I was driven to speak in the Rhondda in South Wales by my brother, Graham. He was a National Union of Public Employees (NUPE) branch secretary and Eileen, his wife, came along, as did two or three of his mates. After the big meeting at an athletics track we popped into a working mens' club. A steward said we'd have to hide Eileen because women weren't allowed in the bar. Eileen said she wasn't hiding. Voices were raised and there was a row. Once we'd thrown the dice, we needed to score a double six. We said we'd come to save the pit and had been speaking to thousands of people, and the enemy was the bosses – not a woman who was on the side of the miners. The argument was heated until somebody behind shouted she could stay in the bar, unhidden. The struggle, as they say, takes many forms.

The donations of food were so huge after a packed meeting in Bournemouth town hall that there wasn't room for me in the minibus going to the next stop in Swansea, so I caught the train. In Swansea we were to march around the city before a rally in the sports centre. We were at the front of the march and I was asked by a young miner who it was in the group at the back, with pink and rainbow banners. 'If I was guessing,' I told the kid, 'they'll be the gays and lesbians.' We walked through Swansea, to applause all along the streets, and into the sports hall.

Ten or eleven of us were sat along the platform and I was at one of the ends. A lad came up and said he was with the gays and lesbians and asked if he could say a few words. I told him: 'You can as far as

I'm concerned' and asked for a note to pass along to the chair, a South Wales NUM official. It was then he added they had a cheque for £1,000 to donate to the funds. 'Don't you worry about speaking,' I said. 'You can have my spot.' We both spoke in the end and he received a fantastic reception after his two or three minutes. Part of the ecstasy of the strike was the involvement of gays and lesbians who knew what it was like to be persecuted politically and supported mining communities under the Tory cosh.

I'd be lying if I pretended all support was well received. Towards the middle of the strike we were told about a lorryload of tinned food arriving in Shirebrook from Holland. Naturally there was great excitement when men hadn't been paid for months. The lorry pulled up outside the Carter Lane School premises where we stored everything and at least twenty of us, including Bill Adams, the chair of Shirebrook NUM, Alan Gascoigne, Cliff Hawley, Ken Walker, Leo Fretwell and many others formed a line as we ferried the boxes into school. Within twenty-four hours the tins were distributed to the Shirebrook mining families and within days most of Shirebrook was rushing to the toilet every few hours. Apparently there were hundreds of cans of tinned bacon that caused the problem and the picket lines were a bit thin the following two days. Nevertheless, after several months on strike, the international aid was a considerable help, as were the contributions of Indian shopkeepers who cleared their shelves whenever they were approached for help. A lot of people were beginning to realise that Thatcher and McGregor were trying to starve the miners back to work.

Towards the end I was invited to speak at the Guildhall in Bath. The writing was on the wall and we knew what was coming as tired and broke miners went back. I told the organisers to book a small room so it wouldn't look empty. They were having none of it, insisting they'd fill the main hall. Try as I might I couldn't dissuade them so it was with some trepidation that I approached the Guildhall. I couldn't have been more wrong. I can still see the massive chandelier in the hall, the size of the glittering light Del Boy dropped in a stately home in *Only Fools and Horses*. Beneath it every seat was filled, with people standing down the sides and packing the back. There were others outside. This was another part of the ecstasy, experiencing first hand how much goodwill there was for us.

Three weeks after the miners marched back to work, I was waiting on the Wandsworth Road in south London for a 77 bus to take me to Parliament, when this big car pulls up and the window winds down. This Derbyshire voice asks:

'Do you want a lift to the Palace of Varieties?' It was what I'd called the place at countless meetings so I thought I might know them, but I didn't recognise the faces.

'Who's that?' I replied. The lad explained they were miners from Whitwell colliery in the Bolsover constituency. 'What you doing down here – the strike finished three weeks ago?' Another of them says:

'We're staying down the road in a film producer's house and we have got his car and everything. He put us up during the dispute and says we can stay until he's back from Tuscany. In any case, there's a cellar full of wine and we're not shifting until we've supped the lot.' That agony and the ecstasy. The least I could do was accept a lift to work. It would've been rude not to.

You can always look back and wonder what we could have done differently. I am not a man to cry over spilt milk. I am who I am.

We can't rewrite history. We took decisions and events happened and that's that. The arguments about a national ballot in 1984 were an excuse for some to withhold support the miners deserved. We didn't want to be dictated to by the Tories and their friends in the media, including bloody Robert Maxwell who owned the *Daily Mirror*. Our opponents might be able to argue miners could be led by the nose for a few weeks. You only stay on strike for an entire year if the cause is yours. The sneery jibe from our enemies that it was about one man, Scargill, was pernicious rubbish.

The struggle was truly heroic, the miners who stayed loyal to the end of the twelve months the bravest of the brave. But they marched back, with their bands and their banners, defeated. I don't like admitting it, but I couldn't join them on the day they returned to work. I was too sad. I never said anything to anybody. I didn't make a song and dance about it. It was too much of an agony that day. I didn't share the romantic view that the struggle was a victory in itself. We had suffered a defeat. The glorious victories of '72 and '74 were wiped out.

In the end the full force of the state had floored us. Courts and anti-trade union laws were used to tie us up in legal knots. Derbyshire was one of the areas sequestrated, with our assets seized by a judiciary that was wielded as a lethal weapon by the Conservatives. When I first went down the pit in 1948 there were 700 coal mines in Britain. Now there are three, and two of those are earmarked for closure. What's been done to the industry is heartbreaking.

*

A fiasco in Libya was to be a public relations disaster for us. Thatcher had begged Libya's Colonel Gaddafi to turn on the oil taps for Britain. There was a huge dose of hypocrisy in her criticism when in the back half of '84 an NUM employee, Roger Windsor, was conveniently filmed embracing the dictator in North Africa and appealing for funds for the miners. I realised immediately, however, it was a PR disaster for us. Gaddafi's goons had, a few months earlier, murdered a policewoman, Yvonne Fletcher, outside the Libyan embassy in London. Thatcher let the killer return to Libya when she guaranteed safe passage out of the country for everybody inside the embassy when the fatal shots were fired. But it was a mistake by the NUM to send Windsor to Tripoli.

How could it have happened? The security services, MI5 and MI6, were all over us like a rash. Telephones were tapped, pickets arriving at ports or steel works to find the police had mysteriously got there first. There was also dark talk of agent provocateurs and spies in our ranks.

Dozens of MPs were to sign an Early Day Motion (EDM) in the Commons supporting Scargill and Peter Heathfield, the NUM general secretary, after Windsor and a group of others sold smear stories to the *Daily Mirror*. The motion, five years after the strike, denounced the 'personal attacks, smears and allegations against national officials of the NUM by unscrupulous elements of the media and two former employees of the union'. It was ignored, predictably, by the same media.

In August 1990, on a hot evening, I spoke in Sheffield alongside Scargill and Heathfield in front of getting on for a thousand people. Peter likened the vilification to the abuse suffered by miners' leader A.J. Cook after the 1926 strike. He wasn't wrong. The sustained campaign against Scargill and Heathfield was dirty, smearing them by accusing the pair of misusing funds, both during and after the strike. Stella Rimington was the first female director-general of MI5 and the first to court publicity, smiling for the cameras and posing as the champion of the great British public. We gave her some publicity she didn't want. Her PR offensive was purely cosmetic, plastic charm for the criminally gullible. With Mick Clapham and Jimmy Hood, mining MPs like me, we put down another EDM. We noted her central role in spying on the strike including 'her deployment of agents provocateurs' – including Roger Windsor. It was, I believe, the first time an alleged MI5 agent was named on the House of Commons order paper.

Windsor, we said, was 'an agent of MI5 under Mrs Rimington, sent in to the NUM to destabilise and sabotage the union at its most critical juncture'. The motion recounted how Windsor had 'staged a televised meeting with Colonel Gaddafi, causing immense damage to the striking miners'. Windsor was paid a reported £80,000 by Robert Maxwell for his treachery, spinning his lies about Scargill and Heathfield. His high five-figure cheque was 30 pieces of silver adjusted for inflation, the Judas kiss the lurid nonsense Windsor made up in interviews. Windsor turned the NUM's Sheffield headquarters into his personal Garden of Gethsemane.

I'd been uneasy about Windsor from the start. I directed the people who collected money for the miners at meetings or on streets to hand it over to Peter rather than Windsor. Heathfield pointed out to me the lay-by off Junction 29 on the M1 where he'd receive huge amounts from supportive unions, the NUM operating in cash because the courts controlled the bank accounts.

I continue to lend a hand to workers in struggles and, looking back, I'm proud of the stands we took. A march in 1972 to free the Pentonville Five – Bernie Steer, Vic Turner, Conny Clancy, Tony Merrick and Derek Watkins – was notable for growing bigger as we made our way from Tower Hill to the prison in Islington. Usually they shrink as people duck into the pub or peel away tired. Not this one. It was in support of the five dockers jailed by Heath's National Industrial Relations Court for striking without the requisite ballot. Our ranks swelled enormously. A bus driver was persuaded to join the protest outside the jail and his abandoned vehicle added to the chaos outside the high walls. From the top of a rickety stepladder I could see thousands and thousands of faces when I spoke.

The threat of wider industrial action forced Heath to send a hitherto obscure legal officer, called the Official Solicitor, scurrying to the High Court, who purged the contempt of the five. The labour movement secured their release and defeated Heath's attempt to shackle the unions. It was a great day.

I witnessed at Grunwick the early use by the police of what became known as kettling. A right-winger, George Ward, exploited the mainly Asian women developing photographs at the film-processing laboratory. He was against recognising the Transport and General Workers' Union and sacked one of the low-paid women involved in the union. The dispute became a cause célèbre between 1976 and 1978, with mass pickets and mass arrests. Riot police were out in force in what was to be a forerunner of the tactics against the miners.

Towards the end I could see the police were breaking us up into groups to be detained, so I escaped. I arrived back in Parliament and many hours later Martin Flannery, a Sheffield left-winger, finally returned. He was spitting tacks that they'd been corralled for ages.

'Didn't you go today?' he asked, puzzled.

'I did, Martin,' I answered, 'but I saw what was happening so got out. I've been here waiting for you.' It didn't brighten his mood.

The only occasion I was arrested and locked up was on a picket with striking workers on *TV-am*, the ITV breakfast show. The station's management locked out technical staff at the Camden Lock studio in north London after a twenty-four-hour strike in 1988. I'd been on a few of their demonstrations and they were pretty placid affairs. Alan Sapper, the leader of the ACTT union involved, made it clear he wanted no trouble.

The bosses couldn't put on news programmes without the camera crews so they'd run a lot of cartoons, including *Batman*. Adam West, the actor who played the caped crusader, was scheduled to sit on the show's sofa. I told the union the only way to secure publicity for the dispute was to stop him entering the building. We stopped him dead in his tracks, more of a match for Batman than the Joker or Mr Freeze ever proved. There was a little bit of an incident, and from then on the police took a more aggressive line, settling a few scores at future pickets.

Not very long after the Batman blockade I was back outside the Camden Lock studios when a police officer unexpectedly ordered me off the road and on to the pavement. I told him I'd been on a lot of marches and pickets and the general rule was to keep the pavement clear for pedestrians. I suggested the cops would be better deployed tacking crooks in the city and drug traffickers. He didn't like that and ordered me on to the pavement again, a little more forcefully than previously.

It was the day after Thatcher had been filmed picking up litter in St James's Park that had been dropped moments before in a stunt about clean streets when she was sacking hundreds of road sweepers. On the road outside *TV-am* was a piece of paper. 'Should I pick it up,' I asked, pointing at what I think was a discarded leaflet, 'or will you?' Before I could say anything else the copper had hold of me and bundled me roughly into the back of a van. He had a cadet hovering near him and he may have reacted to save face with the trainee.

I was taken to Kentish Town police station where they put me into a cell. I overheard one of them saying 'We've got the Beast of Bolsover in Number One' as they tried to decide, in lowered voices clearly not lowered enough, what to do with me. I sat down on the hard bed, wondering if I'd be out for Prime Minister's Questions that afternoon. They'd left me with the newspaper and a pen so I started doing the crossword.

The peephole in the door was pulled aside and I saw a beady eye looking at me. I'd been inside quite a while when the door opened. It was an officer with pips on his shoulder, looking all important.

'Is there anything you want?' he asked, curtly. My reply didn't secure a speedy release.

'I'm struggling with 23 across in the *Guardian* but,' I added, 'as a *Sun* reader, I don't think you will be able to help me in this regard.' The door slammed shut and I thought: That's it, I won't be back in Parliament for Thatcher's questions.

It's boring in a cell. There wasn't much to do after I'd finished the crossword without the help of the copper. I sang 'The Red Flag' to entertain myself and annoy them before I was charged at 2 p.m., and bailed to appear before Highbury magistrates. I hired a barrister and turned up for the case, only to be greeted by a gang of journalists shouting questions about what I had to say.

'What do you mean,' I said, '"What have I got to say?"? – I don't know yet, I've not been in. Wait until I come out.'

The pack chorused: 'The case has been dropped.' It was news to me, if potentially good news.

'Are you sure?' I replied.

'Yes,' they chorused, jostling with their notebooks and pens for a quote.

It emerged a cameraman in the union had filmed my conversation with the arresting officer and it was obvious I hadn't caused trouble or resisted arrest. I was another victim, albeit a minor one, and a lucky one because the case was thrown out, of the police in an era when Thatcher deployed them against trade unionists and their supporters. Too many miners were not so fortunate.

The police were a law unto themselves back then. The Wapping dispute in London was like a rugby scrum after Rupert Murdoch sacked thousands of secretaries, messengers and printers at his newspapers. The police were out of control, again bashing people up and arresting whoever they fancied. The brutality was ferocious and the lies afterwards were atrocious. Murdoch backed

Thatcher and Thatcher backed Murdoch, the Prime Minister delighted to assist him to smash the trade unions as Murdoch's *Sun* and *The Times* cheered her anti-union fatwa.

What the police did at Hillsborough was no surprise for those of us who'd experienced the South Yorkshire force during the miners' strike. Treating working people with contempt was part of the culture and philosophy back then. Thatcher had granted the police a licence to do what they wanted. Blaming Liverpool football fans for the deaths of 96 supporters, Murdoch's *Sun* the chief cheerleader for the smears, was all part of the game as far as the police were concerned.

I'm delighted the families of the Hillsborough dead are finally finding out the truth, just as the miners did. Documents revealing the depth of the lies, and the extent of the cover-up at Hillsborough made grim if unsurprising reading. A part of me likes to hope that in the current era, when the mobile phones in most people's pockets have cameras and pickets and fans can film what happens, it would be harder for bent police to get away with their crimes. That it would be more difficult to beat up miners and printers, or falsely accuse football fans of robbing the dead. Another bit of me isn't so sure.

We have to struggle for justice in this world. Trade unionists know that. The Hillsborough families have proved it. I'll never forget the highs and lows of the miners' strike. And I'll never forgive those who lied and betrayed the miners. We were left with agony when it could've been ecstasy.

CHAPTER THIRTEEN

The jazz singer

In another life I'd love to have been a professional singer or a top-class marathon runner. I inherited my enjoyment of singing from my mother, Lucy, who, as I explained earlier, always had a song on her lips. I was a pub singer as a young man. Weekends I'd be up in the Greyhound and Elm Tree in Clay Cross. Al Jolson, Frankie Laine, Slim Whitman, Guy Mitchell and Dean Martin – I tried them all.

I was invited to audition as a semi-pro club singer, touring the vibrant and potentially profitable northern circuit, but I didn't fancy it and packed in pub singing when I gave up drinking. I'd been wanting to change my lifestyle, never really enjoying alcohol, drinking pints primarily to fit in, when on Boxing Day 1953 Uncle Nip's death was a fork in the road in my life.

I'd wandered into the Elm Tree for a drink and to see my mates. The landlady, seeing me at the bar, asked: 'How's your Uncle Nip doing?'

'What do you mean?'

'He's in a bad way. He was hit by a car and dragged along the street.'

The previous day, Christmas Day, Uncle Nip, whose real name was George, had left the inn after a few drinks and been run over on his way home. I hadn't heard. We had no telephones so even bad news travelled slowly.

I left the Elm Tree for the last time to go to the hospital, but Uncle Nip had died. I'm not puritanical about alcohol by any means. I've had the odd shandy since. I did find, however, I had more time, energy and money. I gave up smoking at the same time, then started again during the 1984–5 pit strike before stubbing out the habit the following year.

I still enjoy singing at parties and socials, and I'm delighted to join in with the elderly when I visit homes in Bolsover. I also love musicals in London's West End. I've been lucky enough to go to the best, such as the Sondheim musicals, *Jersey Boys*, *Blood Brothers* and *Billy Elliot*. There was a scene in *Billy Elliot* of the miners' Christmas party about me being unable to appear as guest speaker because I was already booked. I'd have gone if I wasn't, and sang them a song. Then there are the films – *Oklahoma!*, *Carousel* and *Singin' in the Rain* – that have me breaking into song.

I'm lucky to have sung at the Albert Hall. It was a rally after the end of the miners' strike. I came up with a parody of Ethel Merman's 'I Hear Music' to poke fun at Maggie Thatcher and her mob. I'm happy to say it brought the house down. I still remember the chorus:

I hear Thatcher and there's no one there,
I smell Tebbit and his greasy hair,
All the time he thinks she walks on air,
I wonder why, I wonder why.

Leon's tossing in his sleep at night,
Heseltine has lost his appetite,
Stars they used to twinkle in her eyes,
And now they're telling lies and we know why.

The Albert Hall song followed a skit of 'Shall We Dance' I sang at
the Joan Littlewood theatre in London's Stratford when the traitorous Gang of Four – Roy Jenkins, David Owen, Shirley Williams
and Bill Rodgers – were plotting in 1981 to destroy the Labour
Party, creating a Social Democratic Party (SDP) that sustained
Thatcher in power at the 1983 and 1987 elections. I'll let you
judge how I felt about them. Here is the first verse:

Will they go with a plane on the runway,
Will they fly, will they go,
Say au revoir when they really mean goodbye,
Or perchance when the last drop of claret has run dry,
Will they still be together,
Doctor Death and Shirley Poppins,
Or will this be their last romance?
On the clear understanding that this kind of thing can
    happen,
Will they go, oh for Christ's sake let them go.

I think fondly of my mother whenever I hear or sing old
Gracie Fields favourites, or wartime numbers such as 'Hang out
the Washing on the Siegfried Line' or 'The White Cliffs of Dover'.
As I said, I'd love to have been a professional singer, but it wasn't
to be.

CHAPTER FOURTEEN

The Queen's Speech

The Prince of Wales tried to meet me once, but I wasn't interested. Socialists are for opportunities and fairness, not unelected hereditary privilege. In common with many socialists, I'm opposed in principle to the monarchy. As you can imagine, it came as a surprise to be invited to meet him.

Conservative MP Nicholas Soames was the emissary. He's a grandson of Winston Churchill and has been an equerry to the Prince of Wales. He stopped me at the entrance to the Tea Room in the House of Commons.

'Dennis,' he said, 'may I have a word?'

I was instinctively suspicious, grunting: 'What's up?'

Soames said: 'You know that I'm a friend of Prince Charles?' I did but I acted as if I didn't, saying nothing as I waited to learn where this was leading. Soames is a grandee, a Tory who likes his dinners. He was a farming and defence minister in John Major's government. He isn't exactly quiet and is usually heard a mile off, possessing a foghorn rather than a voice. My suspicions were heightened when he motioned with his head for us to move away from the door, presumably to avoid being overheard. Intrigued by what his game might be, I went with him.

In what was a whisper for him but a normal decibel level for anybody else, Soames said that he'd been looking for me and was glad our paths had crossed. He repeated that he was a friend of Charles. Then he said it: 'Prince Charles would like to meet you.' He wittered on about how the Prince of Wales regularly met MPs to discuss subjects and he was interested in talking to me, as a working-class Labour man and an ex-miner.

'I'm not interested,' I replied sharply. Soames looked a little startled. Maybe he's not used to MPs telling him they don't want to meet the heir to the throne. I don't. I've better things to do. To be fair to Soames, he didn't ask why. Perhaps he was worried the answer I'd give would be home truths he didn't want to hear, and certainly wouldn't be able to tell Charlie boy.

It was unbelievable, really. Soames thought I would fall into Charlie's lap. I have never met a member of the Royal Family and, to be honest, I have absolutely no desire to do so. If Charles is bored with talking to plants, he can find somebody else to pass the time with. It definitely wasn't going to be me. Soames said something about it being alright and our paths resumed their usual directions by diverging.

I've no doubt some of the royals are OK people. Most people in the country, in the world for that matter, are OK. But I don't put people on a pedestal just because they were born into a particular family. The whole deference thing, the hereditary principle, is contrary to my belief in equality, of treating people the same instead of elevating an undeserving few above all others.

Yet I acknowledge most people, at the moment, accept the Royal Family. They are conditioned from the off to revere them. The mass media fawns in front of the royals. Even the *Guardian* – yes, the *Guardian* – a supposedly republican newspaper, published a special supplement the day after William married Kate Middleton in what was billed as an austerity wedding. Some austerity when there were a thousand guests in Westminster Abbey and they drove off in an Aston Martin.

Support swings with the mood of the nation and it's inevitable that one day people will wake up and see the royal charade for what it is. The royals weren't so popular when Fergie was having her toes sucked by a man who wasn't Prince Andrew. The hostile public reaction to the aloof response to the death of Diana was genuine. The royals are trying to ride two horses by being regal and simultaneously posing as common, in touch with ordinary people. At some point they'll be unseated.

Until they are, I don't believe in wasting time on tilting at windmills. Devoting energy to fighting battles which are largely irrelevant to bigger questions is a costly diversion. In politics you have to weigh up the foremost goals. I want to abolish the House of Lords and consistently vote to do so, although I've noticed there are fewer of us these days. But I'm not going to spend all my waking moments thinking of ways to do away with peers when there is a big majority in the House of Commons against me.

The royals fall into the same category. After Diana's death, I went for a stroll in St James's Park. Parliament was on holiday but I was interested to see for myself what was going on after watching the flowers, crowds, grief and hysteria on the telly. I'd never seen so many people in twinsets and pearls. I was stopped by one of the women who angrily told me that the Royal Family should've been down in Buckingham Palace instead of up in Balmoral. There was a revolutionary spirit. The Queen and the royals were momentarily very unpopular. Blair, on the other hand, was held in great esteem. His 'people's princess' performance outside that church in Sedgefield went down incredibly well. A few years later it was the Queen who was popular and Blair on the wane.

I'm not naive enough to believe that out there in Britain there is a majority of people ready, as I am, to abolish the monarchy. That doesn't mean I'll change my views. I'm a republican when the pendulum swings their way, for instance when a baby heighten's the family's popularity, as much as when a royal scandal swings it mine. What's important is the principle and I'm sticking to mine as a republican. Nye Bevan had a phrase about socialism being the language of priorities. Some fights are unavoidable. Other battles we pick. I try to avoid the royals. When the royals don't avoid me, I make my views clear.

The May 1966 local elections were a stupendous year for Labour. Harold Wilson in the general election two months earlier had transformed a majority of 4 into 96. In Derbyshire we won urban districts, the small town councils, across the county. Places such as Matlock and Wirksworth, which we didn't often control, were ours. I went to a meeting in Matlock, the county town on the edge of the Peak District, where the Derbyshire Urban District Council Association gathered to elect a chairman and sort out this and that.

The association met three or four times a year to discuss mutual issues. Each council sent two delegates and I was one half of the Clay Cross duo. The chairmanship had never struck me as worth a row of beans and I went along only because I was asked to attend. At the meeting the Labour people came to me and said: 'Dennis, we're going to nominate you for chair. We can win this.'

I wasn't fussed, replying: 'It doesn't mean much – you're only talking about officiating on formal occasions which don't amount to a row of beans.'

The truth was Labour had been forced to play second fiddle to the Tories for as long as anybody could remember so the party wanted the position to rub Conservative noses in their defeat, depriving them of what they considered theirs by right. Seizing the post symbolised the world was changing, and the true blue Derbyshire county set was eclipsed by working-class pit areas such as mine. I was elected president of the Derbyshire Urban District Council Association, thinking I'd have little to do.

One of the first duties was unexpected: I was invited to a royal garden party in the grounds of Buckingham Palace. I know now these bashes are thrown every year. In 1966 I was clueless. I wasn't exactly a student of the Court Circular. My initial reaction was to laugh and dismiss it as a mistake, that the Palace had sent the invitation to the wrong name at the wrong address. I had a second laugh when I worked out the invitation wasn't to me personally. The invitation was to the holder of the chairmanship of the Derbyshire Urban District Council Association, who hitherto had always been a Tory and would be thrilled to dress up and go with his wife in her big hat to stand on the Buckingham Palace lawn and nibble a crustless cucumber sandwich.

The invitation came via the Lord Lieutenant of the county, a character who puts on a uniform with a sword to be a representative of Her Majesty's Ruritania. I worried a young lass in the office probably sent it out automatically and would be in trouble for failing to strike the position off the list, now Labour held the seat. I read the letter and studied the embossed card with its gold lettering. The envelope contained other bumf and I spotted a car park pass for the Mall which added to the otherness of their world when, as a miner, we didn't have a phone in the house or a bank account, let alone a car.

I put all the royal stuff back in the big brown envelope in which it had arrived and chucked the lot in the dustbin. I had no wish to go to a royal garden party and mingle with people I didn't know and, most likely, would've ended in an argument with if we did talk. That was the end of it as far as I was concerned. Until I went to the Clay Cross council offices to see Joe Rysdale. Joe was the officer who made the council tick and knew the town like the back of his hand.

'Hey, Joe, you'll never believe it. I received this package inviting me to Buckingham Palace for a royal garden party,' I told him. 'Would you credit it?'

Joe was interested. 'You did?' he asked.

'Yes, I did. The bloody cheek of it. They think we've all got cars as well.'

Joe's interest deepened. 'Aren't you going then?' he asked.

'No, I'm bloody not. I've put it in the bin.'

Joe responded again: 'You're not going?!' The excitement in his voice should've alerted me. 'Quick, we've not emptied Wheatcroft Close bins yet. Get me that car park pass in the envelope that you don't want.' Joe was a walking timetable and knew every bin round in the town.

So off I went home to Wheatcroft Close to fish the royal car park pass out of the bin for Jim. What he'd do with it wasn't my business as long as he wasn't doing anybody harm.

The fact is Joe was a big fan of horse racing, liking a bet. And Joe did have a car, unlike me. He'd spend his holidays at the big race meetings. Every year he'd go for a week to Royal Ascot. He was a regular at Cheltenham, where he met all these fellers he knew from Ireland.

In the early 1970s Joe suffered a mini-stroke and wasn't too well. During a summer recess I was doing my front garden when his car pulled up on the side of the road. I went over to the hedge and shouted:

'Hey up, Joe. How are you?'

His voice was weak and Joe replied that he'd been better but was getting along.

'Should you be driving?' I asked him.

He insisted he was OK, though to be honest I wasn't sure.

'By the way,' I said, 'did you ever use that pass?'

He opened the glove compartment where you keep your odds and ends and pulled out the pass. 'It's here, Den,' Joe laughed. 'I use it every year. Gets me straight in to Ascot and Cheltenham.'

A small victory for the workers and a big triumph for Joe. He's long gone now, Joe. I can't think of him, driving into the VIP car park with my old pass, without smiling. I saw a new pass sent out a few years ago and it was the same colour and design as the old. I couldn't believe that despite everything – the Troubles in

Northern Ireland, suicide bombers on London Transport – they hadn't changed them.

MPs are invited annually to one of the Buck House garden parties. The notices are general, going out to all MPs. The Labour Party sends it round with the regular whip detailing how we'll vote in the week ahead. If I'd wanted, I could be nearing a half-century of them. Instead I'm stuck on nought by choice.

In my early days as an MP I enjoyed seeing who was going on the quiet so, on sunny days I'd sit on a bench in St James's Park waiting for them to pass, all dolled up to the nines. You'd be surprised who I spotted. There I would be sitting, doing the crossword or watching the world go by, when I'd catch the eye of an MP who'd go bright red because I'd caught them living a double life. The excuse I heard most often from those joining the Establishment for the day was a variation on a single theme: the missus wanted to go. I do wonder if women MPs who are republicans the other 364 days of the year similarly blame a husband if they weaken and accept an invitation. Poor Willie Hamilton, a Labour MP from Scotland who made more noise than me about the royals, endured a real bashing when it was found out he'd gone to one of the Queen's parties.

On one garden party day I was playing my little game in St James's and it was really nice weather, a gorgeous day. I was doing the crossword and as happy as Larry on the bench as I awaited the procession of Parliamentarians returning from the Palace. Out of the corner of my eye I noticed a man sit down at the other end of the bench.

'Are you Mr Skinner?' he asked in a Scouse accent.

'If you guess again you'd be wrong,' I answered. 'You from Liverpool?'

He was from Merseyside, a construction worker who'd come to London 20 years ago to work on sites and had recently retired. We started chatting and it emerged he'd done some work on the terrace of Parliament overlooking the River Thames at the House of Lords end.

A few MPs walked by and changed colour from the neck up when they saw us sitting there.

'Who are they?' he asked, puzzled at their embarrassment.

'They have been to a garden party at Buckingham Palace,' I said, 'and would've preferred us not to know. If I was to guess they will be heading to the House of Commons and within twenty minutes they'll all be sitting on the terrace having a drink.'

I asked him: 'Hey up, do you want to go on that terrace and have a cup of tea? With a bit of luck we'll beat that lot in their finery if we get a move on.'

We did. Sitting for about an hour, we watched elected Members of Parliament return to the centre of democracy after their day out as guests of an unelected hereditary institution.

He was a nice feller, the lad from Liverpool. I gave him a quick tour of the Palace of Varieties, as I do for many people who visit. I explain the political significance of this statue and that, rather than regurgitating the bland accounts contained in guidebooks frightened to address what people and events were really about. He was impressed by Westminster Hall, the cavernous 11th-century building used when the likes of Nelson Mandela and Barack Obama address both Houses of Parliament. The medieval hammer-beamed timber roof is testimony to the craftsmanship of the workers and has stood the test of time. I showed him the plaque on the steps marking the spot where, in 1649, King Charles I was sentenced to death for plotting to overthrow Parliament in the English Civil War. If truth be told, he'd have stayed longer but I had to get off.

MPs face the arcane rigmarole after every election of swearing an oath to the Queen or affirming loyalty. Tony Banks, the late Labour MP for West Ham who was skilled at delivering witty attacks, was a republican like me and found himself in a spot of trouble after the 1997 general election when the newspapers saw him cross his fingers at the mention of the Queen. Banks was the sports minister and potentially in trouble with Downing Street, so quick as a flash he claimed he was wishing himself luck in his new job by crossing his fingers. I told Banks it was all a nonsense, that we just had to do it in order to take our seats to fight on far more important issues. The whole process reeks of promoting a hereditary monarchy over democracy, Her Majesty's This and Her Majesty's That taking precedence over the wishes of the electorate. My allegiance isn't to Queen Elizabeth II. My allegiance is to the people in Bolsover who vote to send me to Parliament to represent them, not her.

MPs are expected to attend when the Queen or another royal visits their constituency. I make myself scarce, even when I received a message in early 1997 from an officer in Bolsover council informing me I'd been selected to join dignitaries greeting the Queen on a visit to Hardwick Hall in July. The workers built a fine place when they put up Hardwick Hall. It was the 400th anniversary of the house. Bess of Hardwick, who kept marrying rich men for their money and outlived all four husbands, loved having stately homes built and her portfolio included Chatsworth and Hardwick Hall. The Queen wanted to take a peep.

I rang the council office straight away. 'What do you mean, I'm going to meet the Queen?' I asked.

'Well,' said this voice on the other end of the phone, 'there's the chief executive and a few others plus you as the MP, making six in all. It's a great honour. You're very lucky.'

'You think I'm lucky?' I responded. 'You better take me off that list because I'm not going to stand in a line to bow before the Queen. If you've sent out the list to others with my name on, you'll have to send out a new one without me on it.'

The man at the council couldn't grasp that I wouldn't go, maintaining it was a great honour and I was lucky. I know other Labour MPs who are republicans who, when the call comes, hop to it and go to see the Queen. I don't and won't criticise them. But I'm not dancing to the Palace's tune.

I wondered about that invite. It wasn't as if my views on the Royal Family were a state secret. For a while I even thought it might be a trap, or a joke, to see if I'd sneak off to meet the Queen secretly. The skirmish about not showing up for the Queen didn't do me any harm in Bolsover. My majority went up in Labour's 1997 landslide.

I've never gone along with the nonsense of MPs trooping into the House of Lords from the House of Commons for the Queen's Speech on the State Opening of Parliament. The entire panto-mime is Walt Disney rather than serious politics. From the Queen clip-clopping to Westminster in a fairytale coach to Black Rod tipping up in fancy dress to bang on the door, summoning the elected to pay homage to the unelected is a democratic farce. Parliament resisting Charles I then defeating the Royalists in the English Civil War of 1642–51 was a huge statement, culminating in the execution of the King. All the current nonsense, with a government whip held hostage in Buckingham Palace until the monarch's safe return, is treating democracy as an extension of the entertainment industry.

On Queen's Speech days I turn up for work as usual and, from my perch on the front bench below the gangway, I decline to be swept along by the ridiculous pomp. I started cracking jokes to puncture the pomposity. The timing has to be spot on, as the microphone above me is only on for a second or two when Black Rod summons us to follow him meekly to stand before the Queen and her seated peers in their ermine. The point has to be topical if it's to hit home, making a few MPs laugh in the chamber and, more pertinently, deliver a political message to voters reading newspapers or watching the show on TV. To my surprise the Queen's Speech joke has developed into a mini-show over the years.

I called the whole rigmarole the 'coalition's last stand' in 2014, in what I hoped would be Cameron's final Queen's Speech. In May 2012, with the ConDem coalition's austerity plunging the country back into recession, there wasn't much to celebrate around the Queen's Diamond Jubilee. The quip 'Jubilee Year, double-dip recession. What a start!' was a simple statement of the facts. David Cameron and the Queen could put on a circus but, as the Romans would've recognised, bread rations were becoming thinner.

The release of *The Queen* movie starring Helen Mirren in 2006 invited the question 'Have you got Helen Mirren on standby?' I was told BBC presenter Huw Edwards described it as 'cheap but funny'. Cheap? It was free – I didn't charge a penny. Of course I didn't hear him myself because I was in the chamber.

I've urged Black Rod to tell the Queen to pay her taxes and sell up when the country was told to tighten its belt. I wondered aloud why there was no Royal Commission inquiry when it was revealed the Duchess of York had taken money from a dubious American friend of the Duke of York. And asked 'Who shot the harriers?' after a couple of protected birds were blasted out of the sky close to where Prince Harry and his chums were shooting at Sandringham.

I hit the bullseye in 1990 with 'It tolls for thee, Maggie' when Black Rod banged on that door. She was all set to troop off to the Lords, Neil Kinnock walking alongside her, Tory and Labour MPs in file behind their leaders. Yet virtually everybody in that chamber knew the game was up except for Maggie herself and a few blinkered Tories blinded by love for her, devotion leaving them unable to acknowledge she'd rusted badly and was destined for the scrapyard. Equally 'New Labour, new Black Rod' in 1996 chimed with the mood of a country which couldn't wait to see the back of John Major and his miserable malcontents.

A journalist informed me excitedly there were guffaws at the *Guardian* when, with that paper campaigning to end the supremacy of the male line of succession, I said to Black Rod: 'Tell her to read the *Guardian*.'

One year Tory MP Damian Green had been arrested and his Commons office searched over his links to a Conservative mole in the Home Office, the lad leaking documents to embarrass the Labour government believing he might get a job with the grateful Tories. I asked: 'Any Tory moles at the Palace?' Black Rod, a retired general by the name of Michael Willcocks, had struggled to keep a straight face for a fair few years. He broke with protocol, responding: 'I shall miss you, Dennis.'

I'll offer the Establishment a deal: cut the Queen's Speech and I'll stop the mockery. The quips articulate what millions of people in their homes are thinking when they watch a narcissistic spectacle which distances Parliament from their lives, the fripperies of a costume drama emphasising how out of touch the House of Commons, the House of Lords and a woman born to be Sovereign are from everyday life.

Her Majesty's Prime Minister David Cameron, a silver-spoon Tory who is a distant relative of the Queen, couldn't hide his excitement at inviting the Queen to Downing Street in December 2012 to sit with Her Majesty's Cabinet while Her Majesty's Government discussed what horrors it had planned for Her Majesty's Subjects. She had the good grace to look bored before departing, having left a forwarding address for the sixty table mats Her Cabinet had bought as a Diamond Jubilee gift.

Downing Street claimed she was the first monarch to visit the Cabinet since George III in 1781. The BBC and other broadcasters repeated the spin to build up the visit. She was in fact the first monarch since her father, George VI. The truth isn't so dramatic. I remember Dad telling us how George VI, or that 'stuttering old fool' as he called him, met the Cabinet during the Second World War. I was interviewed by Sky News, which wanted somebody who wasn't fawning. They didn't broadcast me but did alter how they presented the visit in later news bulletins, either because of what I'd told them about George VI or because they'd found out themselves and didn't want to be spun by Downing Street.

Slaying little monsters isn't a priority. Nor will I be dragooned into bowing or showing respect to those who haven't earned it.

CHAPTER FIFTEEN

The Iron Lady

No figure in my 40-plus years in Parliament encapsulated the poison and nastiness of the Conservative Party more than Margaret Thatcher. The record of what she did to Britain – deliberately breaking people, communities and industries to impose her brand of casino capitalism, impoverishing a swollen group at the bottom as she rewarded her City friends – was unforgivable. Thatcher ruined millions of lives. Not out of ignorance, or as an unintentional by-product of her policies. But systematically in her war on decent, working people.

If you were of no value to Thatcher, you were chucked on a scrap heap. If you got in her way, she'd steamroller you. If you resisted, she'd try to destroy you. Thatcher was a dictator with a handbag. She didn't care. The hurt she caused didn't bother her. Thatcher wouldn't have recognised the truth if it was sprayed on her eyeballs.

Mrs Thatcher's passing in April 2013 reminded victims of her political and economic crimes over 11 bitter years. I didn't return to shed crocodile tears when Parliament was recalled at great expense. I would never have dreamed of protesting at her funeral; death is the ultimate leveller and all without exception are entitled to dignity in taking a final leave. But it was easy to understand the seething resentment in the country at the gun carriage cortège, the pitiful irony of Thatcher enjoying the trappings of a state funeral when she'd despised the public sector. She wanted the best for herself so demanded the Army when her supporters, if they'd had the courage of her and their political convictions, would've booked G4S and DHL for a cut-price private job. Thatcher went out of her way to divide the country in life, so it was no surprise the country split when she died.

On her death I objected in the House of Commons to the cancellation of Prime Minister's Questions. David Cameron was using her funeral as an excuse to escape accountability in Parliament. I took the opportunity to deliver home truths ignored by the one-eyed Tory press and BBC. It was an occasion when the flood of letters and emails expressing agreement underscored both that voters do watch the Parliament Channel on TV and that your instincts chime with a large audience. The decision to scrap PMQs, rather than delay it until a few hours after the St Paul's ceremony, was history repeating itself. The parallels with Anthony Eden were uncanny. Nearly four decades on, they were proposing a similar mini-break in Westminster. I hadn't changed my view.

In the debate on letting Cameron off the hook, I raised the issue at the heart of why I hate a Tory Party that serves the interests of a narrow elite:

Let's not kid ourselves. We hear talk about the thing that we sometimes suggest has gone away: class. That's what it is: it is about class. It's about the fact that people out there have to live their lives in a different way and that there is one rule for those at the top and another for those at the bottom. It has never changed – I wish it had, but it hasn't.

In a week when benefits for the neediest were cut again, the arrangements for Thatcher had grown like Topsy. What started as a ceremonial funeral embraced the silencing of Big Ben, then binned Prime Minister's Questions. I knew I wouldn't win a vote to restore the session. The front benches had reached an agreement. This was an opportunity to be a voice for those who challenged the Tory gloss on Thatcherism.

I reminded the House how divisive a character Thatcher was. I accept I am too, but I was never prime minister. Nadine Dorries, the Tory MP who went into the TV jungle in the vain hope of emerging a celebrity, opened her mouth to complain. This gave me an opening to rub in the truth that Thatcher's own side kicked her out like a dog in the night when she was considered useless after winning three elections.

To remain in order and sustain the debate under parliamentary rules, the points I made needed to be framed as questions to the leader of the House, Andrew Lansley. So I said one of the questions I would like asked at the Prime Minister's Questions to be abandoned was about scrapping the bedroom tax. Another was about how to stop employers exploiting migrant workers to undercut British staff. I was working up to why Britain is skint. Memories of the 1980s are still fresh in my mind. The financial crash of 2007 and 2008 was a direct result of Thatcherism. She deregulated the City. The last Labour government should've reimposed tough regulation and nationalised banks when they were solvent, not bankrupt. Why did the great economic tsunami sweep the world? It was a rhetorical question. I answered:

Because in 1989, in one of her last acts, Mrs Thatcher talked about the brave casino economy, the big bang in the City and deregulation. That was the moment it began. We never knew when it would turn into a recession, but we knew that somehow or other, that society of instant gratification would cause a recession at some time. That is how it all began.

It was just like that with the share-owning democracy. We could have discussed that tomorrow. Mrs Thatcher, that non-divisive character, sold off all the public utilities. She said we'll sell off all the public utilities – gas, electricity and all the rest – and everybody will have shares. You can buy them off Sid and you'll be able to be part of that great British share-owning democracy. What happened to that? What happened to the share-owning democracy? EDF is now owned by French electricity; EON is owned by Germans; Scottish Power is owned by Spain's Iberdrola; and npower is owned by the German company RWE. Anglian Water has gone to Canada, and Thames Water is owned by the Germans . . . So who owns Orange and T-Mobile? Have a guess. France and Germany. Who owns Cellnet and O2? Spain. Who owns Arriva buses? The German Deutsche Bank . . . Gatwick is owned by South Korea; Cadbury's is owned by the United States; the M6 toll is owned by Australia's Macquarie Bank. On and on it goes. We could, then, talk about bringing the public utilities back into public ownership. The whole concept of Thatcher was to divide and rule. She was also the one who said that there is no such thing as society.

I quote this speech because it captures the essence of my case against Tories in general and Thatcher in particular. Conservative MPs muttered, interrupted, demanded I end. But I was there. The reality of her Downing Street fatwa demands to be on record.

What I am saying is that it is important to remember that the people out there know where Thatcher stood. They have not forgotten it. I am talking about those communities where shipbuilding was destroyed in the early '80s and where the steel industry at Corby and various other places was smashed when Thatcher brought in MacGregor, then brought him back, paying a £1.5 million transfer fee to Lazard's bank for him to shut, it was said, about 20 or 30 pits. What happened in practice? We had 150 pits at the end of the 1985 pit strike, and by the time Thatcher went, there were only 30 left. That is why people out there are angry, and why they demand of us, at least a few of us, to speak the truth on their behalf.

Winding up, I thanked the Speaker, John Bercow, for allowing me to raise issues that were much more important than funeral arrangements.

It is not about personalities; it is all about class. We must never forget that. We should remember where we come from. I remember my own family – with nine kids, who did not have two ha'pennies to rub together – and that is still embedded in my soul. That is why I speak as I do. I do not want to change; I never will. That will not get my hands on the dispatch box, but that is not a luxury that it has ever bothered me to get. It is important to remember that these words of mine do not come out of my mouth because of envy or greed, but because I believe that we have to look after those people who do not have two ha'pennies to rub together. That should be what motivates us every day of the week, including at Prime Minister's Question Time. When the Labour Party understands that as we do here today, it will be better for it.

There is so much else to be hung around the neck of Thatcher. Mass unemployment, dole queues topping three million after she hired actors so the propagandists of Saatchi & Saatchi could produce a poster claiming it was Labour that wasn't working. A poll tax that ultimately did for her, the policy of charging the same council costs to a duke as a dustman too much even for most Conservatives. Council house sales helped create the homelessness crisis with us today, a third of those flogged finding their way to landlords who rent them to the same councils at inflated rates. And, of course, the never-to-be-forgotten miners' strike. Thatcher perfected the Tory art of divide and rule, ably assisted by the SDP splitting the anti-Conservative vote at general elections. Public versus Private, North v. South, Jobless v. Working, Young v. Old – Mrs Thatcher divided the lot. Never was Saint Francis of Assisi so inappropriately quoted as on that day in 1979 when she lied 'Where there is discord, may we bring harmony' as she prepared to rip Britain apart.

She was never the great orator her cheerleaders in the media would pretend. Thatcher was there for a purpose. The right-wing of the Tory Party wanted one of their own and Thatcher fitted the bill. The Mad Monk, Keith Joseph, was the brains. She was the frontwoman for a nasty project.

Labour MPs where I sat on the front bench below the gangway would keep up a running commentary, starting with 'Maggie Thatcher, milk snatcher' for grabbing small bottles of milk from the hands of schoolkids when she was Ted Heath's education secretary, to shouts of 'You're mad' when she stabbed him in the back and became leader. Thatcher was a touch unbalanced. She thought she was more regal than the Queen. After the pit strike in 1984–5 she took to wearing what I can only describe as an Elizabethan collar. I said then she was on her way. Those whom the gods wish to destroy they first send mad.

Tories are intimidated when no respect is shown, and Thatcher was a prize example of that weakness. The groupies who gathered around her skirts, their fawning a plea for attention, would be close to shock when we failed to show her the deference they stupidly believed was their heroine's by right.

I recall once in the Tea Room I went to fetch a newspaper from the bottom end. Thatcher was sitting at a table, surrounded by a dozen braying acolytes. As I passed the odd group, a plummy voice sounded:

'Here's Skinner, he's got all the answers. He went to grammar school.'

This smart-alec Tory clearly didn't know, or had forgotten, that Thatcher was a Grammar Girl. So I stopped.

'She went to one as well,' I said, pointing at Thatcher. 'Do you agree with what they are saying, deriding grammar schools?'

Nobody said a word. There was stunned silence. Thatcher herself didn't reply. The acolytes looked sheepish. It was as if the Bullingdon Club had been struck dumb. I wasn't waiting for them to think of an answer. Attack, as always, was the best form of defence.

'You had to swot to get to grammar school,' I said. The now distinctly unmerry band, including Thatcher herself, said nothing. 'In my case it was a higher grade school and I got a county minor scholarship at ten,' I added. 'Did you, Maggie?'

They were stunned that somebody, especially a Labour MP, was addressing their heroine with a directness they couldn't bear.

On a roll, I filled the silence. 'You studied Chemistry and Physics, didn't you, Maggie?'

A few looked as if they would suffer cardiac arrests when I called her Maggie. Not Margaret. Nor Mrs Thatcher. Certainly not Prime Minister. But Maggie! The pained responses to the faux familiarity were all the encouragement I needed. Running my words together like a racing commentator at the Derby when two horses are neck and neck heading for the line, I continued:

'When a body is weighed in air then in a fluid the upthrust or the apparent loss in weight is equal to the weight of the fluid displaced.' They were gobsmacked. I slowed to conversational speed:

'Do you remember having to learn that, Maggie? What was it? It wasn't Boyle's Law, it wasn't Charles' Law. What was it? Come on, all you public school kids, what's the theory?'

Her apostles looked on open-mouthed, chins dropping so far they were almost on the table. The preening band of Tories uttered not a word. Thatcher sat motionless, bemused. If I'm generous, I'll accept she knew, or used to know, what it was. But she didn't tell them or me.

'I suppose I have to tell you then,' I continued, then announced: 'It was Archimedes' principle.'

I could have left it there. Sauntered down the Tea Room, collected the paper. Returned to my chair and read the thing before doing the crossword. I didn't. I was having too much fun.

'I used to swot, you know,' I told them, 'while my mam was black-leading the grate. Did your mother black-lead the grate, Maggie? Does that Ronald Reagan black-lead his hair?'

For those unfamiliar with the practice, black lead was applied to clean a coal fire's iron grate. Thatcher rarely, if ever, spoke about a mother she didn't like. Until she finally bit on this question. Not on the comment about her mother keeping the house clean, but in response to my impertinent suggestion that Ronald Reagan dyed his hair. In a glorious Freudian moment, Thatcher looked me in the eye and said: 'Oh, no, it's all his own hair.'

The entire crew surrounding her was astounded. Still none spoke. Their faces said it all. I'd baited and caught the Prime Minister. She couldn't hold her tongue when a right-wing Republican President of the United States of America needed defending.

Quitting while ahead, I went for that paper. I was smiling inwardly and outwardly. After the Tea Room encounter, I took to describing Thatcher and Reagan as the Bonnie and Clyde of international politics. I'd heard the stories about her doting on him and him on her. A couple of years later, by the way, the acolytes that day were among the gang who knifed Thatcher in the back.

Thatcher uprooting old English country garden capitalism to shift the balance of power even further away from wealth-creating workers, and towards her reactionary clique, was a scorched-earth policy that left much of Britain derelict. Vast industries were razed to the ground; there were riots on the streets of Liverpool, Brixton and Bristol; the spoils of her war went to City Fat Cats in red braces and Yuppies.

On the left and in trade unions the disrobing of consensus was an opportunity to argue for a fundamental alternative. We had a different vision to landscape that garden. Ours would put every-body to work with spades to blend it along with the natural contours of the population instead of serving the few. Thatcher never smashed the spirit of resistance. No matter how many laws she passed to outlaw trade unionism and stifle protest, we fought her every step of the way. We argued, debated, marched and struck. She could hit us but we never fell down. She never delivered the knock-out blow. We couldn't let her win.

The sole moment I felt hostility to the positions I adopted was shortly after the end of the Falklands War. It was the first and last time I noticed people were avoiding eye contact with me in Bolsover marketplace, looking away rather than engaging me in conversation. A group of us, 32 in all, resisted the wave of jingoism to vote against sending a naval task force. Thatcher's ineptness had lost islands at the other end of the world to a fascist junta in Argentina she'd been happy to cohabit with until they read her mixed signals as a green light for invasion. Spilling blood in a colonial adventure to save her skin was a waste of young lives.

The bloodlust of Cruel Britannia herself and the war party, roared on by a rabid press led by the Gotcha! *Sun*, created a unique hostility. Those of us against military action were denounced as traitors. The Liberal Democrat Cyril Smith denounced us as such outside Parliament. Leo Abse, a left-wing MP from South Wales and a solicitor, wanted us to sue for libel. I wasn't interested in that but Smith was forced to eat his own words. Thatcher was demotic, her incompetence in losing the Falklands packaged as a triumph when the islands were regained – at the cost of 1,000 British and Argentine deaths – to form one of the more enduring myths of Thatcher. She wasn't a great war leader. Thatcher spilled British blood to cover up her error in losing the Falklands in the first place.

The antagonism in Bolsover didn't last long. Normal relations resumed as soon as the public learned a fortune was to be spent on a new airfield for the RAF at Mount Pleasant in the Falklands. People hadn't signed up for never-ending expenditure. The thrifty housewife careful with the shopping money splashed the cash when it came to the South Atlantic.

Public enthusiasm for the war also waned when greater consideration was given to the errors of Thatcher's government, such as withdrawing the icebreaker HMS *Endurance*, which was viewed in Buenos Aires as a sign that London wasn't committed to the islands. A bit of me wondered if the Argentines were lured on to a punch so she could have a little war. I told Tam Dalyell and he raised the possibility on TV!

Thatcher's history on Europe is equally distorted by her gang because they're unable to face the truth of her enthusiasm for a project they have grown to despise. I've remained opposed to the Common Market from day one and voted against entry. She voted to push Britain in without a referendum when Ted Heath and the Tories did the dirty deal. I voted to save Britain in Labour's 1975 referendum. Thatcher voted to stay in. Tories shut their eyes and stuck their fingers in their ears, singing la-la-la to avoid the truth.

Nigel Farage, the Tory con man who leads the right-wing rabble that is UKIP, is pained by the truth as he keeps that flame of Thatcher burning in Britain's second Conservative party. They all, in both the official Tory Party and the unofficial version, cling to Maggie swinging her handbag to demand a few bob back in a rebate, or seek comfort in a sceptical speech in Bruges in the dotage of her premiership.

When I hear Tories and the purple-faced of UKIP go on now about Poles, Romanians and Bulgarians coming to Britain to work, I think back and remember what Mrs Thatcher did. She signed the 1986 Single European Act to create the free market in people. She was championing the eastwards expansion of the European Union into the former Soviet satellites. She wanted the EU to embrace that part of the world to roll back the Iron Curtain, and stick it to Mikhail Gorbachev and Communists. The Single Market was designed deliberately to allow employers to transfer cheap labour across national borders. It wasn't principally about letting workers decide where they'd look for jobs. That's a by-product. The Single Market's main aim was to supply cut-price workers to capitalism. A capitalism with an insatiable appetite for the dozen-a-penny workers she created by stripping away employment rights, by shackling trade unions. The problems we wrestle with today can be traced back to her door.

I remind voters it is her legacy when I take groups around Parliament. Tony Banks, the Labour MP who chaired the arts committee, was the driving force behind the statue of Margaret Thatcher in the Members' Lobby. Her outstretched finger, as if pointing at a fresh batch of meat to be slaughtered and processed to feed the economy she created, serves an unintended purpose. It is a staging post to remind new generations of the horrors she visited upon the British people, or to reflect on that era with those who were there.

On the Meryl Streep film about Thatcher, *The Iron Lady*, I ended up an extra. I played, if played is the right description because it was part of my job for eleven years, an MP heckling her in the House of Commons. I didn't require much direction. It happened by accident really. I bumped into the actor Anthony Head, who played Geoffrey Howe, on the terrace along the Thames. He was having a cup of tea with Dan Norris, a Labour MP in Somerset until he lost his seat in 2010.

We discussed Howe and I said he wasn't regarded as a great orator, or an orator of any kind. The House had been full for Howe's resignation speech when he quit as deputy prime minister in November 1990. We thought he wouldn't live up to the occasion but he did in a quiet way, his 'broken bat' cricketing metaphor undermining her on Europe. It marked the beginning of the final end for Thatcher and she was swiftly history.

The director was toying with including a moment in her last speech to the Commons as PM, when I heckled she was off to be governor of the new European Central Bank, running the fingers of my right hand over the left palm in an exaggerated gesture to indicate she'd coin in the money. There was a silence that felt like an eternity and in reality probably lasted ten or fifteen seconds before she answered: 'What a good idea.' MPs laughed to Tory cheers as she added: 'I'm enjoying this.' No she wasn't. Thatcher was almost in tears.

So an invitation followed and off I went to an industrial estate near Wimbledon in south London where Granada keeps a replica of the chamber. It was a Thursday morning and I arrived very early. I walked into the room and bumped immediately into four or five Tory whips. The look of shock on their faces when I turned up was hilarious. Patrick McLoughlin, a Derbyshire MP who'd worked down the pit during the strike and was a scab, was the chief whip at the time and he and his praetorian platoon were on parade to guard her memory.

The director had decided against the 'good idea' clip but I was to be an extra and was sent immediately to change my shirt. Mine had stripes and they wanted it to be plain. I had lunch in the canteen with a troupe including Richard E. Grant (Michael Heseltine), Michael Pennington (Michael Foot) and John Sessions (Edward Heath), who was absolutely hilarious. He had Heath down to a T, including the shaking shoulders. It was a laugh a minute as we swapped stories, Sessions topping every tale with a funnier one of his own. Every now and again I would glance to see what the gaggle of Tory whips were up to. They were huddled together on a table of their own, listening to the laughter emanating from ours.

Had I lived in a big city and life had turned out differently, I'd have loved to tread the boards. To be an extra on the film was the closest I came. We were summoned to the set with 250 or 300 other extras. I looked over my shoulder and behind me, following, were the Tory Boys who, presumably, had grown bored in their isolation.

The production crew directed me to sit in the front row opposite Meryl Streep, aka Mrs Thatcher, and instructed me to shout improvised insults when the cameras rolled. The Tory Boys tried to sit behind Streep on what would be the Conservative benches. The rows were in dark. Our side was lit up. The embarrassed Tories were sent our way to join the Labour ranks and were seated behind me. I heard the crew instructing the Tories, including McLoughlin who Cameron later appointed transport secretary, to yell abuse at Meryl Streep – to barrack the woman portraying their goddess, Thatcher!

The cameras started recording and I shouted 'Milk snatcher', 'Go now', 'Resign' and a medley of other insults. Directly behind me, I could hear the Tory silly buggers screaming 'Get out' and all sorts at their heroine. If only I'd taken a camera of my own.

I spoke afterwards briefly to Streep, a Hollywood star who supports the Democrats, not the Republicans, and she is the consummate professional. The Oscar winner makes a first-class fist of every film she's in.

I rage against the Thatcher who in her pomp treated the working class like dirt. I was interviewed during her reign by a magazine called *The Face*. The writer had to fill me in on what the magazine covered – style, apparently – because it wasn't on my reading list. I'm told it was quite trendy in its day and perhaps it was. What I remember is going for a cup of tea with the journalist in the back of the Strangers' cafe. The biggest impression made on him was by an elderly lady, in a turquoise evening gown, who butted in to tell me that Edwina Currie, a Tory with a Derbyshire seat, had complimented me on my speeches and performances. I didn't want to be rude, and I wasn't, but what Currie thought mattered far less to me than the misery that she, Currie, one of Thatcher's ministers and unbeknown to us a close friend of John Major, was inflicting on decent people in Britain.

Thatcher, more than any other politician, personified the modern Tory operator. She set out to diminish trade unionism and in the process destroyed a large chunk of the manufacturing base. In its place she created the unregulated casino economy where 'invisible' exports were supposed to balance the terms of trade and, like Ronald Reagan, she promised to balance the books but didn't. Thatcher and Reagan both failed on that score, her hero Ronnie never cutting America's deficit. In fact it soared. Both failed.

Now, in 'modern' Britain, the City of London has become the resting place for the super-rich oligarchs whilst millions of people are up to the neck in debt with pay-day loans, have to rely on food banks and search unsuccessfully for even a low-paid, part-time job. That's Thatcher's legacy.

CHAPTER SIXTEEN

On the right as well as the left

Until I was elected to Parliament, I got about fine on my bike and buses and trains. I didn't need a car so I didn't buy one. Becoming an MP changed all of that.

After 1970, I gradually received more and more invitations to speak all over the country. Most were too far to cycle and difficult to reach on public transport, no matter how long I studied time-tables and wondered about connections, so in 1975 I took the plunge and bought what was to be a string of Rovers. The only remaining problem was I couldn't drive. I manoeuvred around that particular difficulty by receiving lifts in my own car from my children – Dawn, Dennis and Mandy – when they'd passed their tests. It's fair to say they went to a large number of meetings and demonstrations.

During the miners' strike I was driven in the car to many rallies and demonstrations by Pete Darby, a Derbyshire miner friend. He'd been banned from picket lines by a court on the say-so of the police and would be behind the wheel while I navigated, a map on my lap in the passenger seat. We made a pretty good team.

It was Tony Benn who inadvertently prompted me into learning to drive. Tony, who was elected MP for Chesterfield in a 1984 by-election after losing in Bristol at the general election the year before when he was given a difficult seat, asked how I travelled back to London from Derbyshire if I popped up to Bolsover for a mid-week meeting. The last train from Chesterfield, his and my nearest station, was at about 7.30 p.m. There was talk, too, that the Midland line might shut and we'd be cut off.

So in 1990, approaching 60 years of age, I took the plunge and started to learn to drive. I took a few lessons and booked a test early in July. The test centre was in south London. On the big day I felt relaxed. I was doing quite well and thinking, this is going pretty OK. Until, that is, the examiner revealed he used to work in the pits.

'I was a miner like you,' he announced suddenly.

'That's great,' I replied, trying to keep my eyes on the road. 'Where did you work?'

The answer left me cold: 'Nottinghamshire.'

No, not what some miners called Scab County during the year-long dispute! I thought: Oh Christ, just my luck. Flashing through my mind were thoughts of how he'd probably worked during the dispute, presumably joining the Quisling outfit that was the Union of Democratic Mineworkers. His very mention of Notts in the context of the strike felt like the motoring equivalent of going through a red light and over a zebra crossing with pedestrians on it. I thought I hadn't a chance in hell of passing.

His pit bombshell distracted me and I hit the kerb doing the reverse turn. I'd never touched the bloody kerb in the thirty times I'd practised that skill. Then I go and clip it in the test after the examiner's told me he was a Nottinghamshire miner. To my surprise he said: 'You'd better try that again.' It was an unexpected second chance. Feeling even more nervous, I drove forward, then tried the reverse again. This time I did it properly. We continued on the route and when we pulled up outside the test centre I was resigned to being failed by the former Nottinghamshire miner. Except I wasn't. He smiled, then declared: 'You've passed!' I'd passed – first time! What a relief. How unexpected.

Sitting in the car as he filled in a form, I asked him about the reverse turn. I probably shouldn't have but I was curious. The examiner replied I hadn't really messed it up and he could tell from the rest of my driving I was competent and safe to other road users. Warming to him now I had achieved my licence, I enquired:

'When did you leave the pit?'

'Oh,' he said, 'I've been in London nearly twenty years.' The lad wasn't anywhere near the strike, scabs or the UDM. If I'd set the record straight immediately I might never have touched that kerb.

I bought second-hand British Rovers until the car industry was sold off and then went through a series of hands until it was owned by BMW. On Radio 4's *Any Questions?* I was on a panel with a vicar. I joked German jackboots were stamping all over British manufacturing. The vicar wasn't very happy. It turned out he was married to a German woman.

These days there are no Rovers any more. I drive a Toyota Prius. I wanted to buy a model with low carbon emissions to do my bit for the environment. I looked at a Honda hybrid and chose a Prius when the Honda dealer warned me there was a long waiting list. Mine was probably the first Prius in the car park under the Houses of Parliament. The car's about eight years old and still remarkably does 50 miles to the gallon so emissions are low and it's very economical. We can still burn coal in the fire of our Derbyshire home but drive a green car. That's what you might call practical environmentalism.

Passing the driving test and acquiring a licence opened up continental Europe for motoring holidays. Over the years I drove a fair few miles on the right, taking the car on a ferry or rail shuttle. On the first foray abroad I'd intended to stay around Boulogne until I saw the sign for Paris. Calculating the French capital was about 180 miles away, I thought: I bet I can do that. And I did. The trip was my first to Paris since the NUM delegation to a demonstration against NATO and nuclear weapons.

In my heyday I'd take friends to France who otherwise might not have gone because they didn't know their way about. We'd visit the usual places: Notre Dame, the Louvre and Sacré Coeur. I'd drop them off for the Eiffel Tower and slot into the Champs de Mars until they were ready to go to the next landmark. The wife of a councillor friend of mine – he is an ex-miner too – was diagnosed with breast cancer. She was waiting for her operation, so to take her mind off it the four of us – Jill and Eion, Lois and me – drove to Paris. The distraction plan worked. I sang to her 'Under the bridges of Paris with you, I'd make your dreams come true' as we strolled under a Seine bridge. She is now, I'm delighted to record, in good health.

We started to drive further afield, as far as the Mediterranean coast, to places such as Nice, Antibes and Menton, a beautiful town on the French border with Italy. I learned French at school and get by, although if you start trying to speak French to a receptionist in a hotel you find they often reply in better English. Trains are cheap in France, the French not so daft as to privatise the railways. So there came a point when the car would be left at home and we'd catch the TGV to the south of the country, SNCF an example of what we could enjoy in Britain if there was the political will and investment.

My childhood fascination with the war was revived the year we took Lois's parents, Paul and Gloria, to the Normandy beaches. Both her mother and father have passed away, as have mine. Paul, a big bear of a man, was part of the Normandy landings on D-Day, going ashore on Omaha Beach. It's hard to envisage the fear and bravery experienced by the young people fighting to liberate Europe from Hitler and the Nazis. Paul wished to visit the grave of a pal who was killed in action. I went ahead to reconnoitre the cemetery so we didn't get lost on the day. The US equivalent of the British Legion identified the plot in the huge cemetery with its row after row of gravestones. It's the cemetery featured in *Saving Private Ryan*, the final resting place of all those who died on the Omaha and Utah beaches.

We found the headstone. The dead friend was only 18 or 19, an Italian lad from the Bronx. It struck home that he was just a teenager, his life barely started when he was killed. Seeing the German pillboxes on top of the hills, overlooking the Normandy landing sites, you could see why there were so many casualties. It must have been sheer hell. His friend and the rest were sitting ducks for the Nazis.

My days of driving on the right in Europe are probably over. During the summer recess in Parliament I fly with Lois to New

Jersey, her home state. Lois's twin sister, Laura, is a wonderful artist who learned to paint with her left hand after she was in a very serious accident with a lorry in 1979 and badly injured. Laura is fortunate to be cared for by another sister, Joanne, who besides being a good painter is a master chef like her late father and, as Lois will confirm, an exceptional designer. I've a bike I use in New Jersey and will get up early when it's cool and cycle along the canal. It's flat, thankfully, and gives me time and space to think.

CHAPTER SEVENTEEN

The odd couple

Pauline Prescott christened her husband John and me the Odd Couple. I was in digs near King's Cross when I first started going down to London after my election in 1970 but I couldn't stay there forever. We got word the hotel was to shut and be turned into student accommodation as part of a university so I needed to find somewhere else to hang my hat.

John had been a steward on the ocean liners and was a full-time official in the National Union of Seamen (NUS) before he went to Parliament the same year as me. The NUS let him stay in a block of flats attached to Maritime House, its headquarters in Clapham, south London. After the 1973 right-wing Pinochet coup in Chile against Allende's democratically elected left government, the union put up the ousted Chilean ambassador in London. When he moved out, John and I were offered the empty flat over the garages. We were charged the market rent of £250 a month each and paid our way, so the accommodation wasn't subsidised by the union. Lambeth council's rent officer set what was called a fair rent and John was flabbergasted when the

Tory press would suggest we were living there for nothing. They couldn't have been more wrong, and there was no chance of getting them to print the truth.

Maritime House was handy for buses and the Northern Line to and from Westminster. Back in those days I didn't drive, relying heavily on public transport. John would give me a lift occasionally when we were heading in together or returning at the same time. He's always liked Jaguars, John, but he searched for second-hand bargains in *Exchange and Mart* and never spent a fortune buying them.

We lived separate lives and didn't see that much of each other. He was in Hull at the weekends and I went home to Derbyshire. But Pauline found it very funny to think of a couple of working-class men from the north of England living under the same roof in London on weekdays, calling us the Jack Lemmon and Walter Matthau of Westminster. We rubbed along pretty well when we were both in the flat, though there were one or two minor domestic disagreements. TV was a bone of contention if we were both in. He'd want to watch every news and current affairs programme. I'd want a break and liked to watch the football, snooker and boxing.

We discussed politics, of course. John never rebelled, while I did. We shared a fraternal disagreement over John doubling up as a member of the European Parliament in the second half of the 1970s when national Parliaments nominated delegates. I was against the Common Market lock, stock and barrel. John thought it could be changed by engagement. He worked hard on his speeches, did John. He'd stay up late into the night, poring over reports to uncover killer facts to floor the opposition. We'd discuss how to focus on the arguments, shaping a speech as a tree with the central trunk to make the main points and subsidiary arguments growing off it like branches.

We shared that flat until 1988 when I vacated the place in a hurry. The National Union of Seamen was involved in a bitter dispute in Dover. In the March of the previous year, the *Herald of Free Enterprise*, a P&O ferry, capsized as it was sailing out of the Belgian port of Zeebrugge and 193 passengers and crew members drowned. The official inquiry criticised the safety culture in a company dissatisfied with record profits as it tried to squeeze even more cash out of ships.

Seafaring is a tight-knit industry and the loyalty of crews counted for nothing when P&O issued a diktat. The *Herald of Free Enterprise* disaster hit the pockets of shareholders. P&O's response was to inform the NUS it would cut 500 jobs, slash earnings and extend working hours. The crews in the Kent port had no alternative. P&O wouldn't listen to reason, so the workers went on strike. Thatcher's anti-union laws were on the company's side and the NUS was tied up in knots. Once again the courts did the dirty work, fining the union and seizing its assets. The sequestration of the union meant my rent would be going to the courts, so I thought: I'm out of here. I wasn't going to be a sitting duck, handing my money to Thatcher's sequestrators. So I found a flat on my own.

John and I remained friends and, much later, when he was deputy prime minister I'd be part of the team that helped him prepare for Prime Minister's Questions when he stood in for Tony Blair. We knew the snobby Tories would want to catch him out, deliberately trying to embarrass him. John had a habit of tripping over words and he knew they delighted in watching him stumble because he'd landed so many blows on Conservatives over the years. The taunting was a backhanded compliment but his confidence was dented in April 1999 when he mispronounced Milosevic in reply to a question about the Balkans. The Tories sniggered. John, naturally, hated giving them the satisfaction of landing a punch.

He did very well in the circumstances if you rewind his appearances. He'd put in a lot of preparation to be able to cover the entire political waterfront and land a few counter punches. One of John's final appearances at the despatch box was to deputise for Blair in March 2007. Vince Cable, who fancied himself as a player in questions, was standing in for Liberal Democrat leader Ming Campbell who'd succeeded a Charlie Kennedy brought low by a drink problem. On the Wednesday morning a few hours before high noon John was searching for a joke at Cable's expense.

Cable, who went on to be the Liberal Democrat business secretary in the Conservative coalition, had embarked on a personal tour of British political parties. He started out in the Labour Party, scuttled off to the SDP and failed to be elected to Parliament for the SDP–Liberal Alliance before fulfilling a life's ambition to enter Parliament when he was elected as a Liberal Democrat in Twickenham in 1997.

At the meeting I said to John: 'Cable's been in a fair few parties in his time so why don't you say: "He's been to more parties than Paris Hilton?"'

The laughter of the party officials and civil servants at the gathering convinced John it wasn't a bad quip. 'Good idea, Dennis,' said John. 'I'll use that.'

We thought that was sorted and the briefing continued. When it was time for John to go to the chamber, I tried to gee him up.

John was always nervous and it isn't detrimental to feel slightly queasy if it keeps you on your toes.

'Remember, John, you always have the last word,' I told him, 'and remember that Vince Cable joke.'

'I do remember it,' he replied, 'and I've stayed in that hotel.' Hotel? It quickly dawned that John thought we were talking about Paris Hilton, a hotel in the French capital, rather than Paris Hilton the American socialite. He had stayed in the hotel and the joke would've survived if he'd used the agreed wording, despite the misunderstanding, but it could've backfired horribly if he claimed he'd had a good night there! We had a little laugh and it helped break the atmosphere. John's jibe that Cable 'has gone through more parties than Paris Hilton' went down a bomb.

Pauline Prescott's Odd Couple description was revived by some in the party to describe my relationship with Tony Blair. Sunderland MP Chris Mullin was told by Blair after Tony had persuaded him to join the environment department that I'd have been a good minister if I was willing to take responsibility. I've always taken responsibility for my actions. What I wouldn't accept was patronage. The power of patronage grants a prime minister the ability to demand compromises I wasn't prepared to make.

After we won the '97 election and Blair was in Downing Street, a message was sent that he wanted to see me. Bruce Grocott, one of his Parliamentary Private Secretaries and therefore a link with MPs, said Tony was going to talk to various people and I was on the list. Bruce said No. 10 would arrange for me to go into Downing Street. I told him I wasn't having photographers taking pictures of me walking through that black door and he suggested I could slip in, unseen, the back way via the Cabinet Office. My objection was if I met the PM in No. 10 I would meet him on his terms. I had serious things to say about the Labour Party and the Left. We agreed I'd meet him in his office in a House of Commons that was common territory.

When we met I urged Blair not to impugn the motives of those in the party who disagreed with him. By all means tell them you think they're wrong, I said, but don't accuse them of ulterior motives. By and large he stuck to that, and his relations with the party would've been much worse if he'd questioned the integrity of critics.

But of course I was prepared to help a Labour prime minister. Blair thanked me for what he called, with a hint of flattery, the 'brilliant' advice offered before Prime Minister's Questions to identify Tory opponents and for feeding him one-liners to rattle their side and rouse ours. Blair was right when he acknowledged that I didn't agree with many of his policies, but liked to see him whack the Tories. Yet it goes deeper than that. I have an unyielding loyalty to a Labour Party that is on the side of working people. It is the only party capable of improving the lives of the working class.

My absolute belief is that a Labour government is better than a Tory regime every time and the Labour years, with Blair then Gordon Brown in No. 10, achieved much that we are justly proud of. From the minimum wage and improved employment rights to rebuilding the NHS and achieving peace in Northern Ireland after 3,600 had died, the record was good. And we put more money into people's pockets. For instance, I'd proposed a winter fuel allowance for pensioners so they could afford to put the heating on in winter, Blair giving me a nod as acknowledgement when Brown announced it in the Budget.

I was also prepared to vote against legislation I believed ran contrary to the interests of working people and the principles of the Labour Party: academy schools, NHS foundation trusts, privatisation, the private finance initiative (PFI), up to 28 days' detention without charge, welfare cuts and every Common Market treaty.

I'm not starry-eyed. I never believe a Labour government is perfect. Perfection simply doesn't exist in politics and is for the birds. I advise people to vote for the party that is best for them and, in most cases, unless you're a billionaire banker, that choice is Labour. So I was willing to give Tony advice but I was also prepared to speak my mind and vote according to my conscience.

The Iraq War was a prime example of when Tony Blair and I took very different roads. I voted against it on every occasion, with the exception of when I was in the intensive care ward recovering from heart surgery. John McDonnell said in the chamber that my name should be added to the list of Labour rebels because I would've been in the voting lobby if tubes and wires weren't protruding from my body on a hospital bed. A convincing case was never made for military action.

I'd said to Blair at a National Executive Committee meeting that Bush was as thick as two short planks, and he shouldn't go along with him. The PM just looked pained. Most Labour people couldn't stand the sight of George Bush and some of us don't think he was elected legitimately. The 2000 presidential contest in the USA was a farce, and many felt Bush and the Republicans had stolen it from Democrat Al Gore. The result hinged on Florida, where Bush's brother Jed was governor and George Bush received a wafer-thin majority after he was granted every advantage, including decisions on the 'hanging chad' votes – tiny bits of paper hanging from ballot papers marked by punching a hole with a machine. If it was unclear, the decisions went in Bush's favour.

Blair, tragically, ignored the lot of us. My last conversation with him about Iraq was in Speaker's Court before I went into hospital and he went to war. Hans Blix, the former US weapons inspector, led a battalion of experts doubting the existence of Weapons of Mass Destruction (WMD).

'You'd better take some anthrax in your pocket when you go because that's the only way you'll find any WMD,' I said scathingly. Blair laughed the way he would when you told him an uncomfortable truth he didn't want to confront. There were no WMD and the rest is history.

Along with others, I had more luck advising him to postpone the 2001 election because of the foot and mouth crisis. In rural areas, including parts of Derbyshire, strict controls were imposed on people as well as cattle. There was no way you could canvass and hold proper meetings. To have gone ahead with the May date would've been irresponsible. We needed to listen, and be seen to be listening, to those calling correctly for a delay. Blair heeded those of us advocating he postpone it to June. Labour won another thumping majority, if slightly down on 1997, with a 166-seat cushion in the House of Commons. I was concerned the turnout had dropped below 60 per cent, an historic low during universal suffrage. It was a worrying sign that traditional Labour voters were staying at home, feeling some at the top of the party didn't represent them.

At the first meeting of the Parliamentary Labour Party after we all returned to Westminster, I urged Blair to avoid treating Labour

MPs as an enemy or regarding workers in the public services as a problem when they deserved appreciation. I reminded him responsibility is a two-way process. In all public institutions there is goodwill that you can't buy and sell in the City. Goodwill in the NHS is greater than anywhere else. We shouldn't throw it away. Blair listened but I was never sure he really heard what I was saying.

Urging him to cherish and revitalise the party was a constant theme when New Labour too often reacted to criticism as if it was a betrayal. It would've been wonderful if a few words from Tony could have resolved everything but they couldn't, particularly when concerns mounted about the direction of travel on health. Privatising key parts of the NHS was never the answer to our prayers, only sapping the morale of activists. Nor did my relationship with Blair extend to bending Labour's rules to suit him when he wanted Ken Livingstone back in the party fold after he'd run for, and won, the London mayor's job as an Independent in 2000. I'd opposed the way control freaks had rigged the Labour selection against Livingstone and opposed the rigging of the rules to get him back in. There was a procedure, a disputes process, and it should've been followed. Instead pressure was put on me to change my mind and endorse Livingstone's return outside the rules, but I wouldn't budge on principle. As it happened I was outvoted on the NEC and the red carpet was rolled out for Citizen Ken.

The game was replayed in January 2013 when Livingstone came to the NEC and tried to get the same favourable treatment for his friend, Lutfur Rahman, who ran against Labour in Tower Hamlets. Standing against the party in an election is automatic expulsion. There is a five-year disqualification rule and cases are dealt with by a disputes committee. Members are asked to go before the committee and explain why they should be let back in. I wasn't giving Rahman a free pass.

'Another mayor wanting a passport on the high road instead of taking the low road. It's not on,' I told Livingstone. 'That couldn't happen in a trade union. People who make the rules can't break them.' This time others were with me and Livingstone's attempt failed. I was the talk of the town afterwards. Harriet Harman and all the rest of them thought I was one of the beautiful people for the day.

Blair and Brown would demand loyalty from the party without themselves always showing it. We heard endless lectures about the importance of iron discipline when regularly there was no discipline at the top and the Blair and Brown camps were tearing strips off each other. I didn't vote for Blair as leader in 1994. Margaret Beckett received my support for both leader and deputy leader, losing the Number Two role to John Prescott. Nor did I nominate Brown in 2007 when he was elected leader unopposed. I backed John McDonnell then to get him on the ticket. We came up short, as we feared we would, but it was worth a shot.

Neil Kinnock never forgave me for not being his biggest fan. He was selected for his South Wales seat against the NUM candidate and I heard he thought it might be something to do with that. I and the rest of the Left, including Tony Benn, were unhappy with the direction Kinnock was taking the party. His compromises with Thatcher never paid off, as election results proved.

I used to appear regularly on BBC TV's *Question Time* debate but word was sent to the programme that invitations should cease because I didn't speak for the Labour Party as a whole. Kinnock became very petty. I'd been on the NEC since 1978 and seniority put me in the running in the mid-1980s to chair the Labour Party, a great honour and responsibility. The chair served for a year and Kinnock's supporters twice voted to elect others and block me. In a third year Kinnock took the chairmanship himself, an unusual manoeuvre by a leader. The chair presides over the party conference and the concept of a revolving chair was introduced for Kinnock, somebody else stepping in otherwise he would have been introducing his own speech.

Kinnock couldn't stop me in the following 12 months and I was chair in 1988–9. I'd grown up in the male-dominated politics of the NUM and at the Labour conference in Brighton in 1989 I was determined to redress the balance by calling as many women speakers as I could. Joyce Gould, the party's chief organiser, would sit at my side whispering who should be selected on political grounds. I'd scan the hall and invite women who I didn't recognise but had their hands up to speak. By the end of the week 38 per cent, nearly two in every five speakers, had been women. It was a record and I had doubled the numbers called.

On the left, by working hard, you deflect criticism from enemies who might foolishly claim you don't have the party's best interests at heart. I go anywhere and everywhere to back Labour candidates. Before the 1997 election I was in Falmouth and Camborne. The packed audience in Falmouth's Princess Pavilion set me wondering that Labour's Candy Atherton could race from third to first and knock out the Tory MP Seb Coe. People were queuing to get into a political rally. I spoke in my speech of a Falmouth Manifesto which I drew up as I thought on my feet. It was to the left of the party's official document but it did the trick. Atherton won by nearly 3,000 votes and Coe was beaten.

We were looking to defeat John Major's ramshackle Conservatives in 1997 so I wasn't allowed near the marginal seats. Instead I was sent mainly to areas we didn't expect to take. Braintree in Essex was one such constituency. Tony Newton, a Tory minister, had a near 18,000 majority and polled more than half the votes cast in the previous election. I had an inkling that day there'd be a landslide for us. The drive east from central London had been a nightmare. I was late. Cars were coming away from the infant school where the meeting was being held and I thought that must be my audience giving up. I couldn't have been more wrong. They were leaving because they couldn't get in. The school was full, some sitting on tiny chairs overlooked by people down both sides and at the back. You could smell victory. Newton lost.

I've never been sectarian, going only to help left-wingers. I want Labour to win. There was a panic on before the 2005 election and this time the party hierarchy wanted me to go to the marginals. We had 31 successes out of 33 constituencies visited. If there's a by-election, I'll be there. While waiting for a hip operation, I couldn't get out and about but that didn't stop me going to the Ealing Southall by-election during Gordon Brown's honeymoon in the summer of 2007. I sat stuffing envelopes with leaflets in the committee rooms, chatting to party members. We held the seat. I was one of the first in Rotherham to support Sarah Champion when Denis MacShane was forced to resign over his expenses. We won that as well. I went to Eastleigh and we didn't win that but I discovered UKIP's weak point by stationing myself outside that party's headquarters and speaking to voters about how Nigel Farage and his mob weren't putting on their leaflets that they were milking the allowances in Brussels. We didn't win. Nor did UKIP.

Ealing Southall convinced me that Gordon Brown, who'd succeeded Tony Blair early that summer, should call an election before the end of October. I told his team we would win if it was called before the party conferences in September. At Business Questions in the House of Commons, I said we should fight it before a new electoral register came into force. The Tories were in disarray and beatable, Cameron and Osborne unprepared. Usually, when I speak in the chamber, the Tories jeer me. That Thursday in Business Questions, when I called for an early election, the Conservatives sat in scared silence.

Brown didn't call the election and we always looked back, thinking what might have been, after the global financial crash. Brown had repeated the mistake of Jim Callaghan. Had Jim gone in autumn 1978 rather than singing at the TUC about waiting at the church, I reckoned at the time he had a good chance of beating Thatcher. Delaying to tighten an incomes policy, provoking workers to take industrial action to win a decent wage, was the oddest choice he could make.

The last two Labour governments lost office after the prime ministers mishandled the dates of the elections. Never let us hear again any nonsense that it is the Left that makes Labour unelectable.

CHAPTER EIGHTEEN

Posh boys and a dinosaur

Attack is the best form of defence and the sooner you turn the tables on an opponent the better. The beauty of going on the offensive is you're ready for the other side to play the same trick and come after you. If you're fast enough, you'll get in first and put them on the back foot. It's also a useful way of intimidating enemies. And if you're lucky, they'll overreact and damage themselves.

I deploy attack in TV and radio interviews if I reckon the presenter is going to come after me. Robin Day made a big name for himself as a BBC journalist and his bow tie on *Question Time* made him recognisable to the public at large. In 1976 he picked me as one of half a dozen in Parliament to be interviewed for a special series of six programmes on BBC Two on consecutive Sundays. The others were political grandees, the likes of Lord Hailsham, Enoch Powell and Michael Foot. I'd been an MP for only six or seven years and was selected presumably because I was a different cut of cloth.

I remained suspicious of Day's motives and was trying to figure out the catch when I read in a newspaper that he'd received a huge pay rise for presenting *The World at One* on Radio 4 for three days a week. Day was on a pretty packet for that on top of chairing *Question Time*. He was never sympathetic to trade unions and the broadcasting default setting of the BBC and most newspapers was to attack automatically workers who went on strike for higher wages when most of the journalists, and especially the stars such as Day, would never have got out of bed for the pay most people were on.

I cut out and folded the story about Day and put it in my pocket before heading to Broadcasting House to record the interview. When I arrived at Portland Place a flunkey was flustered that I hadn't signed a contract to give permission for the show to be transmitted. I told them that I'd think of writing my signature on the dotted line after we'd completed filming. Refusing to sign was a weapon in my armoury should Day be setting a trap. In the studio I was greeted by Day and as I sat down I pulled the folded cutting from my pocket.

'You'll not need notes,' he said. 'You give concise answers and the intention is to broadcast as we shoot it.'

'I'm sure we'll be alright,' I answered, 'but I'll just put this down.' I placed the cutting about Day's massive pay rise on the table between us, the newspaper story facing his way so he couldn't do other than see what it was about. Day was true to his word and good as gold.

The attack on Day was unspoken but I'd needed to be more vocal in an earlier clash with Michael Barratt, another BBC presenter. He was the face of *Nationwide*, a news magazine on after the early evening news. *The One Show* on BBC One is a sort of successor. *Nationwide* wanted me on after I criticised Sir John Stratton, chairman of the Fatstock Marketing Corporation, for pocketing a pay rise way above that of workers under Ted Heath's Tory incomes policy. I was against shackling trade unions under Labour or the Tories, wage limits forcing workers to pay the cost of an economic mess created by employers. Heath's policy was £1 plus 4 per cent and I criticised Stratton for receiving £1 plus 44 per cent. Fat Cats such as Stratton helping themselves to large dollops of cream when workers on low wages were told to swallow reduced rations strengthened my opposition. This time when I arrived at the BBC I engaged the young man who met me in conversation.

'How do you get round the incomes policy here?' I enquired, in my best innocent voice.

'Oh,' he replied in his cut-glass voice, 'we give people new titles.'

'That's very clever,' I responded. 'By the way – does that include Michael Barratt?'

The lad answered: 'Yes, he's just signed a new contract.' Off we went, the boy as happy as Larry and me eager to get into that studio.

Barratt, unsuspecting, asked about Stratton and, when I gave the Fatstock Fat Cat what for, the presenter tried to pick a hole in my argument by claiming the chairman was an exception. I stopped him dead by declaring, live on TV: 'Oh no, there are people like you at the BBC who have just signed new contracts.' You could tell immediately that Barratt was irritated and couldn't wait to finish the interview and get me off the telly. In the half an hour it took me to arrive back in Parliament the messages of congratulation had started flowing in. The staff in the Commons would pin details of telephone calls on a board. One man who watched rang and said: 'Great stuff. My canary had never opened its mouth and it's now chirping.' Barratt was a flustered little bird. He subsequently attacked me in a column he wrote for a magazine. I bet he was paid extra for that. Not only did Barratt have a new contract but he was moonlighting too!

David Cameron and George Osborne are a couple of posh boys who get angry when you don't show them the deference they think they are entitled to by birth. You could see Cameron was ambitious the moment you clapped eyes on him. The friendly smile is deceptive. Everything about how he dresses, carries himself and opens his mouth speaks of ambition. Dodgy Dave was a new MP and had only been in the Commons a couple of years when Iain Duncan Smith, enduring a torrid time as leader of the Tories after 2001, appointed Cameron as shadow deputy leader of the House.

On Cameron's second week in the post Eric Forth, his line manager as shadow leader of the House, was away, so the new boy was put in charge at Business Questions. The beauty of Business Questions is we may ask for a statement or debate on any topic under the sun. I uttered a few words of mock greeting as Cameron stood there terrified, his hands gripping the despatch box, looking for all the world a lost young gentleman. Cameron tried to explain the Shadow Leader of the House was away but mixed up his words and said the Shadow Deputy Leader was absent. You've a split second to heckle. 'He wants the top job already,' I shouted and we laughed to take him down a notch. Cameron appeared embarrassed. You always remember a debut, it's a big moment no matter what you do. He won't forget he stumbled.

I described Cameron as a media creation on Radio 4's *Week in Westminster* in late 2005 when he was running for the top job, and nothing I've seen or heard since has made me change my mind. He was elevated on the back of a puff of wind and lacked the substance of David Davis, the Tory he beat. The figure the Conservative Party could've picked and overlooked in successive contests was Ken Clarke, who was easily the best candidate

I'd watched Cameron as shadow deputy leader of the House and at local government and education, and he never sparkled. When it suited him, he posed as the heir to Blair. He's dropped the act now and come out as the child of Thatcher he always was. Cameron never had Blair's ability or temperament, let alone the Labour politics. Blair never lost his temper at the despatch box. Unlike Cameron, who struggles to keep his under control.

The Cameron mask slipped when he called me a dinosaur. I'm no shrinking violet and if you dish it out some will come back your way. We used to sing as kids that sticks and stones may break our bones but names will never hurt us. The trigger was relatively innocuous. I'd asked if Cameron would appear before Lord Justice Leveson's inquiry into media standards, given he'd once employed former *News of the World* editor Andy Coulson as a press adviser. Cameron replied he'd be delighted, then Flashman lost control of his short fuse and added:

'It's good to see the honourable gentleman on such good form. I often say to my children "No need to go to the Natural History Museum to see a dinosaur, come to the House of Commons at about half past twelve."'

I held up my hands and shrugged my shoulders, trying to look bemused rather than triumphant. Our side protested angrily. I could see most of the Tories were horrified, although there were a few laughing. Blair knew how to appear prime ministerial. Cameron is petulant. Paul Flynn, a Labour MP only a few years younger than me, raised a point of order immediately after Prime Minister's Questions to ask if it was appropriate to criticise each other on the basis of gender, race, ethnicity, disability or vintage. Another Labour MP, Brian Donohoe, proposed that the PM 'should come back to this place and apologise to Dennis Skinner'.

I wasn't the first MP to be looked at down Cameron's nose. Dave the Sexist displayed a misogynist side in telling Angela Eagle, a member of Labour's Shadow Cabinet, to 'Calm down, dear' and later played the innocent when the Michael Winner slogan was wrapped around his neck. I must be the only dinosaur to ride a bike 12 miles on a Sunday. Once again the postbag ballooned with letters and emails flowed into the inbox on my computer. There must have been 150 of them. Cameron's rudeness had gone down poorly. One of the notes was from a vicar in Cornwall who accused the PM of lying to God!

I was evidently under Cameron's skin because, a few months after the dinosaur jibe in January 2012, he snapped once more in the Commons. In answer to a question about whether Jeremy Hunt should keep his job as culture secretary over close links to Rupert Murdoch, the PM jumped off the deep end. He stupidly whined I had a right to take my pension and added: 'I advise him to do so.' History was repeating itself. The remark was widely condemned as graceless, the insult boomeranging on a hapless Cameron. It was more water off a duck's back and Cameron could carry on undermining himself for all I cared. In fact it was best that he did. The penny must have dropped with him, however, and at the next Prime Minister's Questions he apologised.

'I deeply regret my last intervention, it was a bit sharper than it should have been, I hope he will accept my apology for that,' Cameron said, before adding a smarmy 'He is a tremendous ornament of this House and always remains the case.'

It's not an apology for calling me a dinosaur or giving me pension advice that I seek, but a resignation letter apologising for the pain and damage he has caused to millions of people with the austerity imposed by the ConDem coalition. The Tories imitate the extreme Tea Party in the US. What the Conservatives are doing to the disabled, unemployed, working poor and homeless is unforgivable. The destruction of the NHS, carved into bite-sized pieces ready for privatisation, is criminal.

George Osborne is Cameron's partner in crime. Another of the Bullingdon snobs, Osborne is educated beyond his intelligence. I applied the description to Paul Channon, a millionaire minister in Thatcher's time. It is even more apt for a chancellor of the exchequer clueless of life outside his gilded circle. His skin is as thin as Cameron's, as I saw when he resented the reminder that he'd appeared in a newspaper photograph with a line of white powder and the dominatrix who sold sex and pain. These posh boys don't like it up 'em, as Corporal Jones would shout.

I have a good stab at reading their minds when they are up close. On my 65th birthday, shortly before the 1997 election, John Major congratulated me on becoming a pensioner. In the week of my 81st, I decided not to try and get in at Prime Minister's Questions, to prevent Cameron pulling a similar stunt. I could see him looking, wondering why I wasn't getting up. I wouldn't give him the satisfaction.

I picked up the power of precision questions at union and council meetings and honed it in Parliament. I've always admired people who leave the interrogated no room for manoeuvre. During the 1984 Chesterfield by-election, when Tony Benn stood successfully for Labour the party suffered a few palpitations when the actor Bill Maynard threw his hat into the ring as an Independent. Eric Varley, who'd been energy then industry secretary under Harold Wilson and Jim Callaghan during the 1974–9 government, quit in the January to take a paid job as chairman of Coalite, a company producing smokeless fuels. It was a nice little irony that Benn, who was forced by Wilson to swap Cabinet jobs with Varley, was selected as the Labour candidate. Maynard's sole intention, or so he said, was to stop Benn. Maynard posed as a bit of a left-winger himself, though I remember he was all over the place.

We sprinkled a little stardust on the Labour campaign by drafting in Pat Phoenix who, as Elsie Tanner in *Coronation Street*, was a big shining star on the campaign trail. Pat was mobbed wherever we took her, Benn basking in her limelight when the Tory press, particularly Rupert Murdoch's *Sun*, was painting him as some crazed extremist. Tony Booth, Cherie Blair's actor father, played a part and we had the vicar from *Emmerdale Farm*. Yet it wasn't the Corrie heroine who took the wind out of Maynard's sails.

Tupton Hall's catchment area included parts of Chesterfield and Maynard went to a meeting at the school. My daughter Mandy asked if he was for or against nuclear weapons. He gave one of those rambling answers which give politicians a bad name, attacking Benn's unilateralism without committing himself to the bomb. Mandy wasn't letting him off the hook.

'I've been to the House of Commons and there are only two lobbies,' she said firmly. 'Which one would you go in: Yes to keep nuclear weapons or No to get rid of them? There isn't a third for Don't Knows.'

Flustered, Maynard prattled on a little longer without answering her question. She'd been textbook, leaving him no wriggle room. A lot of people might think of putting a question the way she did then fail to find the confidence to pin a candidate to the spot. I was very proud of her. Maynard? I don't recall him doing another school meeting. Oh, and he lost his deposit in a distant fourth as Benn was elected MP for Chesterfield with a 6,300 majority.

I don't dislike Cameron, Osborne and the rest of the millionaire's row just because they are posh. I oppose them because they are Tories, preying on working people and pursuing policies which deliberately punish the weak. But what I do resent is the fact they were born with every privilege money can buy and rather than using their talents and opportunities to advance those less well off, who came into this world with fewer or no advantages, they look after themselves. When they say 'We are all in this together' the 'we' is the Bullingdon Club boys; and that includes Boris Johnson, defender of the bankers and advocate of a cut in the top rate of tax.

Tony Benn and I came from very different backgrounds but we worked very closely in Parliament and on Labour's National Executive Committee. I came from poverty, the pit and the trade union movement. Tony came from a comfortable background and was part of the English radical dissenting Left. I hesitated to join the tributes in the House of Commons after he died but wanted to place on record the Tony Benn I knew.

He started off on the right of the Labour Party and moved to the left during the industrial disputes of the 1970s. The Pentonville dockers, printers and miners changed his politics. He was shaped by events, as I had been from a young age. Tony's environment was different from mine as a kid. As an adult it became the same.

Tony was clever, industrious and had ability by the bagful. He reinforced his knowledge by keeping lists. He had a pager and a mobile phone before New Labour invented them as forms of political control. He was the type of man who could've built a computer out of twigs and vines on a desert island.

Sport was a blind spot. We were on the Labour NEC together for many years, fighting the Left's corner. I turned up late for the start of a Labour conference.

'You're late,' said Tony.

I said: 'I know I'm late, Tony. There's a reason.'

He said: 'Yes, there's a Tory mayor and you didn't want to be here.'

I replied: 'Well, that's part of it. But the most important reason is that I was watching Cram and Elliott on the telly in the mile of the century.'

He said: 'Cram and Elliott? Are they your delegates?'

Steve Cram and Peter Elliott were the two most famous British middle-distance runners after Steve Ovett and Seb Coe.

Having also watched Formula 1, I asked Tony another sporting question: 'Tony, do you know who Ayrton Senna is?'

'Ayrton Senna?' he said. 'Who's he?'

I visited Tony in hospital shortly before the end. I went to room K, which I was told was his, and it was empty. I feared the worst until somebody quickly said he'd been wheeled outside in his chair and I found him in a lovely small park in the sunshine with a feller who helped him with his TV work. For 45 minutes we talked about the Labour conference Tony had missed, him lighting his pipe three times.

The man I knew was wonderful and a myth is perpetuated when Labour's manifesto at the 1983 election, which we lost heavily – 'the longest suicide note in history' as it was dubbed – is pinned on the Left. We lost that election because the SDP traitors split the anti-Thatcher vote and Maggie surfed on a wave of jingoism after the Falklands. But that manifesto wasn't a product of the Left. By 1983 the Left had lost control of the party NEC. The chair of the election committee was John Golding, a fierce right-winger. Eric Heffer was the sole left-winger on that committee.

Before I spoke about Benn in the Commons a successor, Toby Perkins, the Labour MP for Chesterfield, recalled the famous by-election. The Skinners played their part. My daughter Mandy floored Maynard, and my sister Hazel helped gee up Tony when he was being vilified by the Tory papers. Her married name was Dodson and, prodded by our brother Gordon and me, she invited Tony to a meeting of women voters in her house in Curber Curve, Staveley in the seat. Tony didn't know who she was.

'Dennis,' he told me afterwards, 'it was wonderful. All these interesting women in an ordinary house. Wonderful!'

I intended to tell him Hazel was my sister but never got round to it before he died.

Near the start of the contest I gave Tony advice on several aspects of the campaign. He asked if there was anything else he could do to improve his chances.

'Yes. Put a tie on,' I told him.

'But you've not gone one on,' he replied.

'No,' I answered. 'I live here and you will be the ambassador of a market town.'

The following day he turned up in a tie. As I said when he died, and I reiterate here: How could I do other than love the man?

CHAPTER NINETEEN

Fresh air, roses and revolution

Spring is easily my favourite season, as it is for many people. The awakening of nature, plants bursting into blossom and colour, is a magical sight. To watch life returning lifts the spirit and is the best part of the year. And when you're getting on a bit, as I am, to see it happening gives you a boost.

Every spring I'll pay what you could describe as a pilgrimage to the magnolia tree in Hyde Park. Frank Allaun introduced me to it. A committed left-winger who was heavily involved in CND and MP for Salford East for many years until he left Parliament in 1983, Frank hailed this magnolia as 'the finest tree in London'. He wasn't wrong.

There were no votes until 10 p.m. in those days. I'd be in at 8 a.m. to do the post and get on top of the day. There'd be questions and statements and if there wasn't an important bill or a committee to sit on, or meetings or rallies to attend, I liked to get out of that building on the banks of the Thames. So Frank asked me to go for a walk with him and off we set. We strolled through St James's Park and into Green Park, then into Hyde Park. The magnolia is at the bottom of a bank sloping up to the Serpentine cafe. The tree stands 16–18 feet high and the flowers in full bloom are a radiant white, so brilliant you could mistakenly believe that somebody had painted them on the branches. I've been admiring it for close on 40 years and I'll never tire of visiting this tree.

I love the country and green spaces in towns and cities. I love the fresh air. Most pits, including ours in Derbyshire, were in semi-rural areas. My boyhood was spent in the fields which surrounded Clay Cross, the mines cheek by jowl with the countryside. Within a short distance of the coke works spewing out yellow smoke, and the pit tip growing ever larger as spoil from underground was dumped on top, I'd be in Britton Wood with the best bluebells you'll find anywhere in Britain. Three miles away was the beautiful village of Ashover, the last outpost of the Pennines.

We'd come up shattered from a shift in the bowels of the earth. After eating dinner and having a lie-down on a rug for a rest, some miners went down the pub to relax by sinking pints. Others, including me, yearned for fresh air in our lungs. If I wasn't cross-country running, I'd go walking or cycling. When the weather was warm we'd pick mushrooms. The season ran from April to the end of August or September in the north. After the mushrooms had finished, I'd hunt for blewits – a fungus that's blue underneath with a stronger taste than mushrooms.

We'd tend our gardens, planting flowers and vegetables. Pitmen were green-fingered, proud of what they grew. I had quite a big garden and enjoyed working in it. I'd plant roses, delphiniums, snowdrops, crocuses, tulips and daffodils. You picked up useful little tips on the way. Never, for instance, put tulips and daffodils together. The daffodils will always come out on top and you can wave goodbye to your tulips.

The demands on me that grew when I became an MP, accepting increasing numbers of invitations to speak around the country as I became better known nationally from the mid-1970s onwards, gradually reduced me to admiring other people's gardens rather than cultivating my own.

These days my health means I can't put a spade in the ground, but I continue to appreciate the efforts of those who do. In Easington recently I had a cup of tea in the house of an ex-miner before addressing a Labour fundraiser in the town. His garden was absolutely glorious, a neat piece of London's St James's Park in County Durham. He must have spent hours weeding, hoeing and planting, and it showed.

Growing up as I did in a rural environment enables me to talk easily with farmers in my area about their way of life. I don't doubt the majority vote Conservative. But I'm interested in their battle with nature, farmers praying for a perpetual good weather that never comes. Underground we hoped Mother Nature didn't break the strata and bring thousands of tons of earth crashing on our heads. Above us, farmers were locked in a titanic struggle of their own.

I do my best thinking in the open, fresh air clearing the head. Hemmed in by four walls and sandwiched between a floor and a roof, the mind can be constrained. Outside the phrases for questions and speeches come much more easily, answers to apparently difficult issues are grasped more readily. Quite simply I find an inspiration in the fresh air that is elusive in rooms. Revolution always feels possible on glorious sunny days within the scent of roses.

I fear I might have gone mad if I'd spent most of my time in the Tea Room after arriving in the House of Commons in 1970 instead of exploring London's exceptional parks. They knock spots off, say, the Tuileries in Paris and we should be proud of what our gardeners create. Getting out and about has led me to find mushrooms in Victoria Tower Gardens, the park with Rodin's statue *The Burghers of Calais* next to Parliament. St James's is pretty with its lake and the ducks and all the rest of it. Over the road and behind the Foreign Office, St James's is handy for a little walk when there's only half an hour to spare. Sitting on benches, watching the world go by and thinking, ideas have come to me over the years.

I was watching a pelican in St James's when it suddenly dawned on me that John Patten, a pompous education secretary in John Major's Tory rabble, resembled another bird, a peacock. I went back over the road and prepared questions to lay into the arrogance and contempt he showed towards teachers and Parliament. I said:

He has strutted round the despatch box like a puffed-up peacock on heat. Today, he has come in like a bedraggled battery hen that has laid its last egg. His intellectual elitism has overwhelmed his common sense, and the people in the country know it.

Parks are peaceful places. They're also creative.

Green Park between Buckingham Palace and Piccadilly is a pleasant mix of mainly trees and grass. Regent's Park is good and within it Queen Mary's Gardens must have 12,000 roses including almost every variety there is. Hyde Park remains my favourite of the central London parks with that famous white magnolia, an impressive copse of 55 chestnuts of the sweet variety to roast and eat, not the type that kids pick off the ground to play conkers, all sorts of flowers imaginable, the Serpentine lake and rows of seats to rest and ponder and gaze and ponder very often, or nowadays have political discussions with people who ask: 'Are you Dennis Skinner?'

After I'd explored central London's green spaces, I started wandering further afield. Richmond Park is a bike ride or a tube trip away. The Isabella Plantation, with its stream babbling down the middle of azaleas and rhododendrons, is idyllic, a fantastic mass of colours in May and June. Richmond also has a clump of sweet chestnuts near the old Star and Garter home for injured and elderly servicemen. I'd collect the chestnuts to eat. When I started picking them, I was the only one doing it and would wonder: What will people think, seeing this man picking up nuts from under these trees? That's changed. I now have competition from East Europeans who mop up the chestnuts before me!

There have been occasions over the years when I've been looking forward to a walk in a park when people would ask: 'Are you coming on the march?' And I'd think: Christ, I was hoping to go to Richmond Park today. Naturally, I'd go on the march if it was important. At least it would be in the open air, if not as peaceful as discovering a rhododendron coming into bloom. A few times – not many, but a few – I wished I'd chosen the park.

I recommend Hampton Court not for the famous Maze but for a host of golden daffodils, as Wordsworth would describe them, nearby under a canopy of trees. The daffs come out before the leaves are on the trees, so there's sufficient sunlight in the early part of the year. Or get yourself along to Hatfield House in Hertfordshire at the back end of March to enjoy a vast carpet of bluebells.

Being invited to pay homage to the beauties of Richmond Park's Isabella Plantation on the radio prompted a call from Radio 4 asking if I'd do a longer piece on plants with Andrew Sachs, the actor who played the waiter Manuel, abused by John Cleese in *Fawlty Towers*. It was the early 1990s and they wanted a guide to London's parks for a Saturday morning travel show. I was to be their man.

We met at St Stephen's Entrance to Parliament and I travelled with Sachs and a producer on the London Underground to Baker Street. We got off the tube and walked round the corner to Regent's Park and into Queen Mary's Gardens. It was June and I recall the delphiniums were out. The colours were fabulous, stretching from white to purple. My job was to talk at length about Hyde, St James's, Green, Regent's and Richmond Parks, and Hampstead Heath too. Everything felt fine until a very faint drizzle started after about fifteen minutes. It was hardly discernible, so slight you could barely feel the rain. I was surprised when a BBC lady operating the tape recorder suddenly announced: 'Right, Mr Skinner. We're done.' The interview ended abruptly, rain stopping play.

The finish felt uncomfortable, brusque, because it all happened so unexpectedly fast. We walked back to Baker Street and Andrew Sachs went on his merry way. The young woman doing the recording and I went into a little cafe for a cup of coffee.

Puzzled, I couldn't resist asking: 'Right, what was all that about – why did we stop suddenly?'

She smiled and we both laughed at her candid reply: 'Because of the rain – it was smudging Andrew's cue card and he might not be able to read the script.'

That's showbiz, I suppose, although a Labour politician would probably be lynched if they tried to use such a damp excuse in front of a couple of hundred thousand trade unionists at the Durham Miners' Gala.

My adoration of the great outdoors drove my determination to secure funding to promote Creswell Crags, a breathtaking limestone gorge and honeycomb of caves of huge historical importance. Archaeologists have discovered delicate wall paintings, primitive tools and animal remains dating back to the last Ice Age more than 10,000 years ago. The prehistoric cave art is the most northerly in Europe and it's a Scheduled Monument and Site of Special Scientific Interest. Lottery money was up for grabs and I was fed up with the lion's share going to elitist bodies such as the Royal Opera House or Winston Churchill's grandson, a Tory MP of the same name, who pocketed £12.5 million so the wartime leader's letters and speeches could be saved for the nation.

With Nigel Mills, who has since gone on to manage Hadrian's Wall, we lobbied hard to secure more than £4 million to open a visitor centre and move a sewage works so the pong didn't overpower members of the public when the wind was blowing their way. It took a lot of lobbying and many forms but we got there in the end. David Attenborough opened the new building in 2009. I thought I detected a little frostiness between him and David Bellamy, who was also invited. Later I was told they disagreed on climate change. Bellamy's a sceptic about the impact of people on the climate. Attenborough isn't.

I watch when the buds come out every year. Driving up and down the M1 between Derbyshire and London, I examine the trees and yellow gorse. Spring is traditionally later in the north, autumn earlier in the south. But you also see the seasons changing every year. Part of that is natural, of course. But logic suggests that we, the human race, have an impact on the environment and to deny we must contribute to climate change is nonsensical.

The BBC asked me to make a TV programme on Creswell Crags, a sparkling natural jewel. It was the regional contribution for a national BBC Two series on the wonders of the British Isles screened in 2005. Part of the programme involved me cycling around a lake with swans in the background. It looked easy on the television but they must have made me ride the same patch of path a dozen times. The swans kept swimming away, never in the right place for the cameraman when I cycled past. I was recovering from a heart bypass so not firing on all cylinders. The BBC could've killed me with the retakes.

I'm sure some people think I spend my entire life on platforms at rallies or haranguing David Cameron. I do both, of course. But I love the fresh air and make an effort to be out and about. I rarely miss *Countryfile* on BBC One on Sunday evenings. It's a solid hour on the countryside covering a lot of ground in 60 minutes. The exception was an episode given over to Prince Charles, another free advert for the royals.

So what else does an ageing socialist do in his leisure time? When I'm not roaming the countryside and parks, I, sadly, like millions of others, play around with cryptic crosswords and sudoku. Crosswords are a good way of exercising the mind. I'm competitive, so the challenge of searching for the answers in an anagram or a fragment of Latin is irresistible when the bug bites you and then won't leave. I started doing the crosswords in the *Guardian, The Times* and *Daily Telegraph* partly as a test for myself, and also as a diversion from everything else that was going on around me. There was a spell, I admit sheepishly, when I'd leave a nearly completed crossword in the Tea Room to watch a Tory pick up the paper and struggle to complete the few gaps.

The parliamentary expert was undoubtedly Jim Marshall. I'd catch the train from Chesterfield to London and at Leicester this tall, thin, new MP would get on. He'd see me studying a folded paper, trying to work out words, and after a few weeks he asked how I discovered the answers. I explained about following the clues and Jim took up crossword puzzles. If I mentored him briefly at the beginning he soon became better than me. He picked it up with incredible swiftness. Before long there were Conservatives stopping Jim in the Library to seek his help. He was a real enthusiast. I recounted the story at Jim's funeral after he died in 2004. He was so adept at answering the clues I'm sure he could've been a successful crossword compiler in another life.

When I couldn't get about physically after a cancer operation in 1999, I discovered Freecell. The computer card game relies less on chance than solitaire by requiring the player to think six, seven, eight moves ahead. I'd been up Tottenham Court Road to buy the terminal in an era when MPs weren't given computers automatically by the House of Commons. Playing cards on screen helped me forget my troubles and the pain.

Nowadays I prefer Killer Soduku in *The Times*. It helps keep the mind sharp and at the back of my brain is the memory of my mother dying of dementia. I've this theory that if you exercise the mind you're likely to keep it for longer. Between replying to the day's mail and the start of parliamentary business, most days I'll pop on to the Terrace outside or, in the winter, the back of Strangers' cafe to figure out the numbers with a mug of coffee. It's like a session in a mental gymnasium, a regular workout to keep the brain fit.

And if I can complete the exercise outside, so much the better. We ex-miners appreciate fresh air in our lungs and the sun on our faces.

CHAPTER TWENTY

What's left?

I never stop to think what is around the next corner because life is all about dealing with events; including the consequences and, if possible, finding a way out.

When I was told I had cancer of the bladder, I was shell-shocked for a week or two. I remember gazing at the autumn leaves still blowing around and wondering how many spring blossoms I would see. Fortunately, due to the work of all those in the NHS, since then I have made many more annual trips to Isabella Plantation in Richmond Park plus countless visits to my favourite haunts in the Bolsover area and, until my bike was stolen from a rack at Parliament, I cycled around Hyde and Regent's Parks always humming or singing 'This Is My Lovely Day'.

How could I ever complain about what life has thrown at me when I look around the hospital wards, visiting friends and constituents, knowing that I have been lucky in surviving not only cancer in 1999 but then in 2003 staggering into Chelsea and Westminster Hospital a few minutes before cardiac arrest. I stepped onto a treadmill just in time for the doctor to announce

I would need open-heart surgery almost immediately. A fort-night and three operations later, I was able to leave Brompton Hospital in a wheelchair with Lois and my kids Dawn, Dennis and Mandy by my side.

Within a few weeks I was back in the House of Commons and my first speech outside that year was at the Durham Miners' Gala. I dedicated it to all those NHS workers, from 45 different countries, who gave me the energy, spirit and enthusiasm to address a working class audience of 50,000 and tell them about my Dutch doctor, Nigerian registrar, Syrian cardiologist and Malaysian surgeon who provided me with a United Nations heart by-pass. How can I be other than extremely grateful for all those in the NHS, some of whom I still see on a regular basis each year.

Now, and one artificial hip later, I'm still playing a full part in Parliament and speaking at constituency fundraising events for many of my colleagues. And I still found the time to visit half a dozen old coalfield areas to commemorate the 30th anniversary of the 1984 strike.

How I manage to use up so much nervous energy in a 30-minute speech sometimes amazes me and, with the pulse racing, I sometimes mutter to myself 'Be careful' and I'll lie down in the car to recover before I drive back home. Now that isn't exciting – it's just a little dangerous. So, when you've lived as long as I have and are in the public eye, it remains possible, especially in Derbyshire, to mix with my friends at hundreds of constituency events and nothing pleases me more than to be miles away from the sloppy, all-party embrace at Westminster.

Believe me, when I'm singing to my constituents at an early dementia class in their care home, it's not only 150 miles away from the Tea Room gossip. It is an entirely different world!

When I am in the Clay Cross area with my remaining brothers and our extended family I am just another ex-miner. When I am with my kids and grandchildren Matthew, Tom, Hannah and James, I take a back seat and I'm watching a new generation in a complicated world which I know very little about but, believe me, I'm filled with admiration at the talent and expertise of not only my grown-up children but the four grandchildren as well.

What is more, I never leave the garden barbecues feeling out of breath. I never have to make exciting speeches. Indeed, my presence is all that is needed and I drive back home feeling relaxed. A day spent with my family is, without doubt, a day I look forward to every time. I can safely say that I have never left any of these family 'get togethers' feeling I had sailed close to the wind.

What I do feel is a sense of satisfaction knowing there is a new generation growing up and facing new challenges in a world where the pace of life is changing dramatically compared even with my childhood, the Second World War and a lifetime that has been shaped by the coal-mining community. The day before I wrote this passage I opened an event attended by more than 1,800 people at a Shirebrook school where an attempt was made to set a new record for the most people simultaneously learning how to save a life, including how to put somebody into recovery position, cardiopulmonary resuscitation and dealing with choking. I performed the opening ceremony and, at the end, verified that a new record had been set because the British Heart Foundation had taught nearly 2,000 students, staff and members how to save lives.

We started the morning knowing we had to get more than 1,700 people training on a sports field to set a new record. Rain was threatening and for at least an hour we thought we would be short of participants until, on another exciting day in the Skinner life, we beat the rain and the old record as well. Even when we fear the worst, always remember that there is an uncertainty of life that eclipses everything.

Some months earlier I'd raised with David Cameron the constituency case of David Coupe, 57, a farmer and butcher in Calow in the Bolsover constituency who worked hard all his life until he was struck down by an aggressive cancer. Unable to do his jobs, he applied for financial help.

Mr Coupe was summoned for an examination by Atos, the French private company assessing whether people are fit to work. Mr Coupe endured unbearable pain from ulcerated legs, which left him virtually housebound. He also suffered with diabetes and a heart condition. Heartlessly, Atos deemed he was fit to work and stripped him of his benefits. For 11 months Mr Coupe waited for an appeal while the cancer took his sight, took his hearing and then took his life. During that time he and his wife, Lyn, lived on £70 a week. They went without food and couldn't afford to turn on the heating. It was no way to treat a dog, let alone a dying man. The brutal machine was stripping Mr Coupe of his dignity as well as his income. Before he died, Mr Coupe vowed he would fight to overturn the callous decision as long as there was breath in his body. Cameron had no answer when I hit him at Prime Minister's Questions with details of the case, demanding an ex gratia payment for his widow. As a constituency MP, I can win important battles.

But to win the war we need a Labour Government that will get rid of companies such as Atos, Capita and G4S, because David Coupe wasn't an isolated case. The stories are legion of disabled, sick and ill people passed fit for work when clearly they were incapable of doing a job if any were to be found. Of people passed fit to work one day and dying the next. Of an appeals process with built-in delays, to grind down applicants who were in with a good shout of winning if they lasted the course, because the tests stripping them of benefits were slipshod.

Several months after I'd ambushed Cameron with the mistreatment of David Coupe, disability groups called a day of demonstrations across the country outside Atos offices. They weren't the best-organised protests, if I'm honest, but I'd heard about them so I wandered along to the company's headquarters in Marylebone. There were a few dozen of us. I didn't recognise anybody. Most were disabled, quite a few in wheelchairs, the victims of a ruthless system. After a while a few dozen more arrived from another demo to bolster the numbers. I reckon there were probably 50 of us at the final count. A woman had brought a loudhailer and a few of us spoke, demanding justice and denouncing the discredited Work Capability Assessment, the tests implemented by Atos.

The protest probably didn't look much to the casual passer-by but it was part of a broader, sustained campaign. Within a couple of days Atos announced it wanted out of the contract with the Department of Work and Pensions. We appreciated that the tests were the crux, rather than the firm doing them. But we'd secured a tiny victory after the persecution of people who deserved better than a cold shoulder from officialdom.

Over the years I've heard people ask: 'What's his game? What's Skinner after?' I'm playing no game and I'm after nothing. I represent those at the bottom of the heap, people who deserve better in life than the hand dealt by an economic system operating in the interests of a wealthy few at the top. I've no gods. In politics I'm driven by an unyielding belief, an absolute conviction, that there is an alternative to the current economic madness and that is worth struggling for.

You need stamina in politics to last the course, to be able to keep going when others around you are flagging. It's a working-class trait. You had to get up early to go to the pit. The bus for Parkhouse left Holmgate in Clay Cross at 6.00 a.m. We'd go back on a Monday to confront everything Mother Nature had thrown at the place when we were off over the weekend. Roadways we'd left clear 48 hours earlier would be buckled, the floor rising and the roof falling as the earth shifted. If you could knock the pit back into shape, you were fit for the job. Discipline was required and slacking wasn't allowed. Underground was like being in a gym for eight hours, using all of your muscles. You had to keep your wits about you too or you'd risk injury or worse. We took drinking water and a sandwich down with us, and the conditions were harsh.

The physical demands of politics are a cakewalk after the pit and it makes me smile when you hear that footballers couldn't concentrate in the last 20 minutes of a game or a bowler has been taken off because he's tired after five overs in cricket. Try mining, boys! People talk to me about the stress in politics. Maybe I'm an oddity but it doesn't feel like stress after what we felt in the pit. Stress is being in the cage and you're halfway down the shaft and it stops suddenly, bouncing on the cable. Or hearing a sound like thunder underground when the weight of the rock above comes down on the props and it flashes through your head that they mightn't hold the roof. That's stress.

And you need luck in life. The National Health Service is Labour's greatest gift to the nation. When people ask what the last Labour government achieved, I point to the NHS. We saved the NHS. It was ailing terribly from neglect under the Conservatives. We trebled spending from £33 billion in 1997 to £100 billion in 2010. More nurses, more doctors and more operations in new hospitals.

As I've said, twice the wonderful NHS has saved my life. The first was from bladder cancer in November 1999. I thought I was a goner. I was passing blood and saw the GP who referred me to a urologist in London's Chelsea and Westminster Hospital. A camera was inserted through my penis to check. I thought it was probably a prostate problem but they told me it was a tumour on the bladder. The consultant drew me a diagram to show where it was. I asked if it was malignant. He replied, yes, it was cancer.

I was feeling sorry for myself, wondering all sorts of things. They operated after a week or two. I came round, feeling groggy, and I was lying on the bed surrounded by bags of blood. The surgeon whispered into my ear 'I think we've got it' and I felt this hope tinged with fear. I was called back every three months for regular tests. Either the cancer could come back or it might invade other areas. There was a little group of us who'd turn up at the same time for appointments. I'd study the faces when they came out after seeing the doctor, trying to work out if it was good or bad news. Some people disappeared, never coming again. We never knew if they'd beaten it or died.

I remember the day when I was told they'd see me every six rather than three months. The relief was intoxicating. I walked out of that hospital and the pink blossom on the trees was the brightest, most vivid I'd ever seen. I'd intended to walk to South Kensington tube and before I knew it I was past and on my way to Parliament. I was floating on air. I had been given a new lease of life.

The second debt I owe the NHS was a heart bypass in 2003, around the time of the Iraq War. I was feeling awful, thinking I had flu. Walking past Westminster Abbey I was forced to stop and clutch the railings for support. I rang the GP and received a note on the board in the Commons telling me a telephone message had said to get to the Chelsea and Westminster for the treadmill test at 4 p.m. I boarded the District Line at Westminster for South Kensington.

When I got off at South Ken I felt lousy. I worried I wouldn't make the mile along the Fulham Road to the hospital. Every 30 or 40 yards I needed a rest or a sit-down. Eventually I reached the hospital and after two minutes on a treadmill they had me in a bed, feeling exhausted. I told them I needed to be back in Parliament to vote and they looked at me as if I was mad. I was transferred to the Brompton Hospital for an angiogram. I was hoping stents would be inserted to clear the blocked arteries but I had a double bypass with a vein out of my arm and a piece of my mammary gland. They broke my ribs to gain access to my heart. It was painful, if a lot better than the alternative.

I use my experience of an NHS staffed by people from every continent on earth to shame racists. When Nigel Farage, the UKIP leader, was dragged out of that crashed aircraft in 2010 – incidentally, a Polish-built crashed aircraft – he was rescued by public service workers and cared for by an NHS staffed by the best people from all corners of the globe. Nigel Farage and UKIP are hypocrisy by the bucketful. I'll leave his German wife out of this but I'll take him on for wanting to sack public service workers and stirring up prejudice and resentment against people who come to our country to work hard, including within the NHS. The way to head UKIP off at the pass is to expose the party's deceit, lies and policies. UKIP is a right-wing party that would strip away employment rights including paid holidays, privatise the NHS and cut taxes for the very wealthiest. It would do nothing to help the working class.

I've no time for nationalism. The reason I was in the Commons chamber when the bags of manure chucked by Dom Mintoff's daughter were flying my way, everything magnified in the split seconds, was because I was opposing Scottish devolution. I feared in the Callaghan era that devolution would encourage, not snuff out, nationalism. Devolution was given to Scotland and Wales in the Blair period and the result was Alex Salmond and the SNP demanding separation.

Nationalism is about flag-waving. One of the things I have been careful about in all of my extra-parliamentary activity is steering clear of the Union Jack brigade. I had a bit of an argument with Tony Benn after he appeared at an anti-EU rally in Trafalgar Square surrounded by these right-wingers waving the flag. He said forget it and was apologetic.

My philosophy is hope not fear, and nationalism divides people. When you're fighting capitalism, you want to unite people. All my experience in the pit taught me that the Parkhouse and Glapwell miners in Derbyshire were no different in their zeal to improve their lives than miners in Scotland, Wales, Yorkshire and Kent. In the National Union of Mineworkers and other trade unions we never recognised boundaries. I never regarded Lawrence Daly and Mick McGahey, both Scots, as any different from the mining leaders in Yorkshire and Derbyshire and elsewhere. Most of the Kent miners were anyway from Scotland and South Wales. I have never waved the Union Jack so why should I want to wave the saltire?

I've never lost my competitive streak and it is generally an advantage, although there have been unexpected problems along the way. After my brother Gordon's death his widow, Helen, revealed he wanted his ashes scattered on Kinder Scout in the Peak District. He'd been a miner at Gedling in Nottinghamshire and was forced out of the industry after a year on strike. They loved the outdoor life after his pit shut. Helen and Gordon did the Pennine Way, camping out unlawfully one night in the grounds of Chatsworth House, and walked from Derbyshire to Edinburgh.

Sadly, cancer got Gordon in the end. He planned his own funeral, including Edith Piaf's 'No Regrets' and all six verses of 'The Red Flag'. Gordon sitting at his computer to compose the order of service was one of the bravest, most courageous, acts I've witnessed.

Gordon's ashes were to be scattered at the top of Kinder Scout in the Peak District, scene of mass trespass in 1932 when moorland was largely the preserve of the gentry. The family togged up and set off to reach the top. I was out of breath and struggling near the end. I discovered six months later why the going was tough when I needed heart surgery.

When we got to the top we had a family picnic, talked about Gordon and scattered his ashes before making our way down.

Close to the first anniversary of his death, Helen rang and asked if I remembered that we'd agreed to go up again. It turned out she'd brought back half his ashes, saving them for the second trip. Helen said I needn't go because I'd had the heart op but I insisted on going. So off we set.

We were quickly strung out along the path as I competed with my youngest brother, Derrick, to be first to the summit. Near the top, I noticed a track straight up and more direct than the winding path. So I shot up there. It was heavy going and only 10 or 15 yards from the top I was out of breath and had to stop, wheezing and knackered. There were a couple of park rangers. One of them asked: Are you alright? Should I come down and give you a hand? I replied: 'No, I'm just catching my breath.' Then I added: 'I shouldn't be doing this really – I had a heart bypass six months ago.' I thought the ranger was going to have a heart attack. I made it to the top eventually. And got down. The competitive streak didn't kill me.

It was at Gordon's funeral that I discovered my sister Hazel was suffering from dementia. I'd said a few words in a tribute and Hazel said: 'That's a good speech, Den, you could do it for a living.' I thought it was a joke until one of her three girls pulled me aside and explained it was dementia. I felt terrible that I'd thought it was a joke. Hazel's dementia was a different type to my mother's and she didn't last long. To lose another family member to it was heartbreaking.

The last time I saw Hazel alive was on a Saturday afternoon in Chesterfield hospital. She wasn't communicating so I sang her a couple of songs as I had to my mother. I kicked off with 'People Will Say We're In Love' from *Oklahoma*, then 'If I Loved You' from *Carousel*. Hazel and the rest of the ward joined in. I don't think she knew my name but she was singing like my mother. Her children, the three girls and a boy, were over the moon.

The competitive streak came from my father, who had an in-it-to-win-it approach to sport. His doubts about my road walking as a young miner were rooted in a fear I wouldn't be any good. I always wanted to win in cross-country, football and cricket. And I wanted my side to win. On one occasion I ran up a hill backwards to keep Derrick going in a marathon. I'd gone to Chesterfield to see my youngest brother compete. Another brother Gary, who is very good with his hands and can build a bathroom in a day, was driving. We'd stop at a certain point then drive ahead and wait for the runners. When Derrick was 13 he had a medical condition which saw him grow a full beard. Dad was furious when the Tupton Hall headmaster ignored a doctor's note and kicked him out for not shaving, forcing Derrick to move to Deincourt School. Derrick later went to Sheffield University and he's a Labour councillor on North East Derbyshire who can talk a donkey's hind leg off. On the Chesterfield marathon he was flagging going up steep Somersall Hill. I jumped on the course and ran up that hill backwards, urging him to keep going: 'Another thing: remember your name is Skinner,' I told him. 'You're not packing in.' He didn't.

I want to see another Labour government and to defeat the Tories, Liberal Democrats and now UKIP. I've been in to see Ed Miliband about speaking rhythmically and extemporaneously at Prime Minister's Questions and have discussed politics with him more generally. He's bright, decent and has made a couple of very good conference speeches without notes. I told him the key to success at Prime Minister's Questions is to be a bit more like Jeremy Paxman, focusing on the questions Cameron never answers, so he looks silly. We rehearsed a session on the NHS before he knocked Cameron out of the park in the summer of 2012, leaning forward on the despatch box and changing his tone to express astonishment at Cameron's slipperiness. It was very effective. I wish he would do it more often.

I nominated John McDonnell of the Socialist Campaign Group in the last Labour leadership election but we couldn't persuade enough other MPs to join us so his name never made it on the ballot paper. I knew at the end of the day it would come down to a contest between the two Miliband brothers, David and Ed. David was the first in Parliament. Elected in 2001, I sat and watched him in Environment Questions when he became a minister and noted his total and utter confidence at the despatch box. He had this tendency to swivel round when he was speaking, looking over his left shoulder and then his right instead of ahead. He'd sought advice and I'd given it so when David asked how he'd done that day I replied: 'Be careful or you'll end up doing a pirouette while answering a question.'

Ed was elected in 2005 and when he came to me I told him I was giving him the same advice as I gave his brother, David, including how to think of a speech as the trunk of a tree with two or three branches coming off, retaining a central theme for whatever story he wanted to tell. And if the speech was to be no more than 15 minutes, to write a few notes and learn it rather than reading a script from an autocue.

I wish the TV cameras had been running at Hatfield Main pit on the 30th anniversary of the strike when Miliband engaged a blue-collar working-class audience. The hall was jammed with 300 people of all ages. There were kids crawling under the table. We had miners and retired miners. Ed followed me and spoke their language. Miliband was cheered loudly when he backed an inquiry into the police misbehaviour at the Orgreave coking plant. If he looked awkward eating a bacon sandwich, Ed that day was in his element with working people. This was the type of meeting he should do again and again.

I've argued at the NEC for the leader to adopt bold, popular policies such as renationalising rail. I didn't applaud Ed when he abandoned Shadow Cabinet elections. I prefer democracy to patronage. And I opposed his distancing of the party from the trade unions. I was in a minority of two on the NEC when the constitutional changes were put to the vote. Having lost the vote, I demanded a continuing review in the event of a future financial crisis. Although they wouldn't accept my term 'review', an implementation committee was set up which amounts to the same thing. Bizarrely, Labour is adopting a system imposed by the Tories to rub the workers' noses in it after the 1926 General Strike and reversing the position adopted by the Clement Attlee Labour government in 1946. You can do the maths yourself. In 1927 Labour Party affiliates slumped by 1.2 million to just over 2 million when workers had to opt in to membership. In 1946, when they had to opt out, it soared from 2.6 million to nearly 4.4 million.

However, at election time I believe that Labour voters should remember that though Clement Attlee was never regarded in the same breath as Churchill by a right-wing media that dominated then as now, people voted for a Labour team anyway, to transform the economy. That's what we need today.

Since my first election to Labour's NEC in 1978, rule changes have three times knocked me off the party body. Barring MPs from standing in the constituency section and replacing constituency block votes with individual ballots were two of them. The third, in the summer of 2014, saw shadow ministers, instead of just backbenchers, voting for three MPs to represent the Parliamentary Labour Party on the NEC.

Two years earlier I'd topped the poll. In 2014 we were informed that, although the leadership has four places reserved on the NEC, all Labour MPs, including frontbenchers, would be voting. The turnout soared to 95.7 per cent with 250 of 257 MPs participating. Two hours after the party ballot closed, 30 fewer Labour MPs voted against the Conservative-Liberal Democrat Government's Budget. The result meant I would not be able to attend in early 2015 what is known as Labour's Clause V meeting, a joint session between the shadow cabinet and NEC tasked by the party's constitution to draw up the election manifesto.

I've a few suggestions of my own to boost Labour's popularity and beat the Tories.

To start the ball rolling we should end expensive privatisation instead of paying a fortune to contractors such as G4S, Serco and Capita that make a mess of services in the process. It's time we got back to publicly run, publicly owned services provided in the public interest.

On the railways, the £900m surplus on East Coast trains, operated publicly after the private sector crashed twice, shows us the way ahead. Instead of boosting Richard Branson's profits, a nationalised railway could make a profit and generate the cash to improve every station in Britain.

If we want extra money for the National Health Service and social care, we should levy a Robin Hood tax on speculators in the city. Directing the funds raised directly to health and care, including help for the mentally handicapped, rather than to the Treasury, would be immensely popular. We could start with a low rate and increase it when the tax proves to be popular, as I'm sure it will, by emulating the one per cent National Insurance rise for the NHS when Gordon Brown was Chancellor.

Scrapping Trident would free up billions of pounds for a massive house building programme so everybody has a roof over their head and nobody is homeless. The position on council house sales has to change or local authorities won't build houses if they know they must sell them cheaply after a few years.

The savings from defusing nuclear weapons can also help save local democracy. Councils are being swamped by central government. Powers are either grabbed by Whitehall or transferred to unelected quangos. Ever since the Clay Cross rent rebellion, Whitehall has dictated to communities. We need to reverse the trend.

On the question of utilities – gas, electricity, water – this is the moment to start taking them back into public ownership. We took control after 1945 and right up to Wilson's final government, when he nationalised aerospace with a majority of only three, public ownership was advanced. To cap energy bills is a good idea but a better plan is to control utilities by restoring public ownership in Britain of firms that are currently owned in France, Germany and almost every country on the globe.

Spending on education more than doubled under the last Labour government, which was impressive. Let's stop the growth of faith schools and misnamed free schools – taxpayers fund them so they're not free – by enhancing the powers of local authorities to champion the education of every single child.

We need to end the pay freezes. The people that are carrying the burden of the bankers' ramp are mainly workers at the bottom of the scale. The Living Wage shouldn't be optional. Everybody should get it. But let's not stop at £7.65 an hour outside London and £8.80 in the capital. The trade union campaign for £10 an hour should be Labour policy. A decent day's work deserves a decent day's pay.

We should introduce legislation to outlaw zero hours contracts and private employment agencies. Playing off worker against worker, ferrying into Britain cheap labour to undercut employees, is poisoning community relations. Sticking 10, 12 or 15 eastern Europeans into a house then deducting large sums from their earnings is in nobody's interests except cowboy employers. Reasserting the role of Jobcentres as local labour exchanges will improve wages and conditions.

Trade union rights must be strengthened significantly, including the abolition of sequestration. Industrial action requires two sides to be involved in a dispute, yet it is union funds that are seized.

Rebalancing employment rights in favour of workers and unions is essential if we are to build a fairer economy.

And we must escape the dumb economic mantra about balancing the books. There would have been no Spirit of '45 if Clement Attlee's goal was to balance the books. There would have been no NHS, new Welfare State, new council houses and unemployment wouldn't have dropped to 440,000 in 1950, after only five years of the finest Labour Government ever. In fact the finest Government ever.

We need spending to get people to work and the economy growing. You don't need a crystal ball to see where we should be going. We can find the way ahead by reading the history books.

These are not my policies alone. The issues have been debated over the past 10 or 20 years in the Bolsover Constituency Labour Party where Ann Syrett is the chairman and Gary Ransford, the grandson of a miner who probably knows as much about Labour Party rules as most regional and national officers, has been the secretary for 20 years. The discussions are part of the democratic process, so it's not just me who proposes these policies

So am I competent at my age, 82, to be an MP? I have been extremely lucky, healthwise. I've survived cancer and open-heart surgery. My hip is new. I've no trouble from the hairline fracture of the skull when I was knocked off my bike. I worked out how long I've had off work on the sick and in 44 years it must be a total of 12 weeks and only 8 of those were when Parliament was sitting.

I watch what I eat. I try to stay physically active. I walk a lot and I still cycle. I never see Cameron or Boris Johnson in London's Hyde and Green Parks on a Sunday. The *Daily Telegraph* tried to catch me to get a photograph. I think they wanted to see me on a

Boris Bike or a penny-farthing to present me as a hypocrite or a dinosaur. The bad news for them is I had my own bike. And as I've said, I do Killer Soduku in *The Times* every day to exercise the brain.

I've been reselected as the Bolsover candidate with a record 44 nominations from party branches and trade unions. The policy of the NUM used to be that MPs would retire at 65 and I'd have abided by the rule but it was abolished in 1977 when the union realised mining MPs were stepping down and we needed miners in Parliament to campaign against pit closures.

My partner Lois and I get together with my grown-up children Dawn, Dennis and Mandy and my grandchildren about ten times a year for proper family gatherings. My marriage to Mary ended amicably in 1989 when we separated after nearly 30 years. Mary died a few years ago. We'd mended a lot of our fences and the children asked me to pay the tribute at the funeral. Mary was a committed socialist and a brilliant mother.

So I'm fighting for a new Labour government to axe the bedroom tax, save the NHS, cut fuel bills, create jobs for the young and raise living standards. My personal manifesto will be to the left of that of the party but I'm committed 100 per cent to the election of Labour candidates across Britain.

You learn something new every day in this life. Harriet Harman tells me when I'm trending on Twitter after a clash with Cameron or one of the other posh boys. I'm told there is a spoof account called @BolsoverBeast which MPs are convinced is me. It's not, I assure you. The Labour frontbencher Catherine McKinnell told me she's read the tweets and took some convincing it was some-body else. I don't send emails, either. I read them but prefer to ring people up or send a letter, looking up numbers and addresses in the phone book if they're not included in the email. I feel it's more personal and I've had really interesting conversations as a result. It also helps keep postal workers in jobs.

My earliest memories include political arguments. I recall a dispute over the Royals in 1937. I was five years old. I can picture the scene near our garden gate in John Street. A group of Clay Cross lads were insisting the Royal Family had blue blood. They must have heard it on the wireless or read it in a newspaper. 'What do you mean they have blue blood? No they haven't – they've got red like us,' I insisted. How can one family in Britain be more important than any other?

To this day I believe we're all born equal: it is unfair economic and political systems that make us unequal. The fight goes on to win for working people what they are owed but too rarely get. As a socialist, shaped by the pits and the Second World War, I look forward to participating in the battles ahead. In the run-up to the next election I will be speaking in at least another 20 marginal constituencies at fund-raising events for Labour candidates.

I hope to make them laugh, make them cry, make them think and send them home happy. To achieve all that I will, unfortunately, have to 'sail close to the wind'.

ACKNOWLEDGEMENTS

I could not have even contemplated starting this book without acknowledging all the people with whom I have been closely associated, especially during my formative years.

First of all I remember all those teachers who helped me, along with Mrs Langley, to win a County Minor Scholarship at the age of 10. I thank my parents and the extended Skinner family who supported me through my many early trials and tribulations.

Naturally, winning my first ballot at Parkhouse colliery was a life changer for me when I was able to represent my mates on the NUM area council in the mid-1950s. They trusted me, Lucy and Tony's lad, to speak for them. Later, Clay Cross Labour Party nominated me to stand for the council and I won again. I'll never forget the countless times I was stopped in the street by well-wishers who, for the most part, assured me they were all related to the family.

I also acknowledge the part that Derbyshire NUM played in my life, particularly in those years culminating in my winning the area President's job at the age of 34. A few of my colleagues are still around and I will never forget the debt that I owe to them and other friends in the Notts area coalfield NUM such as Henry

Richardson, who fought and won a ballot to be a full-time official on the platform of being Skinner's underground mole. Henry is still alive and he is and always will be a socialist. Indeed in Bolsover Constituency Labour Party there are many others who like Henry are never afraid to fight for a socialist society. They have nominated me for Parliament 12 times and all they have asked of me is to remain true to my beliefs and principles.

I have received tremendous support from colleagues in other areas of the NUM such as Yorkshire, South Wales, Scotland, Kent, Northumberland and in particular Durham where, in total, I have addressed more than one million people since 1978.

I joined the left-wing Tribune Group when I entered Parliament in 1970. There were just 15 of us. Later I, together with Bob Cryer and others, helped to start the Socialist Campaign Group and I have remained a member ever since. It would be fair to say that at all times I have been much more comfortable with those Labour MPs who accept the need for extra-parliamentary activity, working closely with the trade union movement. That's why on many occasions I have supported John McDonnell for the party leadership even though he has never managed to get the necessary quorum.

When I first took my seat in Parliament I sat on the front bench below the gangway together with Frank Allaun, Ian Mikardo, Tom Swain and, later, Bob Cryer, Harry Barnes, Ken Purchase, Andrew MacKinlay, Terry Lewis, Mick Clapham, Jimmy Hood and, in his last few months in the Commons, Harold Wilson to whom I surrendered my corner seat before he retired in 1983. Today my neighbours are Ronnie Campbell, Ian Lavery, Ian Mearns, John Cryer, Kelvin Hopkins and Grahame Morris. And

ACKNOWLEDGEMENTS

all of them at some time have heard many of my lines when I was testing the response to possible Prime Minister's questions.

My sisters and brothers too were, and still are, a big part of my life, together with Lois, my partner, and my children Dawn, Dennis, Mandy and their partners Dave, Zoe and Ralph who have helped to shape this book from beginning to end.

The book has been especially difficult for me because I did not want to write it at all, but my immediate family have driven me on, and I hope it turns out alright.

INDEX

INDEX